The Reception Year: Learning through Play

Dr Reda J Davin
BA, DEd, HNOD (Preprimary), DFE (RE)
Senior lecturer,
Department Teacher Education, Unisa

Dr Christie JS van Staden
BA, DEd, DKO, THOD
Senior lecturer,
Department Teacher Education, Unisa

www.heinemann.co.za

Published by Heinemann Publishers
128 Peter Road, Sandown, 2196
PO Box 781940, Sandton, 2146, Johannesburg, South Africa
www.heinemann.co.za

First Edition 1997 (published as The Year Before School) ISBN 186863 1929
First published 2005
09
8 7 6
ISBN 0 796209 677
ISBN 978 0 796 20967 2

Typeset by Belinda Bompani (Cherry Studio)
Cover photograph by Guy Stubbs
Printed and bound by CTP Book Printers, Cape

Acknowledgements
While every effort has been made to contact copyright holders of material used, this did not always prove
possible. Copyright holders are therefore requested to contact the publisher in cases where formal permission
could not be obtained.

Contents

Chapter 3 Emergent Literacy:
Language and the beginnings of reading 78

Chapter 4 Emergent Literacy: The beginnings of writing and spelling 109

Chapter 5 Emergent Numeracy: The learner's world of Mathematics

Chapter 6: Life Skills and exploring Science and Technology

Chapter 8 Putting it all together: A practical example of integrating in context

Introduction

It is generally accepted that a child's early years are extremely important in terms of developing his or her full potential as a happy and successful human being. This view is reflected in South Africa's new educational dispensation, which prescribes a compulsory preschool year. Providing a setting where the young learner between five and seven years of age can play and learn is an exciting undertaking. *The Reception Year: Learning through Play* is designed to give you, the teacher, the knowledge and skills to be able to teach and educate the reception year learner.

Although this book focuses on the teaching of the three learning programmes of the reception year (Emergent Literacy, Numeracy and Life Skills), teachers should bear in mind that an *integrated approach* which enhances the development of the whole learner is followed.

The first chapter provides an overview of all the different activities that you should present during the course of the school day. As you work through the book you will encounter chapters on Emergent Literacy, Emergent Numeracy (including Emergent Mathematics and Science) and Life Skills. These chapters provide more detailed guidelines on how to develop the necessary learning programmes for this important school year.

Remember

Remember that when children stop enjoying your teaching, they also stop learning.

Chapter

1

Planning to teach
Reda Faber

OUTCOMES

After you have read this chapter you should be able to:

■ understand the role of outcomes in the teaching and learning process and use these to focus your teaching and learning presentations in the Reception Year class

■ plan a fully-functional Reception Year classroom which, because of its design, provides an exciting environment in which to learn

■ decide on and present a well-balanced daily timetable

■ choose suitable and relevant learning topics and activities that will enhance the young learner's total development. Your choice of suitable activities will also be directed by the Learning Outcomes and Assessment Standards set for the reception year

■ present your weekly and daily planning in such a way that it will enable you to teach in a progressive and meaningful way.

Where do I begin?

The reception year can play an important role in the development of the young learner, but only if the teacher knows exactly what the purpose of this year is. We must know exactly what we want to achieve in order to achieve it!

The first step in becoming an excellent reception year teacher is therefore to be able to *understand* the teaching process and to *plan* in detail what you aim to teach.

During the reception year we focus on setting the learner on a lifelong path of learning, by enhancing the learner's optimum development as a total human being. We include the learner's parents and caregivers by respecting their input into the learner's upbringing and by giving educational guidance to them as they fulfil this task.

To be able to achieve this purpose we need to break it down into achievable goals: this is the reason for Learning Outcomes.

What are the Learning Outcomes for the reception year?

The South Africa National Department of Education has identified certain outcomes which direct all teaching and training in South Africa. These outcomes are the starting point for reception year teaching.

The outcomes can be divided into two broad categories:

1. **Critical and developmental outcomes** are a list of outcomes that are derived from the constitution and are contained in an Act of Parliament (The South African Qualifications Act of 1995). These outcomes describe the kind of citizen we are aiming to create through our teaching effort. Critical and developmental outcomes are long term and direct learners into lifelong learning.

2. **Learning Outcomes** are derived from the critical and developmental outcomes. They are descriptions of the knowledge, skills and values learners should demonstrate at the end of the General Education and Training band (Grades R – 9). These outcomes are also long term (being used from Grade R to Grade 9), but in order to make them more specific for each level, Assessment Standards have been set for each grade, including Grade R. **Assessment Standards** describe the level at which learners should be able to demonstrate that they have achieved each Learning Outcome at the end of a specific grade.

There are prescribed Learning Outcomes for eight **learning areas** (these learning areas are applicable to all school grades — from Grade R to Grade 9):

- Languages
- Mathematics
- Natural Sciences
- Social Sciences
- Technology
- Economic and Management Sciences
- Life Orientation
- Arts and Culture

In the Foundation Phase (Grades R – 3) these learning areas are divided into three **Learning Programmes.** The following three Learning Programmes are used in Grade R:

- Literacy
- Numeracy, and
- Life Skills.

The reception year teacher has to ensure that the Learning Outcomes of all eight of the learning areas are covered effectively in these three Learning Programmes.

If we study all the Learning Outcomes and Assessment Standards for each learning area for the reception year we come up with 23 Learning Outcomes and 91 Assessment Standards. Covering all these Learning Outcomes and Assessment Standards is naturally a very difficult task for the reception year teacher! A practical solution is to group the Learning Outcomes and Assessment Standards according to the three learning programmes. The following is a possible way of grouping the Learning Outcomes and Assessment Standards:

Learning Outcomes for an integrated Emergent Numeracy programme

The main focus of Emergent Numeracy in the reception year is to develop mathematically-related knowledge, skills, attitudes and values necessary for learners' daily lives. At the end of the reception year the learners must have:

- knowledge of basic mathematical concepts (such as 'more', 'less', 'same amount', 'equal'), simple measurement and basic time concepts, by using them in concrete, daily activities

- a number concept of not less than 10, by using numbers up to 10 correctly in daily activities and concrete manipulations

- a concept of his or her position in space by using concepts such as 'in front', 'behind', 'on top', 'under', 'left' and 'right' correctly

- basic and concrete knowledge of scientific concepts such as observation, prediction, classification and comparing, and the ability to use these correctly in concrete, explorative science activities

- an ability to use learning skills such as problem solving, logical reasoning and creative thinking in the concrete solving of simple mathematical and science problems

- the ability to realise in a simple manner that technology develops and that this process must be handled in a responsible way

- an increasingly appreciative and inquisitive attitude towards nature and the laws of nature.

Learning Outcomes for an integrated Literacy programme

The main focus of the Emergent Literacy programme for the reception year is to enable learners to communicate effectively (Department of Education 2003 (a): 44). To achieve this, the reception year learner must:

- be able to communicate with ease and clarity in his or her home language. The learners must be able to communicate and listen in a group situation

- be able to use his or her home language to reason and obtain information

- have an introductory knowledge of an additional language, preferably English (if English is not his or her home language) with a knowledge and comprehension of about 200 to 500 everyday words

- understand the underlying principles of reading and writing within a whole language approach through experiences in a language rich learning environment

- listen with interest and comprehend suitable stories, rhymes and songs (with various themes, including historical and cultural), as well as take part in discussions

- develop the necessary perceptual skills needed for reading, writing and spelling through suitable games and activities

- have a positive attitude towards reading and develop a love for reading as a source of information and recreation.

Learning Outcomes for an integrated Life Skills programme

A Life Skills programme for the reception year is developed to enhance the learner's personal development, knowledge, skills and values necessary for social and economical development. The reception year learner must have:

- a positive self concept and the self confidence to be able to move into the greater school environment of primary school

- developmentally appropriate control over emotions and the ability to express emotions in a socially acceptable way

- the necessary knowledge and physical skills to be independent concerning basic daily physical needs, such as putting on clothes, brushing of teeth, hand washing, toilet routines, and eating with suitable utensils

- insight into and comprehension of his or her own responsibility for person hygiene and knowledge of precautions against basic transmittable diseases

- insight into safety through obedience of basic safety rules in the classroom and home environment

- the ability to have healthy relationships with members of his or her peer group and adults in her or his environment, and an understanding of the right to say 'no' to any form of abuse by others

- basic knowledge and appreciation for the values and norms of his or her community

- appreciation and respect for the needs of all people irrespective of age, gender, ability or culture

- the ability to take responsibility for completing activities presented in the reception year class and to understand, on a concrete level, the difference between play and work

- the ability to understand the importance of learning and to look forward to formal school, and by doing so start on the path of life long learning.

Remember

Remember that the whole teaching effort, i.e. all decisions, presentations and activities, are directed towards reaching the Learning Outcomes.

What about school readiness as an outcome?

As stated above the purpose of the reception year is the development of every facet of the young learner. This includes more than mere 'school readiness'.

School readiness is not a condition that is easily measured or defined. Two important facts are evident when one studies the different views and definitions of school readiness:

- There are different perceptions of school readiness.

- Common to all of these different views is the emphasis on the vital role of parents and other adults on the child's development and school readiness.

As far back as 1977, school readiness was defined (Grové 1977: 10) as a broad term which included three aspects of development, namely:

1. school maturity

2. social maturity

3. emotional maturity.

According to Grové, while maturity cannot be forced, school readiness can be enhanced by helping the child to use his or her senses as effectively as possible and by providing a wide variety of concrete experiences.

Definition

Grové (1977: 10) states that a child is ready for school when he or she can meet the formal demands of school.

This definition of school readiness was (and is) the one most accepted by teachers in the Foundation Phase. This definition is, however, unsatisfactory because it emphasises the *demands of the school* and not the *possibilities of the child*. School readiness is therefore perceived as a *fixed* state. Some researchers describe this viewpoint as 'gate keeping'.

Readiness to learn

An alternative perspective, one which takes the child's development into consideration, can be used in order to overcome the 'closed gate' view of school readiness. According to this perspective, we emphasise *readiness to learn* as opposed to *readiness for school*.

> Readiness to learn can be described as a stage of maturity when an individual is able to understand and grasp those concepts and skills that have been deemed necessary for a child of a specific age to attain.

An individual child's readiness to learn is determined by factors such as:

- *The child's ability to concentrate and pay attention.* This is also dependant on the type of activity the child must concentrate on.

- *The child's own motivation to learn.* This can be influenced by parents and other factors beyond the child.

- *The child's health.* A healthy child has more energy and is more capable of learning.

- *The child's emotional maturity.* An emotionally stable child learns more easily.

- *The child's intellectual ability.* Some children do learn more easily than others. (All children with average intellectual ability can be successful in school.)

- *The environment in which the child grows up.* A child who grows up in an environment filled with opportunities to learn and experience different things has a distinct advantage over the child who doesn't. This does not mean that the home environment needs to be wealthy or in a big city. Rural children can be equally advantaged, or even more so, as long as there are adults around them to help them to learn.

According to the learning readiness perspective, the development of the child is an ongoing process that starts at birth. The child is always ready to learn new skills, knowledge or behaviour. This perspective also stresses the role of the adult (the parent and teacher). It is the adults' task to ensure that, in order for the child to develop fully, he or she is being provided with developmentally appropriate activities and learning opportunities.

Implications for the teacher of the reception class

Because the child is continuously ready to learn we must:

- find out what the child *can* do and use that as the starting point. Rather than waiting for the child to *become* ready for certain activities, the teacher must play an active part in encouraging development

- create an environment full of activities that will challenge the child, starting with what he or she can do at that time

- help the child to develop fully, so that at the end of the reception year he or she is able to learn, know, do and feel what a child of 6 – 7 years (school-going age) should be capable of completing.

The child should then be able to meet the demands of formal school without going through a 'school readiness programme' based on activities which are perhaps boring and not developmentally appropriate.

What if the child is not ready?

As the reception year teacher you have a very important role in relation to learners who may have developmental or learning barriers.

■ Identify any problem areas that may hinder the learner's performance in the first year of formal school, i.e. Grade 1. This is one reason why assessment of learners is so important.

● **Go to:**

Refer to Chapter 7 for more a detailed discussion of assessment in Grade R. Depending on the severity of the barrier, the reception year teacher will either help the learner by giving the child additional activities or (if necessary and possible) refer the child for specialist help. (*Assessment will be discussed in detail in Chapter 7: Assessment of the whole learner.*)

■ At the end of the year, you should inform the Grade 1 teacher, in writing, of any possible barriers to learning experienced by a particular child so that the teacher is aware of this before the child enters their class, and can give special attention to these issues.

Early identification of developmental or learning barriers is the first step to overcoming them. Given the opportunity to develop to the best of their ability, learners should be ready at six years of age for more formal learning. The focus during the reception year is therefore to help each child to develop as well as possible, keeping in mind the uniqueness of each child.

> **Remember**
> **School readiness** is not an isolated outcome. Rather, reception year teachers should aim to help the child to develop as a whole person in preparation not only for school, but for life.

How to teach the young learner

Children learn best by playing and imitating others (especially adults).

Playing:

Children must play in order to learn. No other activity in the child's life is as valuable for the purposes of learning. A reception year programme that limits the time learners spend in play is one that limits the learner's opportunities to learn. This is an important fact for reception year teachers to keep in mind, because the most effective teaching methods take into consideration the way that learners learn. This means we have to use the learner's natural way in our teaching approach.

Play is often regarded by adults (and teachers) as unproductive and its importance and value for the young learner is overlooked. Play is not a mere pastime for learner, but an activity which they tackle with all they have.

The fact that the learners are talking and moving around in the classroom does not mean that there is no discipline in that classroom. You may have to teach parents that play is both invaluable and the best method to use when teaching the young learner.

Imitation

The fact that play is of such importance in the young learner's development does not mean that the adult has no role in the child's life. The child also learns through imitating others. The teacher must take an active part in organising the play and learning activities. The teacher's input is important as it serves as a model for the learner. Plan activities and situations where the learner *can* imitate you.

The role of the teacher in facilitating quality play and imitation in the reception year

Opportunities for quality play and imitation which result in learning do not happen accidentally. The reception year teacher must plan and take certain steps to make sure that the opportunities for play and imitation in her classroom are meaningful.

There are six main factors to remember to enhance quality and meaningful play and imitation in the reception class:

1. Plan for a variety of play opportunities

   In order to achieve all the Learning Outcomes you will have to plan a variety of play activities so that learners can develop in many different areas. Not all activities will benefit all facets of the learner equally. Play must be present in every activity!

   Examples of play activities in the reception year class include:

   Imaginative play: Opportunities to play in the fantasy area in the classroom according to a pre-planned theme.

   Building with blocks and other construction materials. Block play enriched with additional props to link the play to the pre-planned theme.

   Manipulative play activities. Activities including playing with clay, water and mud.

   Suitable games. Games such as memory games and colour/shape/number dominoes. (These are often called 'educational toys'.)

   Play apparatus for gross motor development. Opportunities to ride tricycles and later bicycles, outside climbing and hanging apparatus.

2. Safety is always important

   Make sure that all play materials are in good condition – broken toys or apparatus are dangerous! If there is a potentially dangerous situation, the teacher must supervise at all times and explain the potential danger to the class (this is important as it is working towards realising one of the Life Skills outcomes.)

Example

Using a candle to melt a wax crayon provides a unique drawing experience for the reception year learner. This activity is, however, potentially dangerous and the teacher must supervise this activity diligently.

---

3. Meaningful discipline

   Meaningful play requires that there be discipline in the classroom. The discipline is not aimed to dictate the play or to limit the learner's exploration opportunities. Discipline needs to be meaningful and developmentally appropriate for the reception year.

Meaningful discipline means:

■ Rules are kept to a minimum. All rules are necessary and meaningful for the learners.

■ Rules are applied consistently.

■ Rules are decided in advance and all learners know the rules.

■ The learners know the reason for every rule.

4. Verbalise the learner's play

Perhaps the teacher's most important role in ensuring that learners learn through play is to verbalise what is happening. Observe the spontaneous play in your class and when necessary ask questions about their play and talk about it with your learners. In this way the learner's learn new words and concepts.

> ### Remember
> *Playing with blocks can enhance the learner's mathematical concepts in a playful way. The teacher must however show and tell the learner that there are, for example, **many** blocks. He needs **three more** to complete the high tower. The blocks are **on top of** each over. Without verbalising the learner's plays, the learner will not learn these concepts in a concrete situation.*

5. Give individual attention and emotional support

Some of the learners in your class still have to learn to play, especially with other learners. Your task is to help these learners. If a learner struggles with a particular activity, replace it with an easier alternative and support the learner during the activity, as necessary.

6. Learners need information to play creatively

One of the first prerequisites for being creative is *knowledge*. Your task is to provide the learners with knowledge or information, by using a theme, to enable them to play and act out the theme in a creative way.

> ### Example
> Instead of making a model that learners copy during art activities, rather discuss ideas with them of how to create their own object. Discuss the characteristics of the object, using concrete, real examples (not a model they have to copy) – this gives learners an understanding of what they need to create. Then give the learners the opportunity to make their own creative artwork using the knowledge you have given them.

How do we put this into practice in the reception year class?
The teaching approach we follow in the reception year is an outcomes-based approach, and is also informal and enjoyable!

An outcomes-based and informal teaching approach means that:

■ the school day is not divided into time slots for different, isolated subjects but into time slots for different activities suitable for the young learner. Each of these activities includes a variety of traditional school subjects. This approach is called an *integrated approach*.

■ the classroom and playground are planned to include children doing a wide variety of activities at the same time.

- the themes that activities are based on relate to the learner's world
- the learners are active while they learn, and discovery is recognised as an important learning tool.

The daily timetable of a reception year class

As stated above, the school day of the reception year is not divided into different, isolated learning areas but into time slots for different activities suitable for the young learner. This does not mean that the timetable is not well planned; it simply means that one of the main features of the reception year timetable is that it is not *rigid*. This means that the teacher can (and must) adapt the timetable as the need arises during the day.

Example of a timetable for a reception year class

Time	Presentation	Example of activities
7:45 – 8:15	School starts Group discussion	Teacher greets each learner individually. Religious instruction and/or discussion of the theme of the week
8:15 – 9:45	Free choice of activities inside the classroom	Art activities, block play, educational games and fine-motor activities, books, Science activities, Emergent Mathematics activities, fantasy play
9:45 –10:15	Routine	Cleaning up, toilet routine, refreshments/snacks
10:15 – 10:40	Group presentation	Music or movement activities
10: 40 – 11:45	Free choice of activities outside on playground	Outdoor apparatus, Science activities, gardening, woodwork, playing with mud, sand and water, Art activities
11:45 – 12:00	Routine	Cleaning up outdoors, toilet routine
12:00 – 12:30	Group presentation	Emergent Literacy, Numeracy and Life Skills activities, games and experiments. Story-telling
12:30 — 13:00	Group discussion Routine	Recap of the day; Departure of half-day learners Rest for full-day learners

The different periods in the daily timetable

As set out above, there are eight periods in a day (this applies to the morning programme which ends at 13:00). Although a specific amount of time is allocated to each period, these are only to be used as guidelines. A particular period can last longer, or be shortened, to accommodate specific needs of the class on that day. It is good to keep the periods in more or less the same sequence, however, as learners feel more secure when they know what will happen next. This is especially important at the beginning of the year with learners who are in a class situation for the first time. The eight periods in the daily timetable can be divided into four main groups:

Group discussions

In the timetable above there are two opportunities for group discussions. These are very important events in the reception class timetable. During these periods the teacher discusses any news she may want to share with the group, and gives learners the opportunity to share their own news. The teacher also discusses the theme (topic of the day/week) and introduces any new activity. Although these periods are 'discussions' and therefore less active, the teacher must facilitate the discussions in such a way that all learners have the opportunity to participate. The purpose of these discussions is to impart new knowledge or information to the learners. All the information is part of the overall theme of the week or relevant in some way to the learners.

Remember to keep these discussions short:

■ At the beginning of the year start with a discussion of about 10 – 15 minutes long (depending on the group).

■ The discussion can be lengthened, but should never exceed 30 minutes (this includes any clearing up after a discussion).

Group presentations

In the timetable above there are two opportunities for learners to participate as a group. These opportunities include periods such as music and movement, scientific, mathematical games and activities, dramatisation of well-known stories, rhymes and verses, language games, as well as story time. For children in the reception year, these are very important times of the day as they learn to participate as a group in a situation where the teacher can direct their play so that it helps them to learn. As the learner is still learning to be part a group, these periods should not be very long.

Free choice activities inside and outside the classroom

Plan a variety of activities that the learners can choose from, both inside and outside the classroom. (See examples in the timetable.) Remember to do the following:

■ provide learners with a variety of activities which become more difficult progressively

■ observe the children to make sure that every learner is experiencing a balanced variety of activities. (See Chapter 7 *Assessment of the whole learner, Participation charts.*)

Different activities inside the classroom should take place simultaneously, not one after the other. This provides learners with an opportunity to choose which activity they want to do, and they should decide for themselves the order in which they will tackle the different activities. The same principle applies to outdoor activities.

Outside activities are also very important. *Playing outdoors* in the reception year is not the same as *playtime* in the primary school. In other words, instead of simply a 'break' from the indoor classroom activities, playing outdoors is seen as an important part of a *balanced timetable*. (See the discussion on balance and outdoor activities later on in this chapter.)

Routine activities

Routine activities (arrival and departure, refreshments, toilet routine and rest) are included in the daily timetable, as the young learner still needs help with his or her physical care. You, the teacher, must help the learner to become more independent physically during the reception year.

Guidelines when planning a timetable for the reception year class

The following four guidelines will help you develop a well-balanced timetable.

1. Meet the unique needs of the learners in your class

   It is not possible to provide a timetable for all reception year classes as each class will (and must) have different needs. A good teacher will take the specific group into consideration and plan the daily timetable according to their needs.

   The following are examples of how the unique needs of learners can be taken into consideration:

   - Learners living in high-density population areas (e.g. learners who live in flats or apartments with very little outdoor space) will have different needs from learners who live in rural, farming areas.

   - Learners from disadvantaged communities have special needs that must be accommodated. For example, these learners may have needs regarding language acquisition, and therefore more time for language activities should be included in the programme.

   - Learners whose mother tongue is not English must become familiar with English (in a very informal way). Set aside time for activities to introduce English to the class.

   - If there are any learners who have developmental or learning barriers, set aside time for individual or small group activities for them.

2. Provide activities that will cater for the whole learner

   As the purpose of the reception year is to develop the whole learner, it is very important to provide activities that will help you to achieve this goal. Teachers should strive to develop every facet of the learner, and not focus solely on perceptual and intellectual abilities. For example, learners should be encouraged to think for themselves, appreciate beauty and care about the world around them.

   The learner's **physical development** can be encouraged by arranging:

   - activities which require that the learner use his or her whole body (gross motor activities). This can be accommodated in activities such as movement and Music, as well as opportunities for outdoor play using big climbing apparatus

   - activities that develop the learner's finger muscles (fine motor skills) such as Art and games that use small beads

   - activities such as going to the toilet and eating snacks, all of which help the learner to become physically independent – an important developmental milestone.

The learner's **emotional development**, including aesthetic and moral development, can be encouraged by including activities such as:

- art activities
- story time
- music and movement activities
- religious instruction.

These activities help learners to feel better about themselves, care for others and appreciate beauty in the world around them.

The learner's **intellectual and creative development** can be encouraged by including activities such as:

- *story time* and *music*, which help language development and may also serve as an introduction into a second (or third) language. The timetable should include periods when learners can talk freely both to each other and to you, the teacher

- *scientific, mathematical and educational games*, which help to develop learners' problem solving skills as well as number and concept skills

- *excursions*, which provide learners with an understanding of the world around them

- *art* and other activities where learners are required to think creatively and to develop new ideas.

3. The timetable must be balanced

In order to meet the needs of children in the reception year, a balanced timetable is required. A balanced timetable does not mean an equal amount of time for each activity – rather, time allocated to various activities must be balanced according to the needs of the learners. The order of the activities on the timetable must also be balanced. This means there must be variety in the nature of the activities.

A balance of the following activities must be evident in the timetable:

a) Indoor and outdoor activities

Outdoor activities are often regarded as *unimportant*, or merely *playtime*. Time for outdoor activities in the reception year is very important, because:

- young learners who spend too much time inside a classroom become bored, unruly and difficult to handle

- outdoor activities provide opportunities for learners to use their whole bodies while climbing and running freely

- the learners can learn about the environment in an active and concrete way (e.g. the changes in the seasons).

b) Free choice activities and adult-guided group activities

A good timetable will include presentations, where children can play and work individually according their own choice (i.e. they have the freedom to choose to engage in a variety of activities in the classroom and outside) and group activities under direct adult guidance.

Young learners need to play freely in order to make independent discoveries and to solve problems *on their own*. Young learners who play alone at all times will however not develop their full potential; young learners *need* adults.

Adult-guided activities are those activities where the teacher gives guidelines and helps the child to participate in a specific activity such as music, science, movement, story time and language activities. These are important as they offer a break from active free play and redirect the learners' attention.

c) Group and individual activities

The young learner requires individual attention. The timetable must therefore include times where you can give individual attention to each learner. This can be done during the times when children are engaged in both indoor and outdoor activities. During these times you should also plan specific activities to present to learners with barriers or specific needs.

d) Active and 'quiet' activities

Young learners cannot be busy all the time. They need times to rest or to take part in more *passive* activities. Therefore there should be a balance between activities where learners are running around and being very active, and more relaxing, calm activities.

For example, after intense outdoor activities, you could get learners involved in a more relaxed group discussion alternated with active activities, such as story dramatisation or an active music representation.

4. Take the school into consideration

When planning a timetable you should consider the physical characteristics of the school and classroom. Ask yourself questions such as:

- Is the classroom big enough to divide into different areas?
- If the classroom is small, can more than one classroom be used in which to present different activities?
- Are there times when the children should not play outside as they will disturb the other classes?

The answers to these questions will help you to plan a timetable that will satisfy the needs of the reception year class as well the rest of the school.

When planning the daily timetable you should also take the weather and the time of the year into consideration. Weather extremes such as very hot summers or bitterly cold winters should influence your timetable.

Example

If your school is in Gauteng, plan your timetable so that during summer the learners will play outside early in the morning and in winter they will stay inside until later in the morning, when the outside temperature is more comfortable.

Planning the classroom and outdoor play area

The proper planning of the classroom and of the outdoor play activities is very important for successful teaching in the reception class. Learners require enough well planned space in order to learn through play. As has been mentioned before, a variety of simultaneous activities should be planned. Even a small classroom can offer the learners exciting play opportunities if you are willing to plan with creativity and work hard at making the most of the available space. The best way to plan for a variety of play and learning opportunities is to organise the classroom into *areas*. In the reception class the following areas should be made available:

- block play and big construction area
- Emergent Reading area (book area)
- Emergent Science and Mathematics area
- educational games area
- small construction and fine motor skills area
- Art area
- fantasy play area.

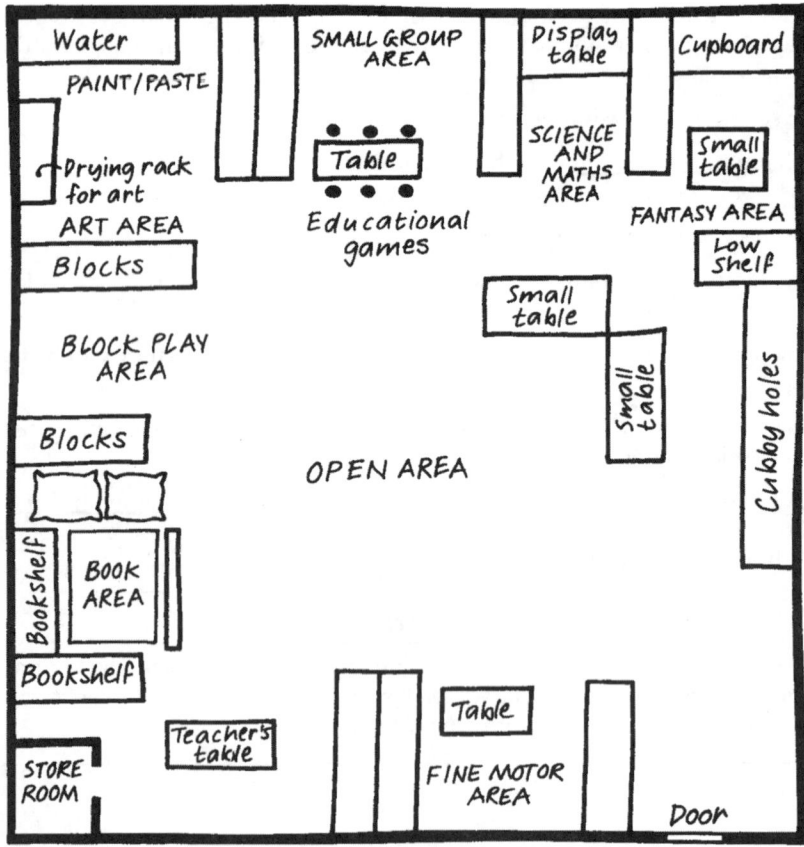

Figure 1.1 – Example of a reception year classroom

Remember
Remember that the most important element for a successful classroom is a relaxed atmosphere! Do not expect a quiet classroom. A successful classroom is humming with activity.

Planning the different areas in the classroom

There is no strict rule when planning the different areas in a classroom for the reception year. The number of areas in the classroom will depend on:

- the size of the classroom
- the number of learners in the group
- the needs and interests of the group.

If the classroom is too small to accommodate all the areas mentioned above, change the areas weekly or bi-weekly in order to give the learners the opportunity to learn from all the different activities.

1. Block play and big construction area

   - This area should be in a part of the class where there is not a lot of traffic, so that the blocks will not be knocked over by passing learners.

   - If possible, learners should be able to leave constructions overnight for further play the next day. This will encourage more intricate constructions by the learners.

   - The area must be big enough so that children can build without being disturbed by other learners.

   - The surface must be smooth so that the constructions can stand firmly.

   - Blocks should be stored in shelves that have the outlines of the different blocks at the back. This will help learners to put the blocks back in an orderly way, as well as to develop their visual discrimination and classification skills.

   - Ideally, there should be enough blocks for meaningful play. Limit the number of learners that can play at any one time, so that the learners have enough blocks to build a *realistic* construction. It is also a good idea to supplement the block supply with cardboard boxes for the learners to use.

   - Extra equipment such as small figures (made from clothes pegs) and toy cars and trucks should be made available. This will encourage the learners to play according to a theme. (For more information on the development of block play, see Chapter 2: *Know the Child.*)

2. Emergent Reading area (Book area)

   - This must be in a quiet part of the playroom (not next to the art area).

   - The book area must be an attractive area that will invite the learners to page through books.

   - The floor covering should be comfortable and inviting. (Ideally this would include a carpet and colourful cushions on which the learners can sit while they page through the books.)

- The books must not be piled in a heap, but should rather be displayed on a shelf. Another inexpensive way of displaying books is to hang a rope from one wall to another and to hang the books over the stretched rope.

- The shelves or rope must be low enough for the learners to see the books and to handle them by themselves.

- The area need not be very big as the learners sit still and do not need to move around. Seating should be available for about five learners.

- If possible, the book area should be screened off from the rest of the class. A low shelf or a screen can be used (even if this is made from cardboard).

- There need not be many books at a time. About ten suitable books are sufficient for a week or two.

3. Emergent Science and Mathematics area

This consists of a display area where real objects from nature and the world around us are displayed. It need not be very big, and is best located in a corner of the classroom.

The following can be included in this area:

- Collections of objects from nature, for example stones, shells, feathers from different birds, seeds, dried flowers and leaves. Keep these in flat boxes with a corresponding picture of the collection on the lid. Learners should be allowed to look at and touch these collections.

- A simple microscope and/or magnifying glass for the learners to look more closely at objects.

- Books on scientific themes that are aimed at young learners.

The following elements are also important:

- An area where *simple experiments* can be carried out. For example: 'Which flower grows best, the one that gets water and light or the one that gets only water?' (See Chapter 5 *The Learner's World of Mathematics*.)

- *Paper and pencils* which must be made available for the learners to use if they want to record their findings by drawing pictures.

- A *bulletin board* for posters, such as a weather poster and a schedule reflecting what the learners should complete daily.

- A *display board* for displaying posters and pictures with a scientific theme.

4. Educational games area

A wide variety of games which develop certain perceptual skills is available, e.g. dominoes and memory games. These games can be either bought or made. Although buying games can be expensive, try to include them in the budget as they help improve the children's:

a) concentration

b) abstract reasoning

c) number concept

d) shape and colour discrimination.

The following considerations are important when setting up this area:

- Depending on the availability of space and tables, games can be played on a carpet or at tables.
- Space allocated for this area must accommodate at least four learners.
- Do not set out all available games at the same time. Have the games on a nearby shelf for the learners to choose from, or put no more than two games at a time on the carpet or table. Change the games at least every second day.

5. Small construction and fine motor area

This area includes activities such as small building blocks, beads and thread, and puzzles. When choosing suitable play materials, keep the following in mind:

- Start with bigger blocks or beads until the learners have the fine muscle control to pick up and use smaller ones.
- Start with puzzles with five pieces and gradually increase the pieces. Provide a *variety* of puzzles for this area. They can be made inexpensively by using pictures and cardboard. Puzzles are very good for the development of visual discrimination and figure-ground perception.

The following considerations are important when setting up this area:

- Activities should take place at tables, as small pieces can be lost easily on a carpet.
- Do not put all available puzzles or blocks out at the same time, but keep some back for later in the year. Try to expose the children to puzzles of varying difficulty levels.
- Check the puzzles and count the blocks every day. Search for missing pieces immediately.
- Later in the year, include the activities of building and threading of beads according to a plan or design. This helps to develop the learners' sense of position in space as well as visual discrimination.

6. Art area

Because four different art activities should be provided simultaneously, it is important to plan this area very carefully.

- The area should have good lighting, i.e. it must either be near windows or have lights overhead.
- There must be water nearby. (Supply water in a nearby basin if necessary.)
- Make sure that you can supervise the whole area, even if you are helping a learner in another area.
- There must be enough space for learners to work comfortably. Remember that some activities can be done on the floor.
- You must be able to clean all surfaces easily. For this reason, do not use carpets as flooring in this area.
- There must be a place for the drying of completed paintings or pasted artwork.
- Learners' work should be displayed throughout the year.

7. Fantasy play area

As a teacher you may feel that a fantasy area is nothing more than simply a play area. In fact, this area is a very important tool in the development and exploration of a child's creativity. In the fantasy area the learner has the opportunity to:

a) talk freely and creatively

b) learn social skills without interference from adults

c) think in an imaginative way (symbolically).

Example

The learner might imagine that a wooden block is an iron. Applying this *new meaning* to objects is very important for the child's intellectual and creative development.

The following are some guidelines when planning a fantasy play area:

- Situate this area in the corner of the classroom to avoid a constant flow of learners through it.

- Put low shelves or a screen around it to create a separate area.

- Change the theme of the area at least once a month or ensure that it fits an appropriate theme. It can be an imaginary house, hospital, shop, post office, hairdresser or doctor's consulting rooms. In order to encourage different themes you should call this area the 'fantasy play area', and not the 'house corner' or 'doll's house'!

- Provide a variety of old clothes and other accessories for the learners to play with. Use your imagination and always be on the look out for any 'junk'.

- Make sure that you provide clothes representing both male and female roles. Provide a variety of props, such as briefcases and old cell phone covers for 'executives', and not only pots and pans and baby dolls.

- The clothes must also represent different cultural groups – for example, provide saris and caftans, and not only western dresses.

- Dolls must represent all colours and ages.

- Provide enough storage space so that the learners *themselves* can tidy up.

If possible, this area must be big enough to accommodate a few learners playing together.

Maintaining discipline in the classroom

Discipline can be a problem for a teacher with a classroom with many areas, and with many different activities happening simultaneously. Keep the following guidelines in mind:

- Decide in advance what rules are required for your class.

- Be realistic when setting up rules. For example, do not expect the learners to be quiet while working, although it is not unreasonable to expect them not to shout.

- Keep the rules to a minimum.

- Apply all rules consistently.

- All corrections must be positive and must be backed up with an explanation.

> **Example**
>
> Do not shout: 'Stop running!' Rather say: 'We walk in the class, because the classroom is small and you might knock the paint over.'

Planning the outdoor play area

Learners need lots of opportunities to use their whole bodies, therefore it is important to allocate time for outdoor play in the timetable of the reception year. The playground for the reception year class needs to be planned as carefully as the classroom.

The playground must provide learners with a variety of opportunities

Plan for the following opportunities outside:

1. Gross motor activities

   It is important to plan for activities where the learners will be using their whole bodies (gross motor skills). The learners must have the space to run, climb, balance and practice coordination. Plan for open areas and climbing apparatus (or even a big, strong tree.)

2. Science activities

   The outdoor area facilitates various 'scientific' discoveries where learners can have direct, concrete experiences of nature. The changes in nature and the growth cycle can be observed on a daily basis by the learners when they spend time outside. It is important to plan for an area where the learners can make a garden and experience how plants grow. Keeping suitable animals (not pets), such as small breed chickens, hamsters and rabbits in suitable cages will introduce the learners in a natural way to the cycle of life.

3. Social play

   It is important for learners to have a big, open area where they can play games freely. This large outdoor play area provides learners with opportunities to form bigger groups that play together.

4. Large constructions

   Provide an area where the learners can make large constructions with big boxes or old blankets. This area provides opportunities for creative play using a theme.

5. Quiet area

   Learners also need time to play alone. Include a quiet corner – for example, a blanket laid out on the grass in a shady area with books to page through.

How to plan for successful outdoor play

Keep the following in mind when planning an outdoor play area:

■ Where possible, include manufactured equipment (such as a jungle gym) as well as homemade equipment (such as rope swings on a tree). Also use natural 'equipment' such as trees for a variety of climbing experiences.

■ Movable equipment (such as sturdy ladders and frames) are very useful in order to rearrange the playground for new combinations of activities.

■ Old barrels, tyres and crates can also be add to the playground. (Paint or stain all wooden equipment to remove splinters and make sure it is safe for children to play on.)

■ Grass and flowers add to the appearance of the playground and give the learners further opportunities to discover nature.

■ Add a vegetable garden and flowerbeds where the learners can create their own garden.

■ Plan for an area where learners can run freely (not near the swings).

■ If possible, include a traffic area with tricycles (small bicycles) or cars made of wire.

■ Plan to present additional outdoor activities everyday (excluding the fixed outdoor play equipment). Activities such as art, woodwork, water play, and reading of stories can be presented by teachers during free play outdoors.

You have a very important role during outdoor play
Outdoor play is *not* the time for teacher to sit down away from the children and enjoy a cup of tea! You are just as involved and on duty (if not more so) as during the other periods in the timetable.

■ Thorough and constant supervision during outdoor play is of the utmost importance.

■ It is the teacher's responsibility to ensure that all equipment is well looked after and safe for use. Rather be without certain equipment than have broken and dangerous equipment which could hurt children.

■ Encourage the learners to explore. Let them try out new ways to do well-known outdoor activities, always keeping safety in mind.

■ *Plan* for every day's outdoor play period – it is an important period in the timetable!

Choosing suitable learning content (Themes and activities)

Without something to teach, there can be no education. The teacher's task is to facilitate the learning of certain knowledge, skills, values and attitudes throughout the year. In the reception year class we use suitable themes to organise the learning content, rather than separate learning areas or subjects.

As a reception year teacher it is your task to choose suitable themes and activities. There are no 'prescribed' themes. Instead the curriculum only provides the guidelines set by the Learning Outcomes and Assessment Standards for the reception year.

Advantages of the teacher choosing themes are:

■ you can plan activities to suit your group

■ themes can be changed if they prove to be unsuitable (i.e. themes are not fixed).

Disadvantages of the teacher choosing themes are:

■ Without prescribed themes you may feel lost, or you may not know where to start.

■ The absence of prescribed themes demands more from you! You have to plan and work out relevant topics yourself.

Choosing suitable themes

Deciding what themes are suitable for the reception year is no easy task. Teachers have to guard against teaching information to the learners simply because 'it is what we usually teach' or '*I think* it will be suitable'.

Here are five main principles to help you choose suitable themes for the reception year. Themes and activities must be:

- linked to the Learning Outcomes of the reception year
- developmentally appropriate
- relevant and meaningful to your group
- multi-cultural and unbiased
- fun and enjoyable.

Each of these principles can be used to 'test' the suitability of the themes and activities. All themes and activities must answer to all of the above principles. Each of these principles will now be discussed in more detail.

Themes and activities must be linked to the Learning Outcomes

When you are deciding on suitable themes and activities for your class the first question must be: 'What do I want to achieve with my teaching?' and 'What must the learners be able to do, know and feel after we have completed the theme and activities?'

In other words: 'What *Learning Outcomes* do I want to focus on?'

Because there is no fixed syllabus, instead of starting with the Learning Outcomes, teachers often ask: 'What can I do with my class?' or even worse 'What themes and activities can I present with the teaching resources that I have in my class?'.

When choosing a theme, always start with the Learning Outcome(s) you want to achieve.

Go to:

In the beginning of this chapter we discussed a grouping of Learning Outcomes for the different Learning Programmes of the reception year.

As each group of reception year learners is different, you should concentrate on different Learning Outcomes for every group. By assessing them you will be able to identify their strengths, as well as the areas in which they need help.

Go to:

(See Chapter 7 *Assessment of the whole learner.*)

Example

After assessing the group at the beginning of the year you realise that the group is exceptionally bright. For this particular group you would focus on Learning Outcomes that include the development of Emergent Writing skills by giving the learners opportunities to experiment with writing words on their own. A theme such as *The Grocery Shop* can accommodate Emergent Writing activities.

The group the year before was not as advanced and had struggled with basic fine muscle control. The Learning Outcomes that you focused on for them was developing the learners' fine motor skills so that they were able to handle a thick crayon/pencil with ease.

A theme such as *All things feel different* can include activities that enhance learners' finger and fine motor skills.

Every theme and activity you present must link directly to an outcome(s). This way you can ensure that your teaching effort is purposeful and directed!

Themes and activities must be developmentally appropriate

When we choose suitable themes and activities we have to take the behaviour and developmental level of the learner into account. When we do this, our teaching will be *developmentally appropriate.* This means that the teaching and learning is in line with the learner's physical, cognitive, social and language development. In other words, the teacher helps his or her group to learn and develop in ways that are compatible with their development and with who they are as individuals.

The teacher must know her class well in order to choose themes and activities that relate to the learners' abilities. The teacher must not select content merely because the learners will need it in Grade 1, but because it fits with their current level of development and interest. It is not only useless but also actually harmful to force learners to master work for which they are not yet physically and psychologically ready.

This does not mean that the learners must only take part in easy activities. While it is important not to present activities that children are not ready for, it is equally important to progress to more difficult themes and activities throughout the year.

Morrison (2001: 279) states four principles of developmentally appropriate practices:

■ Learning must be meaningful to the learners and relate to what they already know. Learners find things meaningful when they find them interesting and can relate to them.

■ Learners do not learn in the same way and are not always interested in learning the same things as everyone else. Teachers must individualise the learning experience as much as possible.

■ Learners should be physically and mentally active. Learners should be actively involved in building, experimenting, investigating and working collaboratively with their peers.

■ Learning should be based on real-life activities as opposed to workbooks and work sheet activities.

Themes must be relevant and meaningful to the learner

The principle that themes and activities are meaningful to your group is closely linked to the principle of developmental appropriateness. Themes must be relevant to the learners so that they can identify with the content.

The following are some ideas regarding themes for the reception year:

■ *The environment where the learner lives:* This is a rich source of ideas for themes.

> ### Example
>
> A theme such as *'Mealie farming'* will be very relevant for learners in Bothaville (a large mealie farming area) but less relevant for learners in Hillbrow (a densely populated urban area).

■ *What is happening in the learner's community:* Activities in the community can also be a source of themes.

> ### Example
>
> The cleaning up of a river by the community can be used to introduce the topic: *'We care for our land'* (Nature conservation).

■ *The topics of the children's play:* Use the topics from the children's play times as themes for your teaching. While it is true that you cannot rely on this as the only source of themes, it will help you to keep your themes relevant for the learners.

■ *The calendar:* Themes can also be selected according to the time of year and activities that are associated with any particular season (for example the harvesting of summer and winter fruits).

Important days such as Christmas, and public holidays such as 'Family Day', can also be used as themes. Always keep your group in mind, especially when using religious holidays as a theme. Make sure that the holiday is relevant for all the learners. You can also use these days to teach the learners about the different cultural groups in our country.

Themes must be multi-cultural and anti-biased

Multi-cultural education should begin with the learner's earliest experiences at school. It is your task to make sure that the learner's experiences are positive and to help to form a positive attitude towards other cultures.

> ### Definition
>
> Culture means the system of shared meanings that a group of people have developed regarding the way they live.

This means that themes selected for the reception year must be representative of all the different groups in the class and in South Africa. Multi-cultural education must:

■ teach learners to recognise and value the *differences* between people

■ stress the *similarities* between cultures

- develop greater *understanding* of different cultures
- aim at developing *respect* between groups.

Example

By using themes such as *Food that I enjoy most* and *Special clothes for special days* the teacher can introduce the class to different cultures and customs. The following are some suggestions for illustrating these:

- Ask caregivers from different cultural groups to send traditional dishes to school or to demonstrate to the group how to prepare a traditional dish.

- Let learners wear traditional clothes to school and let them tell the other learners when these are traditionally worn.

Use traditional holidays as a source for multi-cultural themes. Different cultural groups celebrate the same religious occasion differently (for example, Dutch, British and German people celebrate Christmas in different ways) and different groups also celebrate different holidays (for example, the Muslim celebration of Eid or the Jewish celebration of the Passover). Ask the learners in your group if they have special feast days or celebrations. Ask the parents to visit the school and to talk about their customs to the class.

Remember

*Not all people from the same cultural, gender, age or ability group are the same. Do not treat them as if they are – this is called **stereotyping**. Teach children that while people are **different**, they are also **the same**. For example, we all live in houses, wear clothes and eat food, but our houses, clothes and food may differ as a result of cultural differences.*

Ensure that play materials are also multi-cultural and anti-biased

- Select storybooks that include all groups of people. Also ensure that no book contains stereotypes of any cultural, age or gender group.

- In the fantasy play area, make dolls available that represent all groups. Also include clothes and accessories that represent all groups. (For example, a class that has learners from an oriental background might have a wok, kimonos, and so on in the fantasy play area, while traditional tribal dress might be provided in a class made up of learners of African descent.)

- Photographs and posters in the classroom should represent the diversity of people in the world.

- Games and other manipulative materials should be selected with the aim of including non-stereotyped characters and scenes. If you are unable to purchase materials that reflect an unbiased approach, create your own.

- Books are a rich source of anti-bias material. Before purchasing a new book, think about what you want to achieve with the book. Include books on non-traditional families, different cultures, habits and languages. The emphasis should be on the diversity of people, while simultaneously showing learners that they can relate to people of different cultures.

■ In order for multi-cultural education to be successful, it must be a part of every school day. Learners will learn from your attitudes and behaviour, and therefore it is important that you respect all groups and understand something about their customs.

Themes must be fun!

One of the most important principles when choosing a suitable theme is that the theme must be fun for the learners. If the learners do not enjoy what you want to teach them they will not learn from it. Try to be creative when you choose a theme.

Example

Beware of themes such as *Healthy food*. Rather choose a theme such as *Food I love best!* You can still include a discussion on healthy food, and still capture the learners' attention.

Remember

When choosing suitable themes for learners in the reception year we have to take the young child's behaviour into consideration. Young children:

■ *are **egocentric** (see themselves as the most important people in the world)*

■ *learn best when they use all their senses and are **actively** involved*

■ *experience the world around them as a whole.*

Bearing these characteristics in mind, you should:

■ take the child as your starting point when choosing suitable themes

■ present a theme by linking most (but not all) activities presented during the week to that theme

■ plan themes that are fun!

Using an integrated approach (cross-curriculum)

The integrated approach, using themes, is very suitable for young learners because they learn about the world around them systematically, yet the theme is still treated as a whole.

A theme is chosen by you, the teacher, and is then extended to the learners through the various activities they perform. This theme is used for a day, or a week or two (depending on the theme), and links the different activities.

Most (but not necessarily all) presentations and activities should fit into the central theme. There must however also be activities (e.g. religious stories) which do not link up with the theme and which have been specially selected to satisfy needs of learners in the group.

Using the theme you should plan related activities in all the Learning Areas, but not as separated subjects. Rather, the Learning Areas should be integrated in developmentally appropriate activities for your reception year learners. Plan different activities so that the learners can experience the theme in different ways.

Why do we use an integrated approach?

Many teachers accept the idea of teaching learners under five in an integrated way, but they often feel that five- to eight-year-olds need to learn isolated skills in well-defined school subjects. This is a misconception about the way the child in reception year learns.

The reception year learner still needs to:

- learn through real-life experiences
- use new knowledge in everyday situations – 'book knowledge' is difficult for the reception year learner to retain
- learn new knowledge by exploring it in different ways – e.g. singing, talking about it and doing it
- experiment and become involved with the new information
- be interested in what he or she learns.

By using an integrated approach we achieve all the above and the learner also experiences the school day (or week) as an integrated unit.

How to plan for an integrated approach

The following steps may help you to plan for an integrated approach in the reception year. These steps merely serve as a guide.

STEP 1: Identify the Learning Outcome(s) you wish to focus on.

As mentioned earlier in the chapter, the first step in outcomes-based education is to identify the Learning Outcomes that the learners should achieve.

STEP 2: Decide on a suitable theme for your class.

We have already discussed guidelines for choosing a suitable theme. Choose a relevant and meaningful theme that will help the learners achieve the Learning Outcomes you have already identified.

> **Remember**
> The theme itself is not your 'aim' – it is merely the vehicle you use to help learners achieve the Learning Outcome!

STEP 3: Do research about the theme.

Learn as much about the theme as you can. For example:

- explore the environment of the learners in your group so that you can link the theme to their own world and experiences effectively
- visit places linked to the theme
- read about the theme. Make sure that you know enough about the theme to explain it in simple terms and answer learners' questions about it.

At this stage it is useful to draw a **topic map**. A topic map (also called a spider web) is a diagram of all the related topics and information that you have identify in your research of the theme. Start with the theme in the centre and then expand on all the relevant information.

> **Example**
> An example of an extended topic map on 'Celebrations' – (Hessari & Hill 1989: 50)

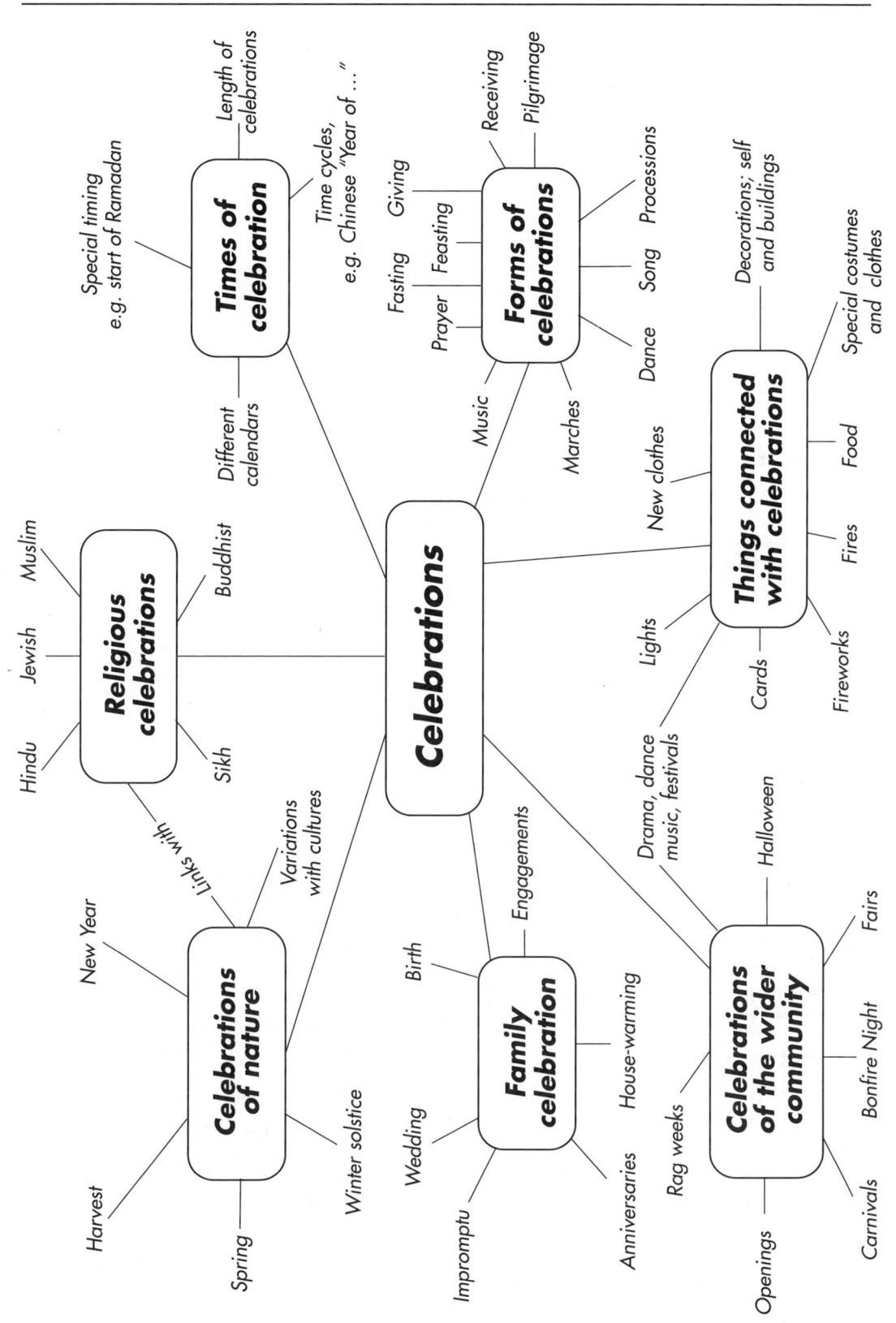

STEP 4: Consider questions your class may ask

When you plan a theme, try and identify possible questions that your class will ask. This will help you to identify the key concepts of the theme, as well as prepare for the following step: selecting activities.

STEP 5: Select appropriate activities

By using the topic map and the questions and key concepts you have identified, you can start to plan suitable activities. Select activities that will answer the questions you have identified. To ensure that you have a balance of activities, use the different learning areas to order your planning. This is also called a curriculum web.

Example

Example of a curriculum web on a theme suitable for the first week of school at the beginning of the year.

Me, Myself And My Family

Me, Myself and My Family

Life Orientation
Discuss the different roles in the family.
Discuss emotions: We can be sad and happy.
What makes us happy and sad?

Mathematics
Count fingers, toes, eyes, nose.
(Also discuss body image.)
Introduce circle, square, triangle.
Weigh and measure learners.
Simple graph of learners' weight and height.

Social Science
Each person has a birthday. How do we celebrate birthdays?
We can be happy – what makes us happy?
We can be sad – what makes us sad?

Technology
Plan and make a simple toy for a baby.

Economic & Management Sciences
Discuss different careers of parents.
Give learners a turn to discuss what they would like to be when they are adults.

Arts and Culture
Art: Draw, paste and paint picture of family.
Cut out and paste facial features from a magazine to form a funny face.
Cut out and paste happy/sad pictures.
Draw outline of bodies on big pieces of newspaper and paint in the features.
Introduce red, blue and yellow – one at a time using finger paint.
Dance and movement: Listen to music and move according to the music.
Play musical chairs.
Clap the beat of each learner's name – body percussion.
If English is the additional language:
Learn the song: 'Head and shoulders, knees and toes.'

Language
Display baby photos and recent photos in the class. Have discussions about how we change and grow.
Make a birthday chart for the class.
Read stories such as *Happy birthday, Sam* (by Pat Hutchins).
Read poems.

Natural Sciences
Name basic body parts.
Observe and discuss differences between older and younger persons (babies and reception year learners; as well as learners and teachers).
Talk about food that we love.

By using the above format, you can ensure that all learning areas are covered in an interesting and meaningful way through the theme.

STEP 6: Gather all the necessary teaching and learning resources

Learning about the theme must be an active investigation for the learners. Provide them with a variety of teaching and learning resources to stimulate questions and discussions.

Collect and plan the following resources:

- appropriate field trips and visits
- props for play in the fantasy area in the classroom
- accessories to add to the block play area
- suitable books to add to the emergent reading area (book area) and science area
- suitable activities for the Science and Mathematics areas
- posters for the Science area and/or table
- recipes for food experiences
- pictures to use in group discussions
- suitable stories, poems and rhymes to read to and teach to your class
- visits by people from the community to talk about the theme (if suitable)

 **Remember**
Plan for spontaneous play opportunities as well. Learners must have time to express through play what they have experienced.

STEP 7: Plan a concluding activity

A concluding activity is an activity that brings all the learning together. This activity can be, for example:

- a mural
- a class book on the theme
- a play
- creation of a hospital/post office/home in the fantasy area of the class
- an activity that involves the whole class – e.g. a traditional meal or celebration
- building a model in which all learners participate.

STEP 8: Assess the success of the theme

Assess whether your group achieved the Learning Outcomes for the theme. Also assess whether the theme was relevant, meaningful and enjoyable for your learners. You can assess the success of the theme by listening to the learners' conversations during activities. Samples of the learners' artwork can also be used to assess what they understood of the theme. All this information will be useful for improving the theme when you repeat it at a later time.

> **Remember**
> *A general guide for deciding how long a theme should be used: No shorter than a week and no longer than two weeks. This 'rule' is not fixed and it will depend on how long the theme can hold learners' interest. It is better to end a theme too soon than to continue when interest has faded.*

Written planning of teaching in the reception year

After you have planned a suitable theme you should plan how you are going to present the theme to your group. You can do this by completing a written weekly plan (an overall summary of all the activities for a week) and then a more detailed daily planning for each separate presentation you are going to present.

Written planning must be done at least two weeks in advance to give you enough time to collect all the necessary resources for the activities.

> **Remember**
> *In the following section we will discuss two possible forms of written planning. But remember, they are only examples of possible ways to complete this important task. Different schools may have different prescribed methods of planning, but the most important thing to note is that written planning must take place.*

A weekly plan

A weekly plan includes all the activities you want to present over a week, including:

- indoor free play (including Art activities)
- group discussions on the theme, Emergent Literacy, Numeracy and Life Skills
- group activities (including Music, Movement and story time).

A WEEKLY PLAN

Group:.. Teacher: ....

Date: .... Theme: ....

Learning Outcomes: ....

Assessment Standards: ....

Assessment Method(s): ....

....

DAY	FREE PLAY	GROUP DISCUSSIONS	GROUP PRESENTATIONS
	Indoors & Outdoors (indicate all activities available)	(indicate type and theme)	Music/ Story/ Movement/ Poems (Title & Source)
Monday			
Tuesday			
Wednesday			
Thursday			
Friday			

Use the planning form above to produce an overall summary of activities you are planning to present over a week period. This kind of written planning will help you to:

- improve your teaching because you will know what you want to achieve, and will have reflected on this before starting the week

- ensure that the theme will develop over the week. The simplest activities can be presented first, followed by increasingly difficult or complex activities over the course of the week.

- have a story, a variety of group presentations and discussions every day

- be focused on the Learning Outcomes for the week

- have more freedom to make changes if something unforeseen happens. Being well prepared will help you to be able to use unexpected opportunities to enrich the learning experiences.

Daily planning

After you have completed the weekly planning you should plan every presentation in more detail. Good written planning should include at least the following:

1. General information

   Include information about:

   a) The class or group for which you plan to present the activity

   b) The type of presentation (i.e. not simply 'Art', but the specific kind of Art activity)

   c) The theme of the activity. This will usually but not always link with the theme of the week.

   d) Length of the presentation. You should ensure that the presentation is neither too long nor too short. Group activities should never be longer than 30 minutes from the beginning until the end (all aspects of the activity included).

2. Learning Outcomes

   The Learning Outcomes you want the learners to achieve.

3. Assessment Standards and assessment method(s)

   Assessment is an important part of every presentation. (Assessment of the reception year learner will be discussed in detail in Chapter 7. At this stage it is simply important to know that you have to plan for assessment.)

   What learners already know about the theme or activity (prior knowledge)

   A teacher must know about what the learners already know about the theme. The presentation must be based on prior knowledge, i.e. it must link to what they already know. Prior knowledge can be based on previous experiences, activities, a story or an outing. Being aware of learners' prior knowledge will help you to ensure that the presentation is not too easy or too difficult and that it will fall within learners' experience of the world.

5. Presentation

   This includes the following:

   a) Introduction, including the lesson outcome(s) and resources required for this part of the presentation. It is important to have a good introduction to capture the learners' interest in the theme. The teacher should introduce the presentation (or new theme or information) by linking it to what the learners already know. The activity should attract the learners' attention and keep them focused on the rest of the presentation.

   b) Core of presentation, including the lesson outcome(s) and resources required for this part of the presentation. This will depend on the type of presentation. A music presentation will differ from movement or story telling, and so on. This is the heart of the presentation and must be well planned.

   c) Conclusion of presentation, including the lesson outcome(s) and resources required for this part of the presentation. It is important to end a presentation in a satisfactory way. A very active activity such as music and movement needs a calming conclusion.

Resources you plan to use in the presentation must add to the value presentation and should be well made and well used. They serve an important purpose. *Teaching resources* are used to help present new information to the learners successfully. *Learning resources* are used by learners to help them understand and learn the new information more easily. The choice of resources depends on:

■ the type of presentation

■ the developmental level and interests of the group.

Remember
Every activity in your presentation must be directly linked to the Learning Outcome(s) you want to achieve. Every activity must have a purpose.

An example of a written presentation plan for the reception year:

(1) General information:

    Group: .... Date: ....

    Type of presentation: ....

    Theme: .... Duration: ....

(2) Learning Outcomes: ....

    ....

(3) Assessment Standards and Assessment Method(s): ....

    ....

    ....

(4) Learner's expected prior knowledge: ....

    ....

(5) Presentation: ....

    Introduction: .... Learning Outcome: .... Resource(s): ....

    Core: .... Learning Outcomes: .... Resource(s): ....

    Conclusion: .... Learning Outcomes: .... Resource(s): ....

Conclusion

This chapter has provided an overall summary of what is expected from you as a reception year teacher.

In the next chapters you will find more detailed information regarding teaching learners in the reception year. You will also find a complete example of a theme worked out for all Learning Programmes and activities of the reception year, in Chapter 8.

May the rest of the book inspire you to become the best teacher you can be. But remember that becoming the best teacher you can be is set in your heart, and not only in the knowledge you have.

Bibliography

Adams, L. 1996. Quality curriculum for quality care and education. In: *International Journal of Early Childhood.* (Vol. 28 no 2) (pp 49 – 52).

Atkin, J. 1991. Thinking about play. In: Hall, N & Abbott, L (Eds). *Play in the primary curriculum.* London: Taylor & Francis. (pp 29 – 36).

Barbour, N & Seefeldt, C. 1993. *Developmental continuity across preschool and primary grades: implications for teachers.* Wheaton: Association for Childhood Education International.

Beaty, J. 1992. *Preschool Appropriate Practices.* Fort Worth: Harcourt Brace Jovanovich College Publishers.

Beaty, J J. 1996 (5th ed). *Skills for preschool teachers.* Englewood Cliffs: Merrill.

Cassel, R N. 1995. Accountability for early childhood education. (Assessing global functioning) In: *Reading Improvement.* (Vol 32 no 1) (pp 32 – 37).

Catron, C E & Allen, J. 1993. *Early childhood curriculum.* New York: Macmillan.

Chisholm, L. 2000. *A South African Curriculum for the Twenty First Century: Report of the Review Committee on the Curriculum 2005.* Pretoria: Staatsdrukkery.

Cole, M & Cole, S R. 1993. (2nd ed.) *The development of children.* New York: Scientific American Books.

David, T. 1996. (2nd ed.) Curriculum in the early years. In: Pugh, G (Ed) *Contemporary issues in the early years. Working collaboratively for children.* London: Paul Chapman. (pp 85 – 101).

Day, D E. 1983. *Early childhood education. A human ecological approach.* Illinois: Scott, Foresman and Company.

Department of Education. (Not dated). *Guidelines for developing learning programmes for Grade R.* Pretoria: Government Printers.

Department of Education. 1996. *Interim Policy for Early Childhood Development.* Pretoria: Government Printers.

Department of Education. 1997(a). *Curriculum 2005. Lifelong learning for the 21st century.* Cape Town: CTB Books.

Department of Education. 1997 (b). Foundation Phase. (Grades R to 3) Policy Document. October 1997. Pretoria: Government Printers.

Department of Education. 1997 (c). Norms and standards for teacher education, training and development. Technical committee on the revision of norms and standards for teacher education. Pretoria: Department of Education.

Department of Education. 1997 (d). Outcomes based education in South Africa. Background information for educators. Pretoria: Department of Education.

Department of Education. 2001. Education White Paper 6. Special needs Education. Building an inclusive education and training system. July 2001. Pretoria: Department of Education.

Department of Education. 2002 (a). Foundation Phase Learning Programme Policy Guidelines: Strenghtening Policy-in-action. Pretoria: Department of Education.

Department of Education. 2002 (b). Revised National Curriculum Statement Grades R – 9 (Schools) Policy: Overview English. Pretoria: Department of Education.

Department of Education. 2002 (c). Revised National Curriculum Statement Grades R – 9 (Schools) Policy: Mathematics. Pretoria: Department of Education.

Department of Education. 2002 (d). Revised National Curriculum Statement Grades R – 9 (Schools) Policy: Natural Sciences. Pretoria: Department of Education.

Department of Education. 2002 (e). Revised National Curriculum Statement Grades R – 9 (Schools) Policy: Technology. Pretoria: Department of Education.

Department of Education. 2002 (f). Revised National Curriculum Statement Grades R – 9 (Schools) Policy: Social Sciences. Pretoria: Department of Education.

Department of Education. 2002 (g). Revised National Curriculum Statement Grades R – 9 (Schools) Policy: Arts and Culture. Pretoria: Department of Education.

Department of Education. 2002 (h). Revised National Curriculum Statement Grades R – 9 (Schools) Policy: Life Orientation. Pretoria: Department of Education.

Department of Education. 2002 (i). Revised National Curriculum Statement Grades R – 9 (Schools) Policy: Economic and Management Sciences. Pretoria: Department of Education.

Department of Education. 2002 (j). Revised National Curriculum Statement Grades R – 9 (Schools) Policy: English - Home Language. Pretoria: Department of Education.

Department of Education. 2002 (k). Revised National Curriculum Statement Grades R – 9 (Schools) Policy: English - First Additional Language. Pretoria: Department of Education.

Department of Education. 2003. The revised National Curriculum Statements Foundation Phase Learning Programme Policy Guidelines. (Draft). Pretoria: Department of Education.

DeVries, R & Kohlberg, L. 1990. *Constructivist Early Education: Overview and comparison with other programs.* Washington, DC: National Association for the education of Young Children.

Dowling, M. 1988. *Education 3 to 5: A teacher's handbook.* London: Paul Chapman.

Draft White Paper on Education. 1994. The Draft White Paper on Education. Pretoria: Government Printers.

Eddowes, E A & Ralph, K S. 1998. *Interactions for development and learning. Birth through eight years.* Upper Saddle River, New Jersey: Merrill.

Edwards, A & Knight, P. 1994. *Effective early years education. Teaching young children.* Buckingham: Open University Press.

Elkind, E. 1996. Early Childhood Education: What should we expect? In: *Principal.* (Vol 75 no 5) (pp 11 – 13).

Essa, E L. 1999. (3rd ed.) *Introduction to early childhood education.* Albany: Delmar Publishers.

Faber, R J. 1996. *Introduction to teaching in the reception year.* Module 1. Unpublished. Study Guide for the Certificate in Reception Year Teaching. Pretoria: University of South Africa.

Feeney, S, Christensen, D & Moravcik, E. 2001. *Who am I in the lives of children?* Columbus: Merrill.

Fischer, J. 1996. Reflecting on the principles of early years practice. In: *Journal of Teacher Development.* (Vol 5 no 1) (pp 17 – 26).

Frazee, B & Rudnitski, R. 1995. *Integrated teaching methods: theory, classroom applications and field-based connections.* Albany, N.Y.: Delmar Publishers.

Gordon, A & Williams-Browne, K. 1995. (4th ed.) *Beginnings and Beyond.* Albany: Delmar.

Grey, J. 1998. Preparing for OBE. A New point of View. In: *The Teacher.* (Vol 3 no 1) (pp 6 – 7).

Grové, MC, Hauptfleich, HMAM & Sonnekus, MCH. 1977. *Perseptuele ontwikkeling. 'n Handleiding.* Pretoria: De Jager-Haum.

Gultig, J. 1997. *Understanding outcomes-based education. Knowledge, curriculum & assessment in South Africa.* Learning guide. South African Institute for Distance Education. Pretoria: Government Printers.

Gultig, J. 1998. *Understanding outcomes-based education. Teaching and assessment in South Africa.* Learning guide. South African Institute for Distance Education. Cape Town: Oxford University Press South Africa.

Hall, N & Abbott, L (eds) 1991. *Play in the primary curriculum.* London: Francis.

Harrod, C. 1998. The very early years. In: *EQ Australia.* (Vol 2) (pp 11 – 12).

Hendrick, J. 1994. (4th ed). *Total learning. Developmental curriculum for the young child.* New York: Merrill.

Hessari, R & Hill, D. 1989. *Practical ideas for multicultural learning and teaching in the primary classroom.* London: Routeledge.

Kagan, S L. 1992. Readiness past, present and future: Shaping the agenda. In: *Young Children.* (Vol 48, No 1) (pp 48 – 53).

Kemp, J. 1994. Failing the first year. Challenges facing South African education. In: *Information update.* (Vol 4 no 2) (pp 17 – 22).

King, E W; Chipman, M and Cruz-Janzen, M. 1994. *Educating Young Children in a Diverse Society.* Boston: Allyn and Bacon.

Kronowitz, E L. 1999. *Your first year of teaching and beyond.* New York: Longman.

Kudlas, J M. 1994. Implications of OBE. What you should know about outcomes-based education in *The Science Teacher* (Vol 61 no 5) (pp 32 – 35).

Lemmer, E M. 1998. Managing quality in education. In: *Outcomes-based education in South Africa.* Pretorius (Ed.) Johannesburg: Hodder & Stoughton. (pp 116 – 129).

Lubisi, C; Wedekind, V; Parker, B & Gultig, J. 1997. *Understanding outcomes-based education. Knowledge, Curriculum and Assessment in South Africa.* A Reader. A pilot module for the SAIDE Study of Education. South Africa Institute for Distance Education and the National Department of Education. Cape Town: CTB Book Printers.

Morrison, G S. 2001. (6th ed.) *Early childhood education today.* New Jersey: Merrill-Prentice Hall.

Moyles, J R. 1989. *Just playing? The role and status of play in early childhood education.* Milton Keynes: Open University Press.

Myles, K. 1997. The outcome of outcome based education. In: *Gifted.* (No 100) (pp. 24 – 26).

Nutbrown, C. 1994. *Threads of thinking. Young children learning and the role of early education.* London: Paul Chapman.

O'Brien, L M. 1996/97. Turning my world upside down: How I learned to question developmentally appropriate practice. In: *Childhood Education.* (Vol 73 no 2) (pp 100 – 102).

Pellegrini, A D & Dresden, J. 1991. The concept of Development in the Early childhood Curriculum. In: *Issues in Early Childhood curriculum. Yearbook in Early childhood Education Volume 2.* Spodek, B & Saracho, O. (Eds.). New York: Teachers College Press. (pp 46 – 63).

Penning, R J. 1986. *'n Didaktiese analise van die informele onderrigbenadering in die preprimêre skool.* Ongepubliseerde M Ed – verhandeling. Universiteit van Suid Afrika.

Read, K & Patterson, J. 1980. *The Nursery School and Kindergarten: Human Relationships and learning.* New York: Holt, Rinehart and Winston.

Reilly, P E. 1983. Learning in the early childhood in *Pre-school Years.* (13:6 – 12).

Republic of South Africa. 1994. Government Gazette. Department of Education. Draft White Paper on Education and Training. Pretoria: Government Printers.

Republic of South Africa. 2001. Government Gazette. Department of Education. Education White Paper 5 on Early Childhood Education. Meeting the challenges of Early Childhood Development in South Africa. Pretoria: Government Printers.

Rhee, Won Young. 1996. How the curriculum can lead to quality care in early childhood education. In: *International Journal of Early Childhood.* (Vol 28 no 2) (pp 69 – 74).

Robison, H F. 1983. (2nd ed.) *Exploring teaching in early childhood education.* Boston: Allyn and Bacon.

Roopnarine, J L & Johnson, J E. 1987. *Approaches to early childhood education.* Columbus: Merrill.

Saracho, O N. 1991. The role of play in the early childhood curriculum. In: *Issues in early Childhood Curriculum. Yearbook in Early Childhood Education.* (Vol 2). Spodek, B & Saracho, O N. (Eds) New York: Teachers College Press. (pp 86 – 105).

Seefeldt, C. 1980. *Teaching young children.* New Jersey: Prentice-Hall.

Seefeldt, C. 1989. (3rd ed.) *Social Studies for the Preschool-Primary Child.* Columbus: Merrill Publishing Company.

Seefeldt, C & Barbour, N. 1990. *Early childhood education. An introduction.* New York: Merrill.

Smidt, S. 1998. *A Guide to early years practice.* London: Routeledge.

Spady, W G. 1994. *Outcome-based Education. Critical issues and answers.* Arlington: American Association of school Administrators.

Spodek, B. 1985. *Teaching in the early years.* Englewood Cliffs, New Jersey: Prentice-Hall.

Spodek, B. 1991. Early childhood development and the Cultural definition of knowledge. In: *Issues in Early Childhood Curriculum. Yearbook in Early childhood Education Volume 2.* Spodek, B & Saracho, O N.(Eds.) New York: Teachers College Press. (pp 1 – 20).

Turner, P & Hamner, T J. 1994. *Child development and early childhood education.* Boston: Allyn and Bacon.

Van der Horst, H & McDonald, R. 1997. *OBE Outcomes-Based Education. A teacher's manual.* Pretoria: Kagiso.

Wilkens, F. 1999. Implementering van Kurrikulum 2005. In:. *Ongepubliseerde simposiumbundel* (pp 1 – 7) SAOU Referate. Skoolhoofdesimposium.

Willer, B & Bredekamp, S. 1990. Redefining readiness: An essential requisite for educational reform. In: *Young Children.* (Vol 45, July) (pp 22 – 24).

Chapter

2

Know the learner

Christie van Staden

OUTCOMES

After you have read this chapter you should be able to:

■ understand and value the different aspects making up the whole child

■ choose appropriate media to enhance child development and foster learning

■ understand how children learn

■ recognise possible developmental delays

■ identify barriers to development and learning

■ plan for the individual needs and abilities of diverse learners.

What you will find in this chapter

As has been mentioned before, a good programme for the reception year should promote all areas of the child's development. In order to achieve this you, the teacher, need to understand the various stages of child development and the expected pace at which these occur. This knowledge will enable you to provide developmentally appropriate activities for the children, i.e. activities which are suitable for a child's stage of development.

Sometimes a teacher or parent may feel concerned about a child's behaviour and wonder whether there is a sound basis for this concern. The most useful way of assessing young children is through observation. In order to be able to observe a child with the purpose of assessing whether or not the child is developing at an appropriate pace, a thorough knowledge of children's normal development is essential. The development of each child varies, but normal development follows certain predictable stages. Interruptions in the pattern and sequence of these stages should put the teacher on the alert. Later in this chapter reference will be made to certain 'red lights' in children's development, and when these occur, special attention should be paid to the child in order to address them.

 Go to:

Chapter 7 *Assessment of the whole child*.

Why the whole child?

In this chapter the focus is on the normal development of the five- to six year old child. In order to put this age group into perspective, reference is also made to other age groups. The development of the whole child as an active, social, emotional, intellectual and creative person is taken into consideration. All of these aspects will have an influence on preparing the child for formal school the following year.

Children are active (physical and motor development)

Growth during the preschool years (i.e. when children are between three and six years old) is less rapid than during infancy, but is faster than in the middle school years.

Normal development in the 3 – 6 year old child

The following is characteristic of the development of a child of this age:

■ By the age of five years he or she is *twice* as tall as at birth and has increased in weight by *five* times. A child's height also follows the pattern of his or her parents' height development. Nutrition is a factor that influences growth.

■ The preschooler (5 – 6 years) looks leaner than the chubby toddler by the end of the preschool period because the increase of body fat slows down at this stage.

■ The preschool child has lost the *top-heavy* appearance of the toddler. The head is more in proportion with the rest of the body. Although the head still appears large, it is more in proportion to the body's length. The trunk is longer and better accommodates the internal organs. That is why the abdomen has flattened and the chest seems larger.

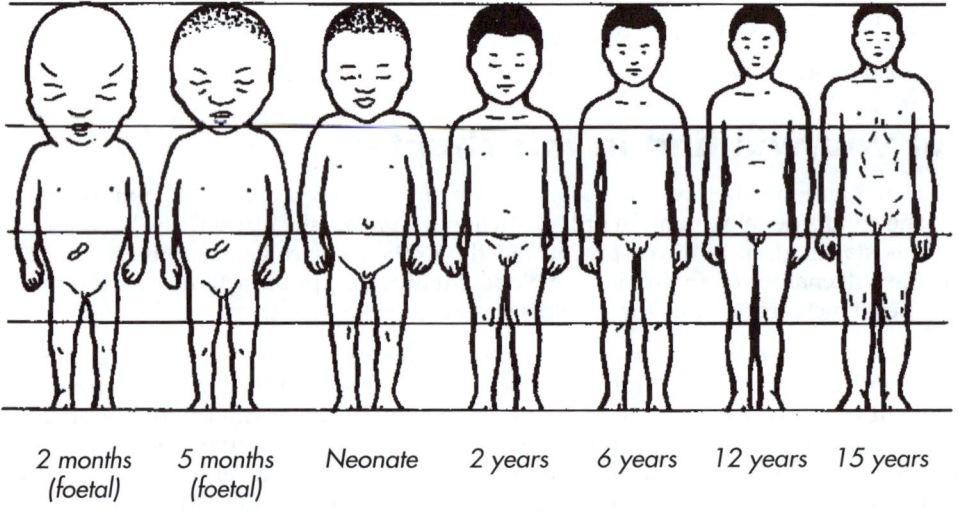

| 2 months | 5 months | Neonate | 2 years | 6 years | 12 years | 15 years |
| (foetal) | (foetal) | | | | | |

Figure 2.1 – The changes in human body proportions (not to scale)

■ His or her neck becomes longer and slimmer and it no longer appears as though the head is sitting directly on the shoulders.

■ The facial features of the 5 – 6 year old child have a more mature look; the eyes appear more widely spaced because the bridge of the nose has begun to form, and the lower jaw has filled out. The shoulders become broader, the fingers longer and he or she develops more obvious wrists.

- By about six years of age the child's brain is approximately 90% of its adult weight. However, brain development still continues at a steady pace. Malnutrition, which has been shown to retard brain growth during the early years, may result in developmental lags.

- In about 90% of children, handedness (the preferred use of the right or left hand) is established by the age of six.

- At about six years of age children will start losing their milk (baby) teeth in the same order as they appeared.

- These are the general trends, but there will be individual differences among children.

Consider Figure 2.1 regarding the changes in body proportions from early in the prenatal period to six years of age.

Normal expectations of gross (large) and fine (small) motor skills

Gross motor skills

A normal *four year* old can:	A normal *five to six year* old can:
Walk backwards toe-to-heel	Stand on one leg (5 seconds)
Bounce and catch a ball	Jump on one leg (5 seconds)
Run three metres and stop	Walk backwards (5 metres)
Push/pull: a wagon, doll, buggy	Run lightly on his/her toes
Kick a large ball towards a target	Throw a ball (15m boys, 8m girls)
Carry a 4kg object	Carry a 5kg object
Bounce a ball with some level of control	Kick a rolling ball
Hop on one foot/four hops	Skip on alternating feet
Perform a somersault	Clap hands, keeping time to music
Climb a jungle gym, use a swing	Skip with a rope
Control his or her body functions	Roll a ball to hit object
	Ride a two-wheel bike with training wheels
	Walk on a balancing beam
	Dress himself/herself
	Have enough stamina and does not tire easily
	Touch right ear with left hand – arm going over head
	At the end of the year, show the difference between left and right
	Can cross his/her middle line

Fine (small) motor skills

A normal *four* year old can:	A normal *five to six* year old can:
String and lace shoe lace	Fold paper into halves and quarters
Cut following a line	Trace around his/her own hand
String 10 beads	Draw a rectangle, circle, square and triangle
Copy a cross, and a square	Cut out simple shapes
Open and place clothes pins (one-handed)	Reproduce letters
Draw a picture of a human with a body (not just the head)	Add finer detail to drawn objects
	Print own name and numerals 1 – 5
Print a few letters	Colour in within lines of own drawings

(Berk 1994, Gordon and Browne 2004, Hendrick 1992, McAfee and Leong 2004, Mwamwenda 1990, Schirmer 1974 and Van Staden 1987)

What does this mean for the teacher in the reception year?

By using the above guidelines the teacher should provide activities which will promote the development of these skills. Provide the following materials and equipment:

Materials and equipment for large/fine motor development

For large motor development	For fine motor development
Tricycles and scooters	Puzzles
Trucks and tractors	Lego and other manipulatives
Wagons	Art materials (crayons, markers,
Climbing structures (trees, jungle gyms)	paint, glue scissors, lots of 'junk')
Crawling through spaces (barrels, culverts, boxes)	Clay and dough
	Musical instruments
Balls (large, small): for catching, running with, kicking, throwing	Dress-up clothes
Rolling tires, hoops	Dolls and doll clothes
Swings (a variety, including belt swings, monkey swings, tire swings)	Unit blocks
	Books
Structures for balancing (loose planks, tires, bricks, slides)	Carpentry materials (hammer, large nails, saw, soft wood, wood stumps, vice, simple
Music with a beat for children to dance to	workbench)
Bean/sand bags and targets	Sand/water toys (home-made: plastic containers, funnels, sieves)

(Turner & Hamner 1994)

Sensory skills

Young children use all their senses to get to know their surroundings. We call this *perception.*

Definition

Perception is the ability to receive sensory (i.e. from the senses) impressions from one's surroundings and relate them to what one knows.

For example, a child who has never touched, looked at, smelled or heard a dog barking will not easily form a concept of what a dog is.

The five senses

Traditionally the five senses include:

- visual (seeing)
- olfactory (smelling)
- auditory (hearing)
- gustatory (tasting)
- tactile (feeling).

In order to make the abovementioned list more complete, we could also add the following senses, as suggested by Montessori (1967):

- *Chromatic:* A broader sense of vision – ability to identify, match and discriminate between colours.
- *Thermic:* One's perception of temperature – things feel hot, cold, warm, lukewarm.
- *Baric:* Recognising objects as heavy or light.
- *Sterognostic:* Recognising objects by touching and handling them without seeing them – e.g. feeling objects in a bag and saying what they are.
- *Kinesthetic:* This involves a whole-body, sensory, muscular response – children learn by *doing* activities such as:
    - using their bodies to act like animals, e.g. walking like a dog
    - counting steps while climbing them.

It is important to keep in mind that the preschooler's sensory organs might not yet be fully developed.

Eyes

The following characterises the development of the child's vision at this age:

- the macula of the retina is not completely developed until about six years of age
- the eyeball does not reach adult size until 12 – 14 years
- the young child is farsighted because of the shape of the eyeball
- at six years of age the child still has 20/27 visual acuity and not yet 20/20 visual acuity – the latter being the perfect vision of the adult

In addition to normal visual acuity, <u>children must be able to distinguish between objects as</u> <u>they later need to be able to distinguish between letters and words.</u>

The child should be able to:

- see differences between objects which are almost the same, e.g. the difference between a square and an oblong (<u>visual discrimination</u>)

- order pictures of situations in a logical way (<u>visual order</u>)

- build a puzzle of at least 25 pieces (<u>visual discrimination</u>)

- thread beads according to a pattern (<u>spatial relationship</u>)

- see specific objects in a picture with a lot of detail (<u>figure/ground</u>)

- rebuild a model built with blocks by the teacher (<u>spatial relationships</u>).

The development of block play

The development of block play follows <u>different stages, as</u> seen in Figure 2.2. This illustration will give you an indication of how the child's concept <u>of space develops through block play</u>.

1. Blocks are carried around but not used for construction. This is found amongst the youngest children.

2. Building begins: horizontal or vertical rows.

3. Bridge-building: blocks with a space inbetween are connected by a third block.

4. Encircling: blocks are packed so as to enclose a space.

5. When the child becomes proficient, he begins to construct decorative symmetrical patterns. They are not yet called buildings.

6. The structure is given a name and fantasy play begins. The name also describes the function of the structure.

7. Structures from their own experience are initiated. The children are stimulated towards fantasy play which becomes interwoven with block play.

Figure 2.2 – The evolution of block play

It is vitally important that you talk to children about what they are doing. Block play is a good opportunity to do this. The key to talking with children about their block play is to use statements that describe what a child has done, or ask open questions that encourage children to talk about their work. Some examples will follow.

Ways to support children at block play

Here are examples of positive and constructive comments you might make about a child's work:

Choice of blocks:

Tasheen, you found out that two of these blocks make one long block.

Arrangement of blocks:

Roy, you used eight blocks to make a big square.

Number and counting :

Amanda, you used more than five long blocks to make this road. How many more will you need to let the road reach the wall?

Similarity/comparing:

Precious, all the blocks in your building are the same. I wonder what will happen if you changed some of the blocks?

Symmetry:

Riaan, you have made a pattern with your block. Can you repeat it and make the same pattern on the other side?

Space:

Yumi, how many animals will fit into this cage? How much larger will you have to make it to make space for another two elephants and a giraffe? Where will the people who visit the zoo park their cars?

Taste

Young children's sensitivity to taste is very high, possibly because they have more tastebuds than adults. Taste buds are scattered on the inside of the cheeks and the throat, as well as on the tongue.

Ears

The following characterises the development of the child's hearing at this age:

- Preschool children get ear infections more easily than older children because the tube which connects the middle ear with the throat (Eustachian tube) is shorter and more horizontal than in the older child and it is easier for germs to enter the middle ear from the throat. When children have problems with hearing, it is wise first to make sure that there is not a medical problem.

- In addition to normal acuity of hearing, children must be able to distinguish among and between sounds.

A child of this age should be able to:

- listen attentively to a story
- remember and carry out at least three instructions (auditive memory)
- retell a story with about six incidents in the right order (auditive memory)
- identify familiar sounds from the environment (auditive discrimination)
- remember the words of songs and rhymes (long term memory).

What are the implications for the teacher?

Children use all their senses throughout the day while they are taking part in activities in the classroom. They should be able to interpret the information which they receive through their senses. A teacher can promote this interpretation by talking to the children in various circumstances throughout the day, and asking questions in order to stimulate the use of the senses. The following are examples of how this can be achieved:

- *Toilet routine:* What does the soap/water smell like, look like, feel like?

- *Science:* What is the difference between fruits, vegetables, leaves, flowers? How are they different in terms of smell, size, texture, taste, form, weight?

- *Songs and rhymes:* Which words start with/end with the same sound or letter?

- *Music:* Listen with a specific purpose. Listen to when the piano starts. Clap rhythms. Indicate high and low sounds. Move with the music.

- *Stories:* Look at pictures and ask questions. Tell stories which the children can retell. Make a tape of familiar sounds and have the children identify the sounds.

- *Mathematics:* It is of little value if children can only identify the different geometric shapes; they should also be able to identify the ways in which they are different. You could say, for example, 'How is the triangle different from the square? Let us count the sides and corners.'

Children are social and have emotions (social/emotional development)

> ### Definition
>
> Social development refers to the child developing ways of adapting to the rules and behaviour of society.

Children do not live on their own; they need other people. Young children need to learn many skills in order to develop socially, e.g. they have to learn how to co-operate and take turns. Socialisation is learned; it does not happen by itself. It is learned in the classroom through the availability of an interested, accepting and communicative teacher. Young children can move away from egocentric ways of thinking (i.e. thinking only about themselves and their needs) only if they interact with other children and experience the fact that other people have viewpoints and opinions of their own.

> ### Definition
>
> Emotional development occurs when the child comes to have knowledge, understanding and a positive acceptance of the self.

Social and emotional development are discussed together because they are very closely related. Healthy social development also promotes the forming of a positive self-concept.

> ### Research
>
> The development of a positive self concept is very important for an understanding of the self and others. Research has shown that the more adequate children feel, the more confident they are about learning and relating to others. The child's self-concept is the foundation on which all future relationships with others will be built.
>
> (Turner & Hamner 1994)

Important people in a child's life (e.g. parents, teachers, friends) gradually help children to form a view of themselves . Thus the self-concept is formed. Much of what happens in the years before school leads to the development of a positive or negative self-concept, and the ability to relate effectively or ineffectively to others. If children feel they are viewed negatively by others they begin to doubt themselves, which will have the effect of them developing a negative self-concept.

> ### *Remember*
>
> *It is difficult for children to feel good about themselves when the message from others is: 'You're different. You don't belong to us.' Prejudice towards others who are of a different race, gender, who have a disability or speak another language, may be found among young children. As the reception year teacher you must intentionally enhance anti-bias behaviour in the classroom.*

Go to:

Strategies for encouraging a culture of anti-bias are explored later in this chapter.

Social skills
Typical five to six year old children can be expected to:

- enjoy group play, competitive games
- like adult companionship
- choose his or her own friends, be sociable
- be aware of rules
- insist on fair play
- accept and respect authority
- ask permission
- enjoy jokes
- have a sense of self-identity
- be sensitive to ridicule
- accept the uniqueness of others
- prefer friends of the same gender.

Emotional skills
The typical five to six year old can be expected to:

- recognise successes and feel pride in his or her work
- recognise and appreciate his or her uniqueness
- persevere with most self-chosen tasks
- show autonomous behaviour and self-discipline by making decisions and choosing activities on his or her own
- develop an emerging awareness of the consequences of behaviour
- be prepared to take a risk and go into a new situation
- be prepared to leave the safety of the home, preschool, and reception year class.

(Berk 1994, Louw 1992 and Turner & Hamner 1994)

What are the implications for the teacher?
The kind of behaviour teachers want young children to acquire is called *prosocial, anti-bias behaviour* which includes:

- sharing
- co-operation
- helpfulness
- mutual respect.

This can be achieved by encouraging the reception year child to take part in group activities with other children, as well as taking turns and sharing toys.

A group Art activity centred around a theme, for example, provides positive sharing experiences.

Example

After an outing to a nearby bird sanctuary, the children can get together and discuss their experience there. They can decide, amongst themselves and with their teacher, what they would like to make to remind them of their outing. They can decide together what Art materials they will need and then plan how they are going to put their group work together.

Teachers must help children to feel positive about themselves. They can achieve this by creating a nurturing, supportive environment in which children feel wanted, secure and safe.

Teachers must provide environments that promote self-respect, tolerance, and mutual regard for *all* children. They must never forget that children model their behaviour on that of the teacher. When children know that a teacher likes and accepts children who are different from the rest of the group, they will do the same. Talk about individual likes and dislikes. Ask different children to choose stories, songs, games and Art activities.

Provide activities where the children will be able to experience success, in other words ensure that you choose developmentally appropriate activities. Make sure there are activities which will allow children to *unload negative feelings or uncertainties in a positive way*. Restless or aggressive children can be calmed down by:

- looking at books
- having a story read to them
- singing a song
- listening to music
- hammering nails into a piece of soft wood
- squeezing soft playdough
- handling finger-paint.

Children often unload uncertainties or find solutions for their problems in art activities such as those already mentioned above as well as, and very importantly, drawing.

In Figure 2.3 a little boy aged five who was being bullied decided to find a solution to his problem in his drawing. He drew himself as a man with a beard and big, red muscles. He explained that when you are grown up you have a beard and you are strong with muscles and nobody can hurt you.

Figure 2.3 –
A child's pictorial solution to a bullying problem

In Figure 2.4 a little girl, also five years old, added legs to her house to show that they had moved and she wished she could take her home with her.

Figure 2.4 – A child's desires expressed in her drawing

Children have minds (intellectual/language development)

Intellectual development – knowledge and thinking – involves the development of a child's ability to:

- pay attention
- remember
- interpret
- classify
- evaluate ideas
- infer principles and deduce rules
- imagine possibilities
- generate strategies
- solve problems.

Let us look briefly at two important areas for intellectual development.

1. Knowledge base

This refers to content – i.e. everything a child knows about a certain topic. This would include:

- facts
- concepts
- understanding
- strategies for using this information.

Knowing the name of a flower or farm animal, the words to a song, understanding the concept *smaller than* as well as the route to school, are all examples of content.

A child's knowledge base also acts as a framework to understanding new ideas. Children build *new* understanding on *old* understandings. New information is easier to remember if it can be tied to information already stored in one's mind.

2. Memory

This is an intellectual process involved in all learning, because in order to learn one must retain (remember) information. The child must pay attention or focus on a piece of information in order to remember it and must not become distracted easily.

The implications of the knowledge base and memory in teaching

The size and depth of each child's knowledge base depends on exposure and experience. The child should constantly be exposed to new knowledge and this can be done by allowing the child to experience things in a concrete first hand way.

Example

For example, to learn about vegetables he or she should:

- have access to *real* vegetables and not only pictures of them
- be able to taste them
- be allowed to make a salad or soup
- be able to classify them according to taste, colour or whether they grow above or beneath the ground.

Before a child can remember something, you need to have his or her attention. When discussing a new theme or Science project there must be time set aside for a discussion without interruptions. Make sure that all the children can see what you are discussing. Mention children by name to ensure that you have their attention.

Characteristics of intellectual development

According to Piaget, a famous researcher on intellectual development, the five to six year old is still in the *preoperational* stage of intelligence. This means that children at this age learn in a certain way and will show the following characteristics:

- They grow in their ability to use symbols.
- They are not capable of operational thinking. (An operation is a reversible mental action.)
- They focus on one thought or idea, often to the exclusion of other thoughts. A child faced with an object which has more than one characteristic such as a large, striped, smooth shell will 'see' whichever one of those qualities first catches his or her eye.
- They are unable to conserve. This means that they cannot understand that the size or quantity of an object or group of objects does not change simply because something in its appearance has changed. (See the example on following page.)

Example

An illustration of a child's inability to conserve

Figure 2.5

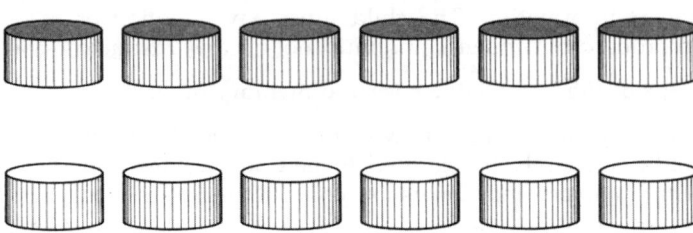

Teacher: Is there a grey lid for every white lid?

Child: Yes, there is one grey lid for every white lid.

Teacher: Now watch what I do.

Figure 2.6

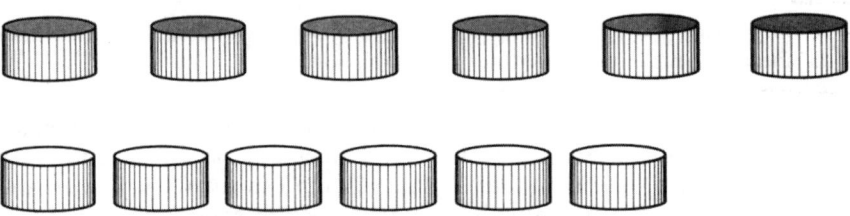

Teacher: Are there just as many grey lids as white lids now?

Child: You've got more grey lids because your row is longer.

In the first part of the example (Figure 2.5), when the lids were matched one for one, the child saw that the two rows of lids were equal. As soon as one row of lids was spread out more than the other row, the child said that the longer row had more lids (Figure 2.6), even though this was not the case.

■ They are _egocentric._ They believe that everyone sees what *they* see and think as *they* think.

 **Go to:**

Look at Figure 4.12 on page [121]. Everybody in this picture is looking to the front because they are looking at the child who is busy drawing.

Research has shown that Piaget underestimated the capabilities of young children. When they are given simplified problems relevant to their everyday lives, their performance appears to be more mature than the levels set in his guidelines.

Children's normal intellectual development pattern

1. Symbolic thought

   By four to five years of age, most children can do representational drawings; some can use written symbols, write their names and some numbers as well as make and interpret graphs with the help of the teacher.

   By six years and older, most children can use written symbols and make and interpret graphs.

2. Classification

   By three to five years of age most children can classify things based on one attribute (e.g. size or colour); place objects in a series based on one attribute; and make a simple line pattern, e.g. ABABABAB. A few can classify things based on two attributes simultaneously, e.g. large blue, small blue.

   By six to eight years of age most children can classify things based on multiple attributes and understand that objects can belong to several classes at the same time.

3. Problem solving

   By three to six years of age most children can spontaneously solve everyday problems by trial and error or by using formulae and rules.

   By six years and older they will:

   ■ make it known that they need more information

   ■ make plans

   ■ use rules.

   With teacher support, children of five years and older can use metacognitive skills such as:

   ■ thinking about the problem

   ■ asking clarifying questions

   ■ planning a solution

   ■ reflecting on learning and errors.

4. Conservation

   By two to six years of age most children cannot conserve; they will state that a group is, for example more, bigger, or longer when rearranged. Current research suggests that preoperational children can conserve number if four or fewer objects are used, but may not be able to explain their answers.

   By six to eight years of age most children can conserve number, length, liquid and mass. They will justify their answers by saying: *You didn't add or take away anything* or *They look different, but they are the same.*

5. Basic concepts

   By four to five years of age most children know the difference between *big/little, tall/short, high/low, thick/thin, outside/inside.* They still experience difficulty with *underneath, below, over* and *under.* Some children know the concepts *full/empty, light/heavy, bottom/top, middle, first, second, third, rectangle, triangle, circle, line.*

6. Colour concepts

   By four to five years of age most children know most colour names.

7. Mathematical concepts

   By four to five most children can match objects one to one.

   By five to six most children can count by rote to 20 and start counting on from a number other than 1 (e.g. 5, 6, 7, 8); recognise and write numbers from 1 – 10; and can use rulers and scales.

   By six to seven children have an intuitive grasp of numbers.

8. Scientific concepts

   By five to six most children know simple scientific concepts based on the observable world: e.g. people, animals, plants, seasons and the weather.

9. Geographical concepts

   By five to six most children can understand their own position in space relative to other things or persons near them; they know words to express spatial relationships. They have difficulty in understanding the geographical concept of a country. They often think a country is the town they live in.

10. Historical concepts

   By four to five most children know the concepts *before* and *after, yesterday* and *tomorrow,* and can identify or tell the sequence in a story. They often have difficulty understanding the concept *long ago* – they think that what happened long ago will happen again now.

Giftedness

It is accepted that it is important to identify giftedness at a young age. This makes it possible for the teacher to cater to this child's special needs, by putting in place the resources needed to make sure that their giftedness is nurtured.

Terman's (De Witt and Van Zyl 1990:114) view of giftedness in the young children is generally accepted. He indicates that 'the gifted – children and adult alike – differ from the non-gifted in degree rather than in kind'.

He argues that greatness is not mysterious or freakish, but stems from an extraordinary ability to exercise sensitive judgement in solving problems, adapting to new situations and learning from performing various tasks and experiencing various situations.

> **Remember**
>
> *It appears that academic and intellectual giftedness are areas most easily identifiable at an early age, in terms of (amongst others) the use of numbers, language and word concepts. Until they are more mature, young children do not demonstrate unusual gifts in the physical and emotional areas.*

How does one recognise gifted preschoolers?

Bear in mind that criteria used to identify older gifted children are not necessarily applicable to the preschooler. The following criteria identified by experts in this field may however be useful for identifying gifted preschoolers (De Witt and Van Zyl 1990, Hallahan and Kauffman 2001, Kokot 1992 and Kruger 1989).

1. Physical criteria

   Gifted preschoolers:

   - are healthy

   - are not necessarily bigger or stronger than peers unless giftedness is in this area

   - may tend to be more cautious than peers on high apparatus, due to their ability to foresee dangerous situations.

2. Cognitive (intellectual) criteria

   Gifted children:

   - usually learn to speak at a very early age – about eleven weeks earlier than other children

   - master advanced concepts in mathematics and language at ages four or five, instead of seven or eight

   - have no problems learning to read. Some show an early interest in reading and teach themselves to read or ask for help in reading before formal schooling. Some show no early signs of wanting to read, but once they start they find it easy to do so.

   - show signs of creativity at an early age in language, games and problem-solving.

3. Social-emotional criteria

   Gifted children:

   - usually show an early acceptance of self

   - might prefer the company of older children

   - have a good sense of humour which might be very sophisticated. Often show a liking for puns, word play and riddles.

   - are usually emotionally stable and better adjusted at home and school than their peers

   - have a highly developed sense of moral and ethical responsibility and are sensitive to social injustices

   - may assume leadership positions in the peer group

   - may display an uneven balance between intellectual and emotional development

   - might show signs of perfectionism and become discouraged and upset if their efforts do not meet their expectations

   - might have invisible friends – the fantasy life of gifted children begins at about the age of two

   - show a strong interest in religious matters, ask questions about God, death and after life

   - demand honesty of others and are generally honest themselves.

What are the implications for the teacher?

Kokot (1992:110) makes the following suggestion about the gifted preschooler: We should not be so concerned with formal identification of giftedness, but

"… be more concerned about challenging all children from where they are, allowing continuous progress and enriching experiences, and letting the children guide us to their next step. Appropriate, stimulating experiences are our best way to nurture giftedness."

Example

Robby came running into the classroom, excitedly. 'Teacher! Teacher! I did it! I put the bird back together. Its bones were lying all around. Look, I made the skeleton of the bird. Let me show you how it works!' Robby puts the bird bones on the table as he thinks the skeleton should look. 'Teacher, will you get me a book from the library so that we can find out about birds and skeletons?' The teacher should nurture this child's interest in birds by getting all the information she can find. This could be done by developing a theme around birds by means of which the knowledge and experience of all the children in the class may be enriched on this subject.

The child has a will (conative aspect)

Definition

The human will can be described as that inward driving force behind all human behaviour.

Each conscious act of the child is performed because he or she wants to, because there is a wish, a desire, a need, a yearning or an aspiration which needs to be fulfilled by means of an action.

This implies that a goal can be achieved by an action preceded by the will to attain the goal. It is your task as a reception year teacher to motivate the child to, for example, want to go to the primary school to learn, to want to be able to read and write, and to do Mathematics.

Children are creative (creative development)

What does it mean when we speak of being creative? We might say that the architect who designs buildings is creative; the artist who paints a beautiful picture is creative or the songwriter who composes a new song is creative. Do we ever think about young children as being creative? What about Lerato when she puts a few stones in the pot and pretends she is cooking meat? And what about Lucinda when she calls a wheelbarrow a *leafcart* and a ring a *fingerbracelet?* According to researchers in this field, people are creative when they have the following attributes:

fluency   – the ability to bring forth many new ideas

flexibility   – an openness to implement different approaches

originality   – the ability to bring forth something new and to see new relationships between things

elaboration – to build further or extend a basic idea.

Bearing these characteristics in mind, one comes to the conclusion that the young child is very creative. He or she makes many new discoveries every day. One must keep in mind that something is a new discovery if it is new to the person discovering it. For example, Lerato used stones in a new creative way; Lucinda created new words by elaborating on the meanings of existing words – she saw new relationships in her own experience of the world. Another child, Sepho, might have discovered (and this would have been new to him) that if you cut a square in half from diagonal corners you create two triangles.

Even though children are creative in many ways, it is in their drawings that children show, in their own original way, what they understand about their world. This is one of the many reasons why we should not confront children with our own examples of subjects or give them colouring books. Children's drawings develop through stages which provide the teacher with clues about the child's intellectual, as well physical (fine muscle control, eye-hand control), development.

Stages of development in children's drawings
(Kellogg, Lowenfeld, Schirrmacher, Van Staden)

Children progress through stages of development in Art which parallel their development in other areas. In the chapters on reading, writing, Mathematics and Science we will refer to these stages in greater detail.

In the period from nought to nine years of age, children's Art develops through three broad stages: the scribbling, preschematic and schematic stages.

Stage 1: The beginning of self-expression – Scribbling

Scribbling is a very important step in the development of drawing and writing skills, just as babbling is an important first step in speech development. Three sub-stages can be identified in the scribbling stage.

Uncontrolled scribbling stage

A baby of 18 months and even earlier will discover that he or she can make marks in his or her porridge. If given a thick marker or crayon this child will taste it, swing it around and make uncontrolled marks on a large piece of paper at random.

Controlled scribbling stage

The toddler at approximately two years of age discovers that these marks can be controlled.

Named scribble stage

Children make a connection between the motions of scribbling and giving these marks the names of familiar objects. They realise that the marks they are making may represent something. This is a big moment for language development.

A fire.
It will not burn you.

Figure 2.7 – Named scribble stage

Stage 2: First attempts at representation – Preschematic stage (± three to four years)

Children begin making forms relating to their lifeworld. These forms are usually incomplete. Children often begin by drawing a human with the head and body depicted as one large circle or oval, to which they add arms and legs. This head-foot man is a universal form drawn by all children who are allowed to make their own drawings and who are not exposed to worksheets and colouring books (see Figure 2.8).

Children in this stage may still be using colour in an unrealistic way. It seems as though the objects in their drawings are floating around at random on the background. This is because they still do not grasp the use of space.

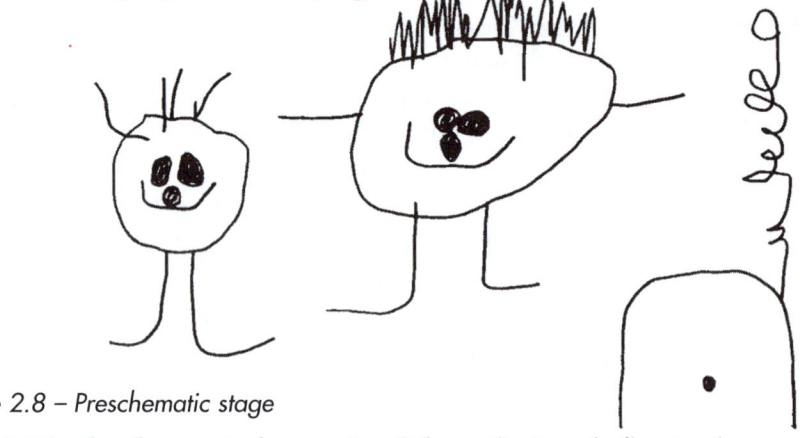

Figure 2.8 – Preschematic stage

Stage 3: The development of concepts – Schematic stage (± five to nine years)

The 'schema' is a child's own individual symbol or pattern for objects such as humans, houses, and trees which develop after much experimenting in the previous stage. A characteristic of this stage is that children start to arrange the objects in their pictures on a base line (see Figure 2.9). The edge of the paper might also be used as a base line without the child actually drawing it. These children start to understand the use of space on a piece of paper – they work on the top and on the bottom of a page, and are able to write more or less on a line on a piece of paper. Children at this stage do not depict a horizon but draw a skyline at the top of the page. By writing the child's name at the top left hand side of his or her pictures, the teacher helps the child to become used to writing or reading from left to right.

Figure 2.9 – Schematic stage

The child discovers a relationship between colour and objects and will start using colour in a realistic way, e.g. green for grass and blue for the sky, although this might not always be the case.

What about colouring books?

What do the experts say? Viktor Lowenfeld, in his book *Creative and Mental Growth* states:

> *"The dependency upon someone else's outline of an object makes the child much less confident of his own means of expression. He obviously cannot draw a cow as well as the one in the colouring book."*

Colouring books and teacher-prepared worksheets give the child little need for problem solving, creative thinking, or decision making. Another person has decided what the objects in his or her world look like.

Compare the elephant outlines prepared by the teacher with the children's own drawings of elephants (Figure 2.10).

Figure 2.10 – Prepared drawings (left) have a limiting effect, compared to the children's own drawings (right)

What are the implications for the teacher?

Colouring books provide children with pictures that adults have drawn; pictures that adults think children will like. But these pictures bear no relationship with the way a young child represents his or her world through drawing.

A question often asked by teachers is whether colouring books teach children eye-hand control by expecting the children to stay within lines. As children move from scribbling to representational drawing it is most natural for them to draw the outlines of the objects they wish to represent. They then colour in the objects in their own drawings with care and purpose.

Language development

Definition
Language refers to a system of international communication through sounds, signs (gestures) or symbols which are understandable to others.

Vygotsky regards language as the foundation of acquiring intellectual skills. He emphasises the need for assisted discovery on the part of the child in the form of verbal guidance from the teacher. For example, discuss with the child how a discovery was made.

Example
Thabo discovers green.
Thabo: Look teacher, I've got green.
Teacher: Can you remember what colours you used to make green?
Thabo: Blue and yellow.
Teacher: Yes, you made green from blue and yellow, and Nicolene also made green from mixing blue and yellow.
Thabo: Blue and yellow makes green.

Language develops rapidly during the early childhood years. When children learn language, exactly what is it that they learn? Language contains aspects that have to do with sound, meaning, structure and everyday use:

Phonology	This is concerned with the *sounds* of speech.
Semantics	This aspect of language is concerned with understanding the *meaning of words* and *word combinations*.
Syntax	This is the set of *grammatical rules* for combining words in understandable units of speech.
Pragmatic	This is the *practical* side of language. To be understood, children must learn to take turns, know how to use gestures, what tone of voice to use, what is considered polite in their social group.

It is expected that the preschooler of five to six years of age will be able to express him- or herself verbally and be able to understand instructions.

The beginnings of reading and writing as the other forms of language expression will be discussed in separate chapters of this book.

The following table may help you understand the normal language development of children.

Age	General language characteristics
three months	The baby starts with all possible babbling sounds and gradually eliminates those sounds that are not used around him or her.
one year	Many children speak single words such as *Mama*.
18 months	Many children use two- or three-word phrases such as *Baby go*. Children may have a vocabulary of 300 words.
two to three years	Object words are emphasised first; action and state words follow on later. A vocabulary of about 900 words is used. They correctly pronounce all vowel sounds a, e, i, o, u.
three to four years	The past tense of the verb appears in their speech. Speech becomes more complex, with more adjectives, adverbs, pronouns and prepositions. Pronunciation improves greatly. Vocabulary is about 1 500 words. They correctly pronounce sounds p, b, m, w, h.
four to five years	Language is more abstract and more basic rules of language are mastered. They produce grammatically correct sentences. Vocabularies include approximately 2 500 words. They correctly pronounce the sounds f, j, sh.
five to six years	Most children use complex sentences quite frequently at this age. They use correct pronouns and verbs in the present and past tense. The average number of words per oral sentence is 6,8. It has been estimated that the child understands approximately 6 000 words. They correctly pronounce the sounds ch, v, r, l.
six to seven years	Children speak complex sentences that use adjectival clauses, and conditional clauses beginning with 'if' appear. Language becomes more symbolic. The average sentence length is 7,5 words. Children begin to read and write. At 7 they correctly pronounce the sounds s, z, voiceless and voiced th.

(Berk 1994, Machado 1990, McAfee & Leong 2004, Mussen et al 1990).

Second language learners

Children whose primary (first) language is not English are very likely to be in your classroom. You may also have several non-English speakers who share a common home language. Read about this situation and how children develop a second language, in the following paragraphs.

The Language-in-Education policy in South Africa specifies that learners' first years of schooling (the Foundation Phase) should be in their mother tongue. The practical situation in South African classrooms however, for a number of reasons, does not often reflect this policy. Just as children have different strengths and weaknesses in many different areas, children learning English as a second language vary greatly. For instance, the depth of children's knowledge of their primary language can vary, whether their primary language is English or any other language. Some children come from language-rich home environments, and bring with them strong language skills in their primary language when they enter the reception year. Others may come from homes where adults may not be very verbal and rarely read books to their children – these children will have a poor foundation on which to build new language skills.

A number of misconceptions about learning a second language can cause unnecessary anxiety in teachers and parents. Study the following table.

Myths about learning a second language

(Genesee, F (n.d.) 2004; Snow 1997)

Myth	Reality
Children who are exposed to more than one language are at a clear disadvantage.	Biligual children are often very ceative and are good at problem solving. Compared to children who speak only one language, those who are bilingual can communicate with more people, and read more.
Learning a second language confuses a child.	
Learning a second language as a preschooler will slow down children's readiness to read.	They do not get confused, even when they combine languages in one sentence. Mixing languages is a normal and expected part of learning a second language.
When children are exposed to two languages, they never become as proficient in either language as children who have to master only one language.	The opposite is often true. Bilingual children make the transition to decoding words very well.
Only the brightest children can learn two languages without encountering problems. Most children have difficulty because the process is so complex.	As long as they are exposed consistently to both languages, children can become proficient in both languages.
	Nearly all children are capable of learning two languages during the preschool years.

Important research (Snow, Burns & Griffen as cited by dodge, Colker & Heroman 2002) with regard to the prevention of reading difficulties has found the following:

Children's continued learning in their primary language should be suported, while at the same time, their ability to learn to speak English (or any other second language) should be fostered. The research on brain development shows that the preschool years are a key time for learning languages. The following are two important findings:

- Children who develop a sound foundation in their first language are more efficient in learning a second language.

- Concepts and skills that are learned in the first language will transfer to the second language.

Being exposed to rich experiences in two languages is a great asset. All children can benefit from learning another language.

It is helpful to know which stages of acquiring English as a second language children are likely to go through, if you have such children in your classroom. As in all areas of development, children vary in their approaches to acquiring English as well as the rate at which they acquire the new language. Consult the following table for the stages of learning a second language:

Stages of learning a second language

Stage	What you might see
Home language use	Children use only their home language with teachers and other children.
Non-verbal period	Children limit (or stop) the use of their home language as they realise that their words are not understood by others. This period can last from a few months to one year. Children may use gestures or pantomime to express their needs.
Early speech	Children begin using one- and two-word phrases in English, and start naming objects. They may use groups of words such as 'stop it', 'fall down', or 'give me', although they may not always use them appropriately.
Conversation	Children begin to use simple sentences in English, like the ones they hear in their environment. They may begin to form their own sentences using the words they have learned. Like all young children, they gradually increase the length of their sentences.
Use of 'academic' language at school	Children begin to acquire English associated with specific content knowledge while they continue to develop social language.

You may see characteristics of more that one stage in a child at any time, and the length of time children remain at a given stage varies. Be aware that children may mix their languages – this is perfectly normal and no indication of a language problem.

An inclusive educational approach

Inclusion is about equal participation for all. This means that all learners are included at all sites where education takes place, which includes all races, cultures, genders, religions or people with disabilities. Inclusion is one of the key principles of the Revised National Curriculum Statement (RNCS) and means that you as the educator should aim to create a learning and teaching environment where every learner in class is seen as a unique person with individual social, physical, emotional and intellectual needs.

According to the Education White Paper 6 on *Special Needs Education: Building an Inclusive Education and Training System*, all teaching, learning and assessment should embrace the following:

■ All learners can learn, each one in his or her own way and at his or her own pace, if they are given the opportunity and necessary support.

■ All learners should take part in the various Learning Areas offered within the GET band. In the Foundation Phase (Grades R–3) this comprises the three Learning Programmes (Literacy, Numeracy and Life Skills) integrated with the Learning Outcomes and Assessment Standards of the eight Learning Areas (Language, Mathematics, Natural Sciences, Social Sciences, Arts and Culture, Life Orientation, Economics and Management Sciences, and Technology).

■ Schools (i.e. in this context, Grade R classes at public primary schools, community-based sites and independent schools) create conditions for all children to succeed.

■ Support for learners should be based on the levels of support needed for overcoming individual barriers to learning and development and not on the categorisation of learning according to their abilities or disabilities.

Children are the same; children are different

Although children all over the world have universal developmental characteristics, the *social settings* and *cultural contexts* in which children live significantly shape their development and contribute to each child's uniqueness. Knowledge about these factors is important in order to ensure that learning experiences are meaningful, relevant, and respectful of children and their parents.

Definition

By **social settings** we mean the significant people in children's lives who influence their development.

By **cultural context** we mean the values, behaviours, languages, dialects, and feelings associated with being part of a particular group.

Cultural and ethnic groupings

It is beyond the scope of this book to provide selected characteristics from each cultural group you might find in South Africa. As an early childhood educator, the best way to learn about the diversity of the children at your site is from the families of these children. Increasing your own awareness, knowledge, and comfort level of working with children and adults from different backgrounds will help you to understand the values, behaviours, languages and traditions of the children you will be teaching.

Definition

The following are words we will be using in the rest of this section, and how we interpret them:

- *Bias* – any attitude, belief, or feeling that results in, and helps to justify, unfair treatment of an individual or group because of their identity.

- *Anti-bias* – an active approach to challenging prejudice, stereotyping, and bias.

- *Stereotype* – an unjustifiably dogmatic (fixed) impression or attitude regarding the characteristics of certain groups of people, e.g. the belief that all women are weak and all men are strong is a stereotype.

- *Prejudice* – an attitude, opinion, or feeling formed without sufficient prior knowledge, thought, or reasoning.

- *Racism* – any attitude, action, or institutional practice that subordinates people because of their colour. This includes handling one ethnic group's culture in such a way as to withhold respect from, demean, or destroy the culture of other races.

Strategies to facilitate an anti-biased culture in your classroom:

- Encourage active participation from all families.

- Incorporate the home culture into the classroom and curriculum (e.g. sing songs from all cultures; tell stories from all cultures – take note that these should not contain stereotypes).

- Use culturally relevant curriculum materials (e.g. use pictures reflecting all cultural and ethnic groups).

- Identify and dispel stereotypes.

- Create culturally appropriate learning environments (e.g. place objects, clothes or utensils of many different cultures in the fantasy area in the classroom).

- Use various grouping patterns.

- Use all the languages represented by learners in your class for labeling objects, for example on the interest table. (Tip – choose different colours for different language groups in your class and use the colour system consistently, e.g. write English labels in red; Xhosa labels in green; Sotho labels in purple; Zulu labels in brown and Afrikaans labels in black).

- Learn some key words of all the languages spoken in your class.

- Simplify your own language use.

- Provide story books where people from all ethnic backgrounds are seen to be assertive, overcome problems, make decisions, take on a variety of family roles, and display a wide range of emotions.

Gender

A person's *sexual identity* (which is biological) and *role identity* (which is cultural) make up your *gender identity*. Children need to acquire a gender identity with the support of adults, in order for them to understand that their gender is based on their anatomy and not how they dress, feel and express themselves. Facilitate learning in such a way that they will go beyond the stereotyped gender roles, e.g. only girls do the housework and boys work outside the house. Other forms of gender stereotypes are the belief that certain jobs are reserved for certain genders, and that boys are expected to be the 'rough and tumble type', while girls are 'well-behaved'. You should challenge all these stereotypes, making children aware of them.

Strategies to facilitate an anti-biased classroom culture with regard to gender identification:

- Choose topics in which both girls and boys may be interested.
- Provide props from block play, and clothes and toys in the fantasy area, which both girls and boys would use.
- Choose storybooks without gender bias, where men and women are seen in a variety of roles, displaying the ability to make decisions, solve problems, care for family members, and work outside and in the home.
- Acknowledge that family groupings are varied (e.g. a family can consist of a father and child, two children and a grandmother).

Different learning styles

You may have noticed that children in your class have different learning styles. This means that you sometimes need to make adaptations to your teaching style, so that it complements your learners' learning styles. Read the following paragraph to find out more about this.

Every person has a preferred way of learning. Some children learn by looking (visual learners); some learn better by listening (auditory learners), while others need to handle something physically before they understand it (kinesthetic learners). Since not all learners learn in the same way, teachers should be aware of all styles of learning.

Auditory learners, who learn best by listening to sounds and words, solve problems by talking about them. They can follow verbal instructions and explanations. The more opportunities you provide these listeners to hear and verbalise concepts, the more they will learn.

Visual learners, who learn best by looking, are drawn to colour, shape and motion. They think in images and pictures, taking in what they hear and see and transforming them into images in their brain. For example, Thabo says, 'I see a picture in my head and draw a line around it.' Children who learn by looking need to make visual representations of their thoughts and feelings in order to learn.

Kinesthetic learners learn best by moving. They generally have good co-ordination and are confident in their bodies. Touching and feeling things and changing ideas into movement all act to boost their memory and understanding. For example, Susan twists, turns and falls down while imitating the autumn leaves falling to the ground. Jannie stomps around imitating the elephant he heard about in the story. Presheen tests the strength and sounds of the waste material he wants to use for covering the top of his drum, while Sipho jumps softly and then more vigorously on the trampoline to reach the ball hanging from the tree branch.

Strategies to cater for the different learning styles in your classroom:

Rather than expecting children to adjust, teachers should make sure that they present information in such a way that 'listeners', 'viewers' and 'movers' can all be successful learners.

- **Auditory learners:** Build their knowledge by describing in words what they are doing, e.g. 'You cut the square into two halves from the corner to get triangles for sails for your boat.' Ask them open questions (questions where more the one answer could be correct) to explain what they are doing, e.g. 'How did you make this bird feeder?'

■ **Visual learners:** Ask them to draw pictures of what they understand about experiments (how a rainbow is made). They learn best when you show them how things are done, rather than just telling them verbally, e.g. 'Your tower keeps falling over; let's put the large block underneath and smaller blocks on top and see if this will work better.' Or 'Let's make a graph of all the different colours of the clothes you are wearing today.' 'Mpo, draw a picture about how happy you are that you have a new baby sister.'

■ **Kinesthetic learners:** Provide them with opportunities to move while expressing themselves or their learning; for example, when learning about an object, they could learn by handling the object, feeling its shape and texture and finding out about its properties.

Research about the brain has revealed that the more ways you allow learners to explore a concept, the more likely it is that they will remember what they learn. This means that in addition to meeting the needs of all children with different learning styles, you can maximise learning by creating different kinds of learning opportunities for all children – the listeners, the viewers, and the movers – and all of them will benefit from being exposed to all the learning styles (Dodge, Colker and Heroman 2002).

Children have problems and special abilities

As a reception year teacher you need to facilitate learning for all kinds of children, including those who have disabilities or special needs. These disabilities or special needs may cause barriers to their learning or development. Some children may have physical or learning disabilities, while others may have special gifts or talents. You need the skills to provide learning opportunities for all of them.

> ### Definition
> The word 'disability' is defined as an inability to do something or a diminished capacity to perform in a certain way (Hallahan & Kaufman 2000:6).

Although you are not expected to have in-depth knowledge of every disability, you do need to find out about the specific needs of the learners in your classroom in order to help them overcome these barriers to their learning and developing. As an early childhood educator, you will nurture and interact with these children in the same positive manner as you would with every other child, because children with special needs are more alike than they are different from other children. They have the same basic needs to be loved and cared for adequately, to be treated fairly, and to be successful.

Barriers to learning and development (i.e. factors that prevent learners from learning according to their full potential) could be:

1. Factors that emerge from within the learner because of disabilities:

   a) *neurological* (e.g. cerebral palsy; communication or speech disorders; perceptual disorders; motor disorders; attention problems)

   b) *physical* (e.g. paralysis or skeletal or muscular weakness; health impairments; chronic illnesses; sensory impairments (visual, hearing); cognitive impairment).

2. Factors that emerge from within the learner because of special abilities:

   a) *gifted children* are characterised by a high level of academic ability

   b) *talented* children show excellence in such areas as Art, Music, Drama or Sports.

Intellectually gifted children progress faster than their peers academically and often have large vocabularies, a deep interest in books and reading, a wide range of interests, and a desire to learn. They often become bored and restless if not challenged according to their ability, or they may hide their abilities in order to fit in with others.

3. Societal:

   a) severe poverty

   b) bias against race, gender, culture, language and/or disability and ability.

4. Systemic   School environment

   For example, overcrowded classrooms, inadequate facilities for Grade R classes, poor teaching, lack of basic and appropriate teaching and learning support materials (e.g. textbooks), unprepared indoor or outdoor environment for learners with physical barriers (e.g. ramps for wheelchairs or lack of space to negotiate a wheelchair; paintbrushes which are hard to handle for children with motor disorders) etc.

5. Curriculum practice

   a) unsuitable, developmentally inappropriate planning of Learning Programmes and activities

   b) unsuitable teaching strategies and practices, because of untrained/ill trained teachers for the reception year

   c) focusing only on one or two domains and not stimulating all domains so as to develop the whole child.

6. Health

   a) lacking a healthy, balanced diet

   b) no access to clean, uncontaminated water to drink and bathe

   c) insufficient or unsuitable exercise to develop a healthy, toned body.

7. Barriers to healthy brain development (Thompson 2001):

   Inadequate stimulation limits the number of synapses (connecting points) formed in the brain. If not used, the synapses do not develop, leading to a child experiencing difficulty in learning and in developing healthy social and emotional relationships. The following barriers lead to unhealthy brain development:

   a) exposure to hazardous drugs through mother or self (e.g. alcohol, sniffing glue, heroin); viruses (e.g. HIV), and environmental toxins (e.g. lead and mercury)

   b) diet lacking iron and folic acid

   c) chronic maternal stress, which releases toxic hormones affecting the development of brain structures in the baby

   d) head injuries from child abuse and neglect.

Developmental red lights

Through research the following characteristics of possible problems ('red lights') have been identified. These should be used in conjunction with what we know about the child's normal growth and development in order to identify a problem.

Developmental red lights are used to identify behaviours that should make a teacher stop, look and reflect, as these behaviours are signals of a problem a child might have. The following categories of red lights are intended to guide your observation of children in the reception year.

Red lights for major developmental areas

(Kokot 1992 – adapted from Hallahan and Kaufman 1991, Kapp 1991, Louw 1992 and McAfee & Leong 2004.)

Motor development – large and fine motor skills, and perceptual skills

Pay particular attention to the child who:

- presents changes in his or her physical conditions (changes in skin tone, weight, amount of energy)
- is particularly unco-ordinated
- has lots of accidents
- trips and bumps into things
- is awkward getting down/up, climbing, jumping, getting around toys and people
- stands out from the group when performing structured motor tasks, e.g. walking, climbing stairs, jumping, standing on one foot
- avoids physical games
- relies heavily on watching own or other people's movements in order to do them
- may frequently misjudge distances
- may become particularly unco-ordinated and off-balanced with eyes closed
- uses much more of his or her body to do the task than the task requires, compared with children of the same age (peers)
- dives into a ball (as though to cover the fact that he or she cannot catch it)
- uses tongue, feet, or other body parts excessively to help
- produces extremely heavy colouring when colouring, tracing, writing
- keeps pulling the knees and feet under the body, or thrusts his or her rump in the air when playing wheelbarrows
- makes extraneous and involuntary movements
- holds the other hand in the air or waves while painting with one hand
- does chronic toe walking
- shows twirling or rocking movements
- shakes own hands or taps fingers
- involuntarily finds touching uncomfortable
- flinches or tenses when touched or hugged
- avoids activities that require touching or close contact

- may be uncomfortable lying down, particularly on the back

- reacts as if attacked when unexpectedly bumped

- blinks, protects self from a ball even when trying to catch it

- compulsively craves being touched or hugged

- clings to, or lightly brushes, the teacher a lot

- always sits close to or touches children in the circle

- is strongly attached to sensory experiences such as blankets, soft toys, water, sand, paste or puts hands in food

- has a reasonable amount of experience with fine (small) motor tools but whose skill does not improve proportionately

- can still only snip with scissors or cuts extremely erratically

- cannot colour within the lines of a simple self-drawn object

- frequently switches hands with crayon, scissors, paintbrush

- tries not to, but still gets paste, paint, sand, water everywhere

- is very awkward with, or chronically avoids, small manipulative materials

- finds it very difficult to build new but simple puzzles, draws a person with a body, and who, for example, may take much longer to do a task, but still does not compare favourably with his peers

- shows a lot of trial-and-error behaviour when trying to do a puzzle, mixes up top/bottom, left/right, front/back on simple projects

- repeatedly crashes rather than builds blocks or other types of construction

- still does more scribbling than drawing, despite having lots of experience at drawing.

Social-emotional development

Recognising children with emotional or behavioural problems is not easy. For a problem to be considered serious, behaviours must be demonstrated to a marked degree over a long period of time in a variety of settings. Pay extra attention to the child who, compared with other children of the same age (or six months younger or older):

- has frequent mood swings

- is unable to communicate with others and take care of his or her daily needs – i.e. presents a picture of helplessness

- does not recognise the self as a separate person, or does not refer to the self as 'I'

- has great difficulty separating from a parent, or separates too easily

- is anxious, tense, restless, compulsive, refuses to get dirty or messy, has many fears

- seems preoccupied with own inner world and whose conversations do not make sense

- shows little or no impulse control; hits or bites as a first response

- cannot follow a classroom routine

- expresses inappropriate emotions at inappropriate times (laughs when sad, denies feelings); facial expressions do not match emotions
- cannot focus on activities (short attention span; cannot complete anything; flits from toy to toy)
- ignores or resists others' demonstrations of love or affection
- relates only to adults and refuses to share adult attention; consistently sets up power struggle; is physically abusive to adults
- consistently withdraws from people; prefers to be alone; experiences no depth to relationships; does not seek or accept affection or touching
- treats people as objects; has no empathy for other children; cannot play on another child's terms
- is consistently aggressive, frequently and deliberately hurts others; shows no remorse or is deceitful in hurting others
- uses defence mechanisms in response to feelings of anxiety
- experiences physical or mental withdrawal
- uses projection: distorts reality ('He did it, not me')
- displays displacement: substitutes someone else for real source of anger (angry with baby sister, and so torments the dog or other children)
- demonstrates denial: pretending that a dead parent is still at home
- exhibits repression: child really does not remember what happened
- suffers from regression: returns to an earlier or more infantile form of behaviour (e.g. starts thumb-sucking and carrying around a 'blankie' again).

Speech and language development
Pay extra attention to the child who:

- is struggling with the articulation of words
- omits certain sounds from speech ('ca' for 'car')
- is difficult to understand
- mispronounces sounds
- substitutes certain sounds for other sounds ('wabbit' for 'rabbit')
- seems to have something abnormal about his or her mouth (excessive under/overbite, has difficulty swallowing)
- has difficulty placing words and sounds in proper sequence ('aminal' for 'animal')
- has a history of ear infections/middle ear disorders.
- who has dysfluency (stuttering) or who displays excessive:
    - repetition of sounds, words (m-m-m-; l-l-l)
    - prolongations of sounds (mmmmmmmmmmmm)

- hesitations or long stops during speech, accompanied by tension or struggle behaviour, excessively putting in extra words or sounds, such as 'um', 'uh', 'well', a click of the tongue, or humming)

- shows two or more of these behaviours while speaking: hand clenching, eye blinking, swaying of body, pill-rolling of fingers, no eye contact (but remember that in some cultures it is a sign of respect not to look your elders or superiors in the eye), body tension or struggle, breathing irregularly, tremors, rise in pitch, frustration, avoidance of talking.

- who has problems with his or her voice. Note the child who

  - speaks in a sing-song voice

  - speaks in a monotone

  - speaks extremely quickly or extremely slowly

  - has a breathy or hoarse voice

  - has a very loud or soft voice

  - has a very high or low voice

  - has a very nasal voice.

- who has problems with language (ability to use/understand words):

  - does not appear to understand when others speak, even though their hearing is normal

  - is unable to follow one or two-step directions; communicates by pointing, gesturing

  - makes no attempt to communicate in words

  - has a small vocabulary for his or her age

  - uses parrot-like speech (imitates what others say – *echolalia*)

  - has difficulty putting words together in a sentence

  - uses words inaccurately

  - demonstrates difficulty with three or more of the following: making a word plural, changing tenses of verbs, using pronouns, using the negative, using posessives, naming common objects, using prepositions.

Hearing development

Even a mild or temporary hearing loss in a child may interfere with speech, language, social and academic progress. If more than one of these red light behaviours is observed, it is likely that a problem exists.

1. Speech and lanquage

   Look for the child:

   - whose speech is not easily understood by people outside the family

   - who demonstrates an unusual pattern of stressing words in sentences

   - whose grammar is less accurate than other children of the same age

   - who does not use speech as much as other children of the same age.

2. Social behaviour (at home or at school)

   Look for a child who:

   ■ is shy or hesitant in answering questions or in joining conversations

   ■ misunderstands questions or directions; frequently says 'Huh?' or 'What?' in response to questions

   ■ appears to ignore speech ('only hears what he wants to')

   ■ is unusually attentive to speaker's face or unusually inattentive to speaker; or turns one ear to speaker

   ■ has difficulty with listening activities such as story time and following directions

   ■ has a short attention span

   ■ is distractable and restless; tends to shift too quickly from one activity to another

   ■ is generally lethargic or disinterested in most day-to-day activities

   ■ is considered to have a behaviour problem – too active or aggressive, or too quiet and withdrawn.

3. Medical indications

   Look for the child who:

   ■ has frequent upper respiratory tract infections, congestion that appears to be related to allergies, or a cold for several weeks or months

   ■ has frequent earaches, ear infections, throat infections or middle ear problems

   ■ has had draining ears on one or more occasions

   ■ breathes through his or her mouth, or snores

   ■ is generally lethargic, or has poor colour.

Visual development

These include visual skills, acuity (the ability to see at a distance) and disease.

1. Eyes

   Be aware of the child who:

   ■ has watery eyes

   ■ has a discharge from the eyes

   ■ lacks co-ordination in directing the gaze of both eyes

   ■ has persistently red eyes

   ■ has eyes which are sensitive to light.

2. Eyelids

   Take note of the child who:

   ■ has crust on lids or among lashes

   ■ has red eyelids

■ frequently experiences styes or swelling of the lids.

3. General behaviour and complaints related to vision

Be concerned about the child who:

■ rubs his or her eyes excessively

■ experiences dizziness, headaches, nausea when doing close work

■ attempts to 'brush away' blur

■ has itchy, burning or scratchy eyes

■ suffers from double vision

■ contorts face or body when looking at distant objects, or thrusts head forward, squints or widens eyes

■ blinks eyes excessively

■ holds book too close or too far away

■ is inattentive during visual tasks

■ shuts or covers one eye

■ its head

■ its eyes which appear to cross or wander, especially when tired.

If more than one of these red light behaviours is observed, it is likely that a problem exists.

● **Go to:**

Taking care of these problems is discussed in Chapter 7.

General *strategies and adaptations to use in an anti-biased way with children with barriers to learning and development (adapted from Hernandez 2001):*

■ Consult specialists in the field of the particular barrier and/or provide guidance for finding medical help for medical problems.

■ Provide consistency and structure – this helps learners with barriers to thrive.

■ Use audiotapes for learners who cannot read successfully.

■ Provide visual reminders (pictures, maps, charts) for learners who have difficulty paying attention.

■ Give directions in small steps.

■ Find the special interests and strengths of each learner and use this knowledge when planning activities for these learners.

■ Arrange seating so that every learner can see and hear comfortably.

■ Demonstrate new materials, equipment, and activities.

■ Children with gifts or talents need to be challenged and stimulated.

Be sensitive to the barriers that prevent learners from learning and developing.

Specific *strategies and adaptations to use in an anti-biased way with children with barriers to learning and development:*

■ Adjust tables so that wheelchairs will fit underneath or equip the wheelchair with trays; provide taller chairs so that other learners will sit comfortably at this table.

■ Provide bolsters or firm cushions in a box to provide support for children with mobility impairments, so that they can do activities on the floor.

■ Pair learners with impairments with able learners so that they never feel abandoned.

■ Use puzzles with knobs for children with visual or motor disabilities.

■ Slip a sponge haircurler over the handle of a paint brush for a better grip for learners with motor disabilities.

■ Include objects that a visually disabled child can feel, e.g. sand in the paint. Demarcate a section on the table with a border where these learners can work. Always put the paint out with colours in the same order.

■ Be aware that a child with a hearing handicap should not sit close to loud areas or sounds, as these interfere with a hearing aid.

■ Children with disabilities should be made to feel positive about themselves in their life world. They should not be depicted as victims in pictures, toys and stories (e.g. one of the characters in a puppet play could wear glasses).

■ Prepare the learners in your class in advance if a disabled child is going to be included in your class. For example, tell an unbiased story about a child with a similar disability.

■ Provide books where adults and children with disabilities take part in all aspects of life: sport, school, family life, etc.

Adaptations for gifted children:

Provide challenging and stimulating experiences for gifted children. They are often eager to explore a topic or situation in greater depth, and approach subjects that interest them with a high level of enthusiasm and intensity. Here are a few suggestions regarding how adaptations may be made:

■ Create an environment that promotes investigation, inquiry, and independent exploration.

■ Follow the child's interests. If the child is interested in fossils, aeroplanes or insects, help him or her explore these topics by providing books, web sites, and other resources. It is not necessary to involve the whole class, but do include others who become interested.

■ Teach to the child's strengths. If a child is advanced mathematically , don't waste his or her time by teaching him or her to recognise number symbols. Find out what the child knows and offer challenging problems to solve. Boredom can be a gifted child's greatest enemy.

■ Have realistic expectations. Keep in mind that being gifted in one area is no guarantee that a child is gifted in all areas of development. The mathematically gifted child may be socially or physically at an average or even low level of development. Treat these children as individuals, and plan experiences that will appeal to their individual strengths.

Conclusion

The concept of the whole child approach also includes the uniqueness of the person. Although the different areas of development (physical/motor, social/emotional, intellectual, and creative) have been discussed separately, they cannot be isolated from one another. They each make a valuable contribution to the total child. The child should also not be seen in isolation, but as a member of a family which is part of a community set in a broader socio-political context.

In Early Childhood Development, a culturally relevant curriculum is anti-biased, discards stereotyping, celebrates diversity, and is inclusive of all children. An appreciation of diversity and individual differences, while focusing on similarities, is important in today's world. Such an approach will help prepare children to develop, live and work together.

Bibliography

Berk LE. 1994. *Child Development.* Massachusetts: Allyn & Bacon.

De Witt MW & Van Zyl E. 1990. *Empirical education: Preprimary education.*
BEd Study guide for OPP 402-B. Pretoria: University of South Africa.

Geneese F (n.d.) *Bilingual acquisition.* Retrieved 7 May 2004 from
www.earlychildhood.com/Articles/index.cfm.

Gordon AM & Browne KW. 1989. *Beginnings and beyond: foundations in early childhood.*
Albany, New York: Delmar.

Hallahan DP & Kanfrau JM. 1991. *Exceptional children: Introduction to special education.*
Englewood Cliffs, NJ: Prentice-Hall.

Hendrick J. 1990. *Total learning: Developmental curriculum for the young child.* New York:
Macmillan.

Hendrick J. 1992. *The whole child* 5ed. New York: Merrill.

Kapp JA (ed). 1991. *Children with problems: An orthopaedagogical perspective.* Pretoria: Van
Schaik.

Kokot SJ. 2001. *Understanding giftedness: A South African perspective.* Durban: Butterworths.

Kruger ACM. 1989. *Identifisering van die begaafde voorskoolse kind.* Unpublished MEd thesis.
University of Pretoria.

Louw DA. 1992. *Menslike ontwikkeling.* Pretoria: HAUM.

Lowenfeld V and Brittain WL. 1987. *Creative and mental growth.* New York: Macmillan.

Machado JM. 1990. *Early childhood experiences in language arts.* Albany, New York: Delmar.

McAfee 0 & Leong D. 2004. *Assessing and guiding: Young children's development and learning.*
Boston: Allyn & Bacon.

Morrison GS. 1995. *Early childhood education today.* Columbus, Ohio: Merrill.

Mussen PH, Conger JJ, Kagan J & Huston AC. 1990. *Child development and personality* 7ed. New
York: Harper & Row.

Mwamwenda TS. 1990. *Educational psychology: An African perspective.* Sandton: Heinemann.

Penning RJ. 1993. *Didactics and literature for young children.* Study guide for DIDLIT-Q. Pretoria:
University of South Africa.

Schirmer GJ (ed). 1974. *Performance objectives for perschool children.* Adapt Press.

Smart MS and Smart RC. 1997. *Children: Development and relationships.* New York: Macmillan.

Snow, CE. 1997 The myths about being bilingual. *NABE News,* 29, 36.

Turner PH and Hamner TJ. 1994. *Child development and early education.* Boston: Allyn & Bacon.

Van Staden CJS. 1987. *Die aard en struktuur van kleuterkuns: 'n Didaktiese perspektief.*
Unpublished MEd dissertation. Pretoria: University of South Africa.

Chapter

3

Emergent Literacy: Language and the beginnings of reading

Reda Davin

Literacy is a basic skill every person needs. In this chapter we aim to help you to develop the necessary skills and knowledge to be able to enhance the young learner's Emergent Literacy skills.

OUTCOMES

After you have read this chapter you should be able to:

- explain the importance of language for formal teaching and learning
- critically discuss the *whole language approach* to the teaching of Emergent Literacy
- understand that the development of Emergent Literacy entails more than mere school-related activities
- develop the learner's language by presenting suitable activities that will enhance the learner's listening and speaking skills
- encourage the learning of an additional language by presenting activities that will develop the learner's use of the language in a meaningful and playful way
- use suitable children's literature as a means to introduce the learning of reading and writing
- understand the teaching of sight vocabulary and letters as part of an Emergent Literacy Programme
- critically discuss different views regarding reading instruction and develop a suitable approach for the reception year
- help the young learner who is eager and able to start with reading instruction on an individual basis.

Why Emergent Literacy in the reception year?

Language is of basic importance for the normal and complete development of every human being. Although any language is difficult and complex, children learn to speak their home language with ease in only four to six years. Why children learn language so easily is a question that linguists (scientists who study language) cannot fully answer and there are different theories about this matter.

 **Go to:**

Also read the section on language development in Chapter 2 *Know the child*.

> **Remember**
> Although the child's acquisition (i.e. ability to use) of his or her first language is more or less complete by the age of six, language is never fully developed. Our use of language should grow and change as we mature. The child (and later the adult) should learn new and more complex words, and improve his or her communication skills, throughout his or her life.

There is general agreement on the importance of good language usage for the Grade 1 learner. In Grade 1 the learner must be able to:

- listen and understand instructions from the teacher

- communicate with his or her friends and teacher

- use words to communicate what he or she is thinking (no one will know what is going on in the mind of the child unless he or she is able to put his or her thoughts into words).

No learner will able to do these things without the use of good, understandable language. During the reception year you will not start teaching the child to read text or to write sentences – you have a far more important task! This task is helping the young learner to develop all the necessary language skills needed to be able to learn with ease, and to be able to learn to read *with understanding*, to spell *correctly* and to write *creatively*. This should all be done in a playful and enjoyable way.

We are going to present activities that will help the learners to enjoy the more formal learning processes in Grade 1 with understanding and ease.

What is the purpose of an Emergent Literacy Programme?

The main purpose of an Emergent Literacy Programme in the reception year is to help the young learner to communicate effectively either in spoken or written/visual form (Department of Education 2003 (b): 41).

During the reception year attention must be given to the following: listening skills; language use (syntax and structure); emergent reading skills, in the form of experience with well-known words in context; exposure to emergent writing; and reasoning skills (based on Department of Education 2003 (a): 34 and Department of Education 2003 (b): 41).

There are six Learning Outcomes for the Emergent Literacy Programme in the Foundation Phase (Department of Education (2003 (b); 43)). They are:

- listening
- speaking
- reading/viewing
- writing
- thinking and reasoning, and
- language structure and use.

Each of the Learning Outcomes is broken down into several Assessment Standards. These Assessment Standards will guide you in presenting activities that are relevant as well as developmentally appropriate for the individual reception year learner.

Go to:

In Chapter 1 we discussed Learning Outcomes for an Emergent Literacy Programme in the reception year.

In the rest of this chapter we are going to discuss how you can achieve these Learning Outcomes in a playful and enjoyable way!

It all starts with language!

Young children learn language in three main ways:

- listening to other people using language
- imitating other people's use of language
- expressing themselves (i.e. using language).

Effective teachers use their awareness of how children learn language to further enhance their learners' language development. Children need the following in order to develop their language skills:

A role model: A person that provides them with a good example of how to use the language.

A rich language environment: Young learners must hear correct language being used in different circumstances.

Opportunities to use language: Learners need to have time to talk to friends and adults (e.g. the teacher) freely and creatively.

> **Remember**
> As the teacher, you should use correct language and full sentences when you talk to your class.

The whole language approach to Emerging Literacy

Just as we use the way the young child learns as our starting point to decide on a suitable teaching approach for the reception year, we use the way the child learns language as our starting point in adopting a suitable approach to teaching language. Based on the fact that children need to hear and use language, we propose that the following should be the main characteristics of an integrated approach to teaching language:

- emphasis on exposure to language in a natural and informal way
- emphasis on the fact that all language skills relate to each other – i.e. listening, speaking, reading, spelling and writing
- use of **mostly** the same activities to develop these skills. (There is also a link between language and all the other sections of the daily timetable.)

This approach is called the **whole language** approach.

> ### Definition
>
> A whole or integrated language approach means that all language activities (reading, writing and speaking), learning and people (learners, teachers and parents) are included. All language arts are interrelated in a theme and activities that are presented throughout the school day.

What are the implications for the teacher?

The beginnings of reading, writing, spelling and the learner's overall language development cannot be separated. Each of these aspects of language helps to further the others. An Emergent Literacy Programme must therefore be part of an all inclusive, integrated language development programme. Language development is part of every activity during the day. As a teacher you should therefore:

- use the child's spoken language (including any errors) as the foundation of what you teach

- respect the child's language and use it as a cornerstone for any emergent reading or writing activities (e.g. if the child's home language is Zulu, they should learn to read and write in Zulu before learning to read and write in English)

- ensure that all young learners experience feelings of success – this will ensure that they enjoy language and all related emergent reading and writing activities

- make reading, writing and language experiences a part of every activity in the timetable and ensure that young learners use words or symbols in an enjoyable and meaningful way

- encourage risk taking – errors are part of the natural process of learning

- use materials which are familiar to the learner, such as well-known stories, songs and rhymes

- read stories, rhymes and verses to the children every day

- set aside time for activities in which the child can experiment with reading and writing independently.

Language activities (including emergent reading, writing and spelling) should not be presented in separate or 'special' language periods. Emergent Literacy activities should be presented throughout the day as an integral part of many different activities.

> ### Example
>
> The timetable for the reception year is full of language opportunities:
>
> *Music time*, with the emphasis on learning new songs and enjoying old ones;
>
> *Story time*, with activities such as puppet shows and the dramatisation of stories by the young learners;
>
> *Discussions*, on topics about the world around them, during which time young learners can hear and use language freely.

Reasons why there should be no formal language periods in Grade R

Research has shown that formal language periods for young learners are of less value to the child than opportunities for the spontaneous use of language.

■ Formal language periods are of less value because language is closely linked to emotions. It is far better for the young learner to speak when he or she feels motivated to do so than to talk for (sometimes) unclear reasons!

■ In formal language periods the language usage is of lower quality and quantity than in activities requiring spontaneous language usage. Fewer topics are introduced during formal language learning and the learner uses fewer words and sentences. The language used is also less creative and more rigid.

■ Formal language periods can hamper certain learners' language development. For example, shy learners find it stressful to speak in front of a group.

■ It is more important that learners learn to speak *fluently* (i.e. confidently) than that they learn to speak *correctly*. Formal language periods tend to place the emphasis on correctness, and this negatively impacts on learners' fluency.

■ The main purpose of language is social interaction. This is achieved most effectively in an informal, social setting and not in a formal, group exercise.

■ The teaching of isolated skills (such as a separate period for reading) is neither creative nor enriching for a learner's language development.

What influences the young learner's ability to learn to read, write and spell with ease?

Learning to read, write and spell correctly does not happen overnight. It takes place gradually and as part of the child's total language experience. Developmental factors such as the learner's physical, perceptual, intellectual, language and emotional development as well as the learner's home and school environment all affect the learning process.

We will discuss each of these factors separately, but it is important to bear in mind that in real life all the factors interrelate with each other.

Physical factors

Certain physical factors can hamper a learner's Emergent Literacy:

■ As with all other learning activities, learners who are healthy, well nourished and get sufficient rest will be more likely to reach their full potential, and will find it easier to master the necessary skills of reading, writing and spelling.

■ Learners with normal visual (seeing) and auditory (hearing) abilities will also find the learning process easier.

■ Learners with delayed speech or who experience any deficiency in their language skills may require special attention when they start with the formal process of learning to read and write.

Perceptual factors

In order to be able to read and spell it is necessary to understand the connection between the written and spoken language. To be able to do so, learners need certain perceptual skills, such as the ability to:

- focus on one thing and pay attention to detail (observation)
- see the similarities and differences between letters (visual discrimination)
- hear the differences between sounds (auditory discrimination)
- observe an object in relation to other objects around it (position in space).

Remember

Some learners may be able to see and hear without difficulty, but still have problems hearing and seeing similarities and differences in sounds and words.

How important are perceptual activities for Emergent Literacy?

Emergent reading, writing and spelling involve more than teaching the child *pre-reading* and *writing skills*. Traditionally, pre-reading skills were thought to be developed through the use of workbooks and activities that were aimed at developing perceptual skills. Current views however see emergent literacy as depending on far more than merely perceptual skills. The ability to hear and see differences in objects and sounds is regarded as less important that the interaction with language and books themselves.

The child does not learn to speak by repeating boring and senseless perceptual activities, but by hearing and using language in context (i.e. by using language in a way that is meaningful to the child). In order to learn to talk, young learners need opportunities to hear and experiment with language in a language rich environment. They start to speak because they want to communicate with people in their environment.

Remember

*Young learners start to read and write because they want to **communicate** and make **sense** out of printed language.*

Intellectual factors

Reading, writing and spelling are intellectual processes. To be able to read and write, the learner needs intellectual skills such as comprehension (understanding), problem solving and reasoning skills. This explains why people who are severely intellectually challenged struggle to learn to read and write. Learners do not need to have a high IQ to be able to learn to read and write. What they do need is an intellectually stimulating and language-rich environment.

Language factors

Learners need to understand and use a language before formal reading and writing instruction in that language can take place. This is one of the main reasons why instruction in the learner's home language is advised. Learners also need experiences of drawing pictures, and then talking about their pictures. These skills all serve as a basis for understanding the printed word.

Emotional factors

Learners may be physically, linguistically and intellectually capable, but still have difficulty in understanding and mastering reading and writing. How learners feel about themselves, other people, the school and learning in general can affect their ability to learn to read, write and spell.

The learners' environment and experiences

It cannot be overemphasised that learners need a language-rich environment with plenty of informal exposure to books, other suitable printed materials and the spoken word to be able to learn to read and spell with ease.

Promoting language development as part of an Emergent Literacy Programme

Language is a basic cornerstone of all learning, and well developed language skills are very important when one starts to learn to read, spell and write. However, you may have children in your class whose language fluency is less advanced than others, because they may not have had many opportunities for speaking and listening or communication in general. Before these learners can become involved in formally learning to read, spell and write they need opportunities to develop their basic language skills.

Three basic skills that you as the teacher should give attention to are:

1. Listening skills
2. Speaking skills
3. Communication skills

In the following sections we are going to discuss each of these as separate skills. It is important to remember that this is only to make our discussion easier. In the daily timetable all the skills (listening, speech and communication) and the introduction to English (or another additional language) are integrated in the different presentations and activities.

Apart from developing these skills in the child's home language, you may have to introduce the learner to English (if it is not the learner's home language) and/or any other language that is the medium of instruction but not the learner's home language.

1. Listening skills

It is important that you as the teacher help and guide your class towards listening with attention. Listening is very important for learning, but because young learners are distracted by the many noises and sounds around them, they are not always sure *how* to listen or *what* to listen to. It is the teacher's (sometimes difficult) task to help the child listen to what is important and ignore all the other sounds and noises that surround him, and in addition to this, to listen with understanding. Learners can *develop* their ability to listen attentively for longer periods.

> **Remember**
> Listening is more than merely hearing. It is the ability to hear and interpret what has been heard.

What you can do to help young learners to listen

Provide the child with opportunities to *listen* and not just to *hear*. Here are some suggestions:

■ Tell stories and recite nursery rhymes and easy verses. (Because stories and rhymes are such important tools for the development of language and reading, they are discussed in more detail later in this chapter.)

■ Give the young learners simple tasks and instructions that they must remember and complete. Start with only one task or instruction, and then increase the number of instructions, so that eventually the child can listen to and remember five related instructions.

Example

Princess, please get a mug from the storeroom. Fill it with water, and then water the plant in the classroom as well as the one on the verandah. When you have finished, bring the mug back to me.

■ Make a tape recording of easily recognisable sounds from the environment and let the young learners sit and listen to them. Allow them to identify each sound, and then ask them questions about what they have heard, e.g.:

– Is the car coming nearer?

– Do you think the dog is barking at thieves or is the dog barking because it is happy that his or her owner has come home from school?

This is an important activity, as the child needs to listen with attention to be able to interpret what he or she hears.

■ Give learners opportunities to listen to and interpret music. Listening to music is an activity that young learners love. Help the child to listen by playing games involving music.

✳ Example ✳

■ Play the well-known game Musical Chairs. Play or sing a song that the young learners can dance or move to. When the music stops, the young learners must sit down. The child that sits down last is out. Repeat until you have a winner.

■ Play a piece of music or sing a song. The young learners then have to listen to the song and say whether it is a happy or sad song (musical interpretation).

■ Play music or a song with different parts. As the music changes, the young learners must change their interpretation of the music. The song or piece can change either in:

beat (e.g. with some parts being slow, and others fast)

volume (e.g. with some parts being soft, and others loud)

tone (e.g. with some parts being high, and others low)

The learners should move or dance with the music. Instruct the learners to either move fast or slowly; stamp their feet or dance on the points of their toes; stretch their bodies or be on the ground.

---

2. Speaking skills

As a teacher, you play an important role in the development of your learners' speech ability – you are their role model. The less developed the child's language, the more important the teacher becomes to their language development. The child hears and imitates the teacher's pronunciation, sentence construction, vocabulary and general language use.

You can improve a child's speech skills by:

■ always using simple but complete sentences. Talk to your class in such a way that the children understand your words, without using 'baby' language. Use simple, correct language.

■ verbalising the learner's actions and play

> ### Example
> Beauty is building with blocks. She asks you for some more blocks. You could either simply give her extra blocks without any conversation, or you could say to her:
>
> 'That is a very complicated tower. Who is going to live there? Is the tower nearly finished? Do you need a lot more blocks or only a few?'

■ use new words in appropriate situations (see the words *complicated, few* and *more* in the above example)

■ provide your group with real experiences that they can talk about. By having new experiences and talking about old ones, children learn new words in context.

> ### Example
> Take your class on outings to museums, the zoo, a fire station, etc. Also provide them with everyday experiences – such as a walk around the block, or posting letters in the post box. Talk about these outings afterwards. Let them draw, build and play what they have experienced.

■ encourage spontaneous conversation during the day, especially during free play activities and outdoor play

>
> ### Remember
> *Do not expect young learners to be quiet during activities such as art. Encourage them to talk to each other while they are working.*

■ accept the child's language and his or her pronunciation of words. Remember that there are different dialects and different ways of using language. This is especially applicable to the child with poor language development and the non-English speaking child.

Go to:
Read the section on *Learning a second (or third) language* later on in this chapter.

■ Provide opportunities that encourage speech. The dramatisation of stories and rhymes is an excellent activity.

How to help young learners to dramatise stories or rhymes

1. The young learners must <u>know the story or rhyme very well before they can dramatise</u> it. Use a story or rhyme that your class has enjoyed. <u>Retell the story at least four times</u>.

2. Make (or help the young learners to make) <u>simple props</u>. Masks or characteristic pieces of clothing are all that is needed.

3. Start dramatising the story or rhyme by <u>telling the story</u> or saying the rhyme <u>while the young learners play out the action</u>.

4. The young learners <u>should not have to say any lines until they feel ready</u> and comfortable to do so. As they feel more comfortable with this activity, they will start to say part of the dialogue, while you read or tell the rest.

5. Your <u>aim is</u> to encourage the young learners not only to <u>play out the story, but also to change its storyline and to create new stories (creative language usage)</u>.

Example

When dramatising the story of *The Three Little Pigs* you need only four props: one mask for each of the pigs and a mask for the wolf.

Figure 3.1 – Examples of very simple masks which can be used as props

Attach strings to tie the mask around the head. Egg carton cut-outs can be used effectively as noses.

Remember

Although it is important for learners to listen and respond to the teacher's use of language, the <u>best method for language development is more indirect</u>. Provide <u>opportunities when learners can model, imitate and respond to your example</u> through activities such as the dramatising, retelling and role-playing of stories.

3. Communication skills

The <u>reason for acquiring language is to be able to</u> *communicate*. To achieve this, the child must be able to <u>use language in a social setting</u>. It is important to plan for <u>opportunities for communication</u> between child and teacher and between children themselves.

To help you communicate effectively with the child, keep the following guidelines in mind:

- Ensure that you talk *with* and not *to* the child. Avoid situations where the child is always in the position of listener, while you do all the talking.

- It is important to create an atmosphere where the child feels secure and relaxed and is not afraid to make mistakes.

- Do not talk only to the talkative, bright young learners. They are the easiest to talk to, but the quiet, reserved child may be the one most in need of your conversation.

- Use a friendly tone and speak at a moderate speed. Use correct English, but ensure that the child can understand the words you use.

- Do not speak down to the child. Use proper language with full sentences.

- Talk about things the young learners are interested in. Choose topics from their environment.

Go to:

See *The integrated approach* in Chapter 1 *Planning to teach.*

- Do not correct learners' language. Rather repeat what the learner said, correcting their mistake in your sentence. If you correct the child directly they may become self-conscious about talking, and this may in turn reduce the amount of talking they do. Your goal should be to encourage your children to talk, even if everything they say is not grammatically correct.

Keep the following guidelines in mind for creating opportunities for communication between children:

- Plan the classroom in such a way that the young learners have opportunities to talk. Have different areas where small groups of learners can work together.

- Encourage conversation between the learners. Do not ask or expect the children to keep quiet during free choice activities.

- A fantasy area in the classroom encourages learners to play together and to talk to each other.

- Ensure that you have play materials such as toy telephones, puppets and masks in your classroom. These materials will help the learner (even the shy child) to talk freely with a friend and later to use creative language.

Remember
Learners need time, a place and support to practise language.

Plan opportunities for communication in the daily timetable

The whole language approach emphasises planning for opportunities to use language throughout the day. The following ideas may help you to achieve this:

- learners need large blocks of time in small groups to encourage spontaneous talking

- plan for opportunities for conversational time, such as informal discussions

- provide a variety of activities that promote interaction between learners, such as art and fantasy play

- in your timetable, include several short periods for teacher-facilitated group activities such as story time, reading and listening to poems and music.

Research into the effect of television on language development

The influence of television on the child's language development is a topic that has been debated for decades. Research has found that while children who watch a great deal of television are exposed to language, they are in fact cut off from interaction with the speaker. Children who watch a lot of television can acquire *vocabulary*, which is naturally a positive outcome. However, children for whom television provides the *only* exposure to language do not acquire the ability to create and comprehend many sentences. The fact that language doesn't develop based on television exposure alone contradicts the idea that mere exposure is all that is required to trigger language development. Children must also have the opportunity to test their ideas about language by interacting with other speakers in everyday settings.

Learning a second (and third) language

Because South Africa has eleven official languages, young learners are expected to learn languages other than their own. Many learners in reception year in this country find themselves in classes where the medium of instruction is not their home language. This has significant implications for the reception year teacher.

Learning a second (or even third) language need not be a major trauma for a learner. Exposing learners in a natural and enjoyable way to a second language can be an enriching experience for them. A second language can be learned easily if learned in a meaningful, functional way.

Acquiring two languages simultaneously

Research has shown that young learners can learn two languages at the same time. The two languages can be learned in a parallel manner. The depth of knowledge of one language may differ from the other or the two may develop equally. The simultaneous acquisition of two languages may mean a mixing of the two, as heard in young learners' speech when they use words or structures of both languages. Learning two languages does not harm the acquisition of either language.

(Gordon and Brown 2004:492)

The child will learn a second language in the same way as learning a first language if given enough opportunities to hear and speak the language.

Many learners in South Africa enter a school without being able to speak and understand the language of instruction. Although there is general consensus that learners must be taught in their home language for the duration of the Foundation Phase, this is not the reality in many reception year classes. However, young learners usually learn a second (or even third) language with ease if, through natural exposure in the classroom, the child has experiences in both languages (the child's home language as well as the language of instruction, which is usually English). This is unfortunately not always possible, as the reception year teacher may not be able to speak the child's home language. The teacher must, in cases like these, be very sensitive to the child's emotional needs.

Guidelines for teaching children who do not speak the language of instruction

■ Your first goal is to help learners to *speak* the language of instruction. They will learn to speak the language if the materials and activities they encounter are related to their experiences and interest. Language learning should relate to their immediate needs in the school and community.

■ Use parents or other volunteers to explain certain aspects of the day in the learner's home language.

■ If possible, ask older children who speak the learner's home language, to help you explain certain information to the learner.

■ Place learners with the same home language together in pairs (for some, not all, activities) so that they can guide each other.

■ Find books and magazines in the learner's home language that they can page through.

■ Label the objects in the classroom in both the language of instruction and the children's home language.

Remember
Use different coloured paper for each language when labelling objects. Keep to the same colour throughout the year.

■ Try to learn a few key words and sentences of the child's mother tongue. The fact that you can communicate with him or her (even in a very limited manner) will make the child feel more safe and comfortable.

■ Give these young learners lots of emotional support. The children may feel lonely and scared at the beginning of the year. You should therefore give them lots of support without the use of language. (For example, hug them when they draw beautiful pictures; or put the pictures up on the wall as a sign of your approval.)

■ Do not correct these young learners' language. Give them time to complete what they are saying and do not complete a sentence for them.

■ Speak at a moderate speed and articulate words correctly.

■ Give these young learners many opportunities to speak freely with the other young learners and with you.

Go to:
See the guidelines under *Communication skills* above.)

■ Use full sentences and give clear instructions, e.g.:

CORRECT   Use the red crayon

INCORRECT   Use that one

■ Try to understand these young learners even if their grammar is incorrect.

- Activities such as songs, rhymes and chants are very useful for children learning a second language. As the young learners say or sing the songs and rhymes together they will feel less threatened because they are part of a group. Language issues such as pronunciation of words are being practised in a fun way.

- Meaningless pronunciation drills must be avoided. All activities must provide opportunities for enjoyable and meaningful learning.

- You should be alert to possible cultural or other misunderstandings due to the learner's initially poor grasp of the language.

When teaching a second language, remember the following tips:

- associate words with concrete objects

- dramatise actions to aid understanding

- provide opportunities for learners to participate in a variety of experiences

- increase learners' vocabulary by providing opportunities for learners to touch, name, label and talk about concrete objects and experiences

- teach and enact prepositions such as under, beside, on, in and out

- learn songs, games and rhymes with gestures and actions

- take learners on outings (field trips)

- use as many audio-visual resources as possible, such as puppets, pictures, magazines and newspapers, films and videos to enhance concrete experiences

- provide activities and opportunities for spontaneous play

- provide many opportunities for the learner to be exposed to the second language – this will ensure better acquisition.

> **Remember**
> The speed at which young children learn a second language differs from child to child – do not force or push a child beyond his or her competence level. Ensure that all activities and the level of language used are appropriate in terms of the child's developmental level.

The beginnings of reading

The ability to read is very important in today's world. A person who is unable to read cannot function properly in society. Our society values literacy because it forms the basis of one of the most important forms of communication in the modern world – the written or printed word.

According to research, learning to read is less difficult than learning to speak. When a child learns to read, she merely builds on what she already knows of the language.

How do children learn to read?

Research has established that young learners learn to read in much the same way as they learn to speak – through interaction with their families and other significant individuals. The child becomes aware of print and is self-motivated to use the printed or written word in order to make sense of their environment. (Maxim 1989:527)

The process of learning to read therefore follows very much the same process as learning to speak:

- by observing others while they are reading and writing
- by experimenting with reading and writing
- by constructing their own written products for others to read.

When is the child ready to learn to read?

Before young children can learn to read with ease they must be:

- able to speak and understand the language they are reading. They must have a good vocabulary and be able to carry out tasks and instructions given in the language.
- interested in books and stories. Stories and books must be part of the child's everyday environment.
- able to focus their attention on pictures and talk about what they see (tell stories about the pictures).
- able to complete and retell well-known and favourite stories. (They must be able to remember them by heart.)
- able to recognise letters and words that they see every day.
- interested in words and letters.
- motivated to learn to read and believe that reading is easy and enjoyable.

In the reception year, all of the above factors must be developed, not as separate skills, but with an integrated, *whole language* approach.

Reading is not only the deciphering of symbols as words – it is also about understanding the meaning of the words. Young learners should understand that written words (letters) are permanent symbols for the spoken word.

Children's literature as a means of introducing the learner to reading and writing

Two of the most important resources for a teacher to enhance the young learner's emergent reading and writing skills are *stories and rhymes*.

If you can only afford to buy one resource for your class, ensure that you buy *books*. No reception year class should be without good books. Make sure that you have an ample supply of good story books, picture books, science books, counting books, and books with poems and rhymes. If you are on a very tight budget, buy only a few books and then add to these by joining a library or a teacher resource centre from which you can borrow books weekly.

A particularly effective pre-reading strategy is to tell the learners a story and at the same time to show him or her the written text and corresponding pictures in a book. The benefit of this method is that it:

■ instils in the learner a desire to learn to read

■ enables the learner to observe the process of reading and to form an idea of what reading is

■ allows the learner to spontaneously discover the value and function of the written word.

How to choose good stories for young learners in the reception year

Although any story will help the learner to develop an understanding of the reading process, good stories are also important for the learner's language and intellectual development as well as appreciation of literature. When taking time to read a story, spend the time well by reading a *good* story.

The following guidelines will help you to choose a good story book:

■ The learner should be able to identify with the characters in the book.

■ The events experienced by the characters should relate to experiences in the learner's life.

■ The characters must not be *stereotyped*. Stereotyping means that all individuals belonging to a particular group are presented as having the same characteristics. Racism, sexism and stereotyped images of old age are all examples of stereotypes that are avoided in good storybooks.

> ### Stereotyping
>
> Stories in which people from one race are presented in a degrading way are never acceptable. Also avoid stories where mothers are always in the kitchen or doing housework, and fathers are always the breadwinners. Ensure that the work and roles of males and females presented in stories reflect the reality of everyday life. For example, in the real world, some cooks and ballet dancers are male, and some doctors and engineers are female. Males also cry and feel sad and females can be strong. Not all grannies spend all day knitting, and in fact many grannies and grandpas are still working very hard in important jobs despite their advanced age. These kinds of realities should be present in story books.

■ The story should have an interesting plot.

■ The story can include adventure and excitement, but not excessive violence and fear.

■ The characters in the story must be convincing – even if they are fantasy characters. The way that they act must suit the character's age and personality.

■ The writing style must allow the learner to experience the atmosphere of the story.

■ A good story has humour, exaggeration and word play. It leaves the learner with good feelings.

■ The structure of the story must be logical, with no flashbacks.

■ The story should have a happy ending.

Stories are an important tool for encouraging the learners' development and should therefore be a part of the daily activities in the reception year timetable.

How to use stories as an activity for Emergent Reading

■ Point to the text when you read stories to your group. Indicating where you are reading will help the learners to understand that the meaning is in the text that you are reading (and not only in the pictures).

■ Give your group an opportunity to retell the story. Help them retell stories by prompting their memory with questions such as 'What happened next?' or 'Did it happen before this?'

■ When young learners repeat well-known stories that the teacher has repeatedly read to them they often remember the story (or parts of it) word by word.

■ Young learners imitate the reading process by 'reading' the words, although this is not really reading – they are merely repeating words they have heard and memorised in the correct sequence. When a learner begins to do this, it is a clear sign that he or she is ready to learn to read words.

■ Read storybooks with few words and useful, interesting pictures, so that learners are able to remember the story easily and 'read' (retell) the story with the help of the illustrations.

> **Remember**
>
> *At this stage most (if not all) of your learners will not be able to read. Their 'reading' is often in fact telling the story, using the pictures to guide them. If you read a story repeatedly to them (not on the same day, of course), some learners will learn the words by heart and they will 'read' the story fluently. This is not actual reading, but an imitation of the reading process, and is an important precursor to learning to read.*

What to do if the learner does not have previous experience with books

The experience of pleasant and regular exposure to books is a very important way to introduce young learners to reading – the more exposure they have to books, the better. Children should ideally be exposed to books from a very young age. The parent or caretaker should start introducing the child to books and stories in his or her baby years. Part of your task as a reception year teacher is to inform parents about the importance of reading books to their children from a very young age.

Naturally, this ideal is not always achieved. Many children grow up in circumstances where books and reading are not everyday activities. Factors such as the illiteracy of parents and poor economic circumstances can deter parents from buying books. You then have the exciting task of giving the learner the opportunity of 'discovering' books in the reception year.

■ Start with books containing only pictures of well-known objects (i.e. no text). You could even make your own picture books by cutting and pasting pictures from magazines. Do not use baby books, but rather use picture books that will be of interest to the five to six year old child. Counting books such as *I Hunter* by Pat Hutchins are suitable.

Go to:

Picture books will be discussed in more detail in the next section.

■ Give learners lots of opportunities to page through books and to talk about the pictures.

- Start by telling them short, simple but interesting stories. Good examples are:
  - *Miffy*: a series by Dick Bruno. (Some of Dick Bruno's books are also available in African languages and Afrikaans.)
  - *The pepper pig*: a series by Anne Clulow. (Illustrated by Joan Rankin and published by Human and Rousseau.)
  - The *Jaws* series and *Jaws Starter* series with tiles such as *Ayo and his pencil* and *Chika's house*. (Published by Heinemann Publishers.)
- Retell stories often so that learners can start to help you to tell the story.
- Help the learner to listen and understand by gradually reading longer and more difficult stories. Discuss the stories with them, asking questions to help with their understanding of the story.

> **Remember**
> Stories with lots of repetition and humour are most suitable as these two elements help the learner to listen, take part and comprehend.

Songs, rhymes, verses and chants as an introduction to reading and writing

Songs, rhymes, verses and chants are all important for reading and writing as they develop the learner's vocabulary, and help him or her to practise difficult sounds in a language (e.g. *ch*, *th* and *s* in English). They also help to develop the learner's auditory memory (i.e. remembering what you hear). When choosing songs or rhymes for your class, keep the following guidelines in mind:

- The theme of the song or verse should fit in with the young learners' interests and environment. Many popular songs and rhymes originated in England and deal with subjects which are not familiar to South African children, such as kings and queens, or the notion of a snowy Christmas. It is preferable to choose songs and verses about subjects that learners can relate to.
- Children enjoy playing with words and repetitive phrases. This also helps learners to memorise the verse or song.
- A song or verse must have a strong, natural rhythm. In a song, the words must fit naturally to the music.
- The rhyming of words adds a musical, singing feel to the piece. It also makes a song or verse more enjoyable.
- Children always enjoy humour – especially overstated humour.
- When choosing a song, remember that the young learner's voice can sing with comfort between the notes D to C (above middle C). The song must not have large intervals (gaps) between notes (never more than five intervals).

Using songs, rhymes and chants

Remember the following when using songs, rhymes and chants:

- Start with short songs and verses if your class has not been exposed to these before – e.g. only two lines with a repetitive phrase.

■ Never teach a song or verse to your group on a *line by line* basis. Start by saying or singing the whole song. Repeat it a few times.

■ Repeat the song or rhyme during the day whenever there is a spare moment.

■ Encourage your class to say the verse or to sing with you when they feel ready to do so.

■ Encourage the young learners in your class to say the verse or to sing alone, but never force them to do so.

■ Singing and reciting songs and verse must be fun activities.

Chants, rhymes and songs can also be used to introduce the learner to the *written word*. Write down the words of a song, rhyme or chant. Then as the learners *say* the word, they will also *see* them.

Because the young learners are able to *recite* the verse fluently while looking at the written words, this activity has the additional benefit of acting as an example in terms of *reading* fluency.

Looking and talking about pictures as a means of introducing the learner to reading and writing

Creating opportunities for your learners to look through good picture books is very important for Emergent Reading. By interpreting pictures (i.e. saying what they see in the pictures) or telling a story from pictures in a book, learners start to realise that pictures can represent the spoken word. When learners first hear stories, they do not realise that the printed text and the telling of the story go together; they believe that the story comes from the pictures.

Authors of good books for young children will convey the story through the pictures in the book. When you reread favourite stories, you are helping your class to realise that authors convey meaning in text and pictures, and in this way they will be using reading principles to figure out and construct the meaning of the written words and pictures.

Pictures and illustrations

Picture books are important to use as part of an introduction to a reading programme. The learner must be provided with opportunities to look at good picture books and to tell stories to friends by means of pictures.

Telling stories by using pictures is a very important activity in an introduction to a reading programme. The learner realises that a symbol (in this case a semi-abstract symbol) can be used to represent the spoken word. The pictures are interpreted by the learner (he or she is able to retell the story), and later he or she will progress to interpreting letters (written words).

Guidelines to help you to identify good picture books and illustrations:

■ All good storybooks for reception year learners are books with illustrations. In these books two art forms are combined: literature and visual art. Pictures thus have to be of a high aesthetic standard.

■ Illustrations in a book must complement the story – there must be no discrepancies.

> ### Example
> If the story tells of a girl in a red dress, the girl in the picture must be wearing a red dress.

- The illustrations must help the learner to understand the story better. Illustrations can help the learner to understand new topics. For example, pictures about children in other countries will help the learner to understand the way they live.

- Pictures must give learners more information about the story. For example, illustrations can be used to show the passing of time in a story.

- The learner must be able to tell the story by looking at the pictures.

- The illustrations must be of a high standard to help create a certain atmosphere in the book.

- The size of the objects in the pictures must be correct. For example, a dog must not be larger than a cow!

- In realistic books the illustrations must be factually correct and show detail. However, in fantasy stories the artist uses his or her imagination. (For example, the pictures in a fantasy story may include purple trees and dogs larger than cows – as long as they fit in with the storyline.)

Using pictures in picture books as an introduction to reading

The value of picture books is that they introduce the learner to a symbolic representation of words. Help the learner to interpret these symbols by means of the following activities:

- Show a small group of learners (not more than three) a picture with lots of detail and then ask them questions about the picture.

 **Go to:**

See the Example and Figure 3.2 on page 98.

Figure 3.2 – A picture can be used to ask young learners leading questions

Ask the class open-ended questions about the picture. (Open-ended questions have more than one answer, rather than one correct answer.)

- What do you think is happening here?
- What do you think will happen next?
- Why do you think the two boys are fighting?

Also ask questions which require that the young learners find fine detail in the picture:

- How many boys are playing soccer in the picture?
- Find a girl with a floral dress.

- Display the books you have read to the class in the book area. Encourage the young learners to retell the stories to their friends.
- Use the illustrations in a book to redraw about three to four of the main events. Let the children find the correct sequence of the illustrations and use them to retell the story.
- If you use any other media to tell stories, such as a flannel board with pictures, encourage your learners to use these to retell stories.
- Never correct children if they tell the story differently from the original story – this is also an excellent activity for creative language.

Other picture activities which can be used as an introduction to reading and the value of writing

1. As a resource during discussions

   Pictures can be used in nearly all presentations to illustrate certain aspects of a lesson. When you use pictures as a teaching resource, include time for the learners to discuss the pictures. This can be done during or after the activity.

   > ### Example
   > When you use pictures as resource for telling a story, put the pictures and flannel board out the next day. The learners can look at the pictures again and retell the story.

   When you use pictures as a teaching resource, revisit the guidelines regarding good pictures books, as these also apply to teaching resources. The following is also relevant:

   - Pictures should include a diversity of people.

   - Do not only use pictures that represent stereotypes, such as mother working in the kitchen and father going to work.

   - When pictures are used to illustrate aspects of nature (reality), they must be factually correct.

   > ### Example
   > Do not use a picture of a moon with a human face drawn on it during a discussion about space.

   - All pictures must be neatly cut out and glued onto a piece of cardboard. Do not use floppy, untidy pictures.

2. To enhance learner's participation during the school day

   - A weather chart

   It is highly recommended that each classroom has a weather chart, on which the learners fill in a suitable symbol according to the day's weather. This is one of the best activities to introduce learners to the concept that a symbol (i.e. a picture of the sun, clouds, blowing wind and rain) represents words.

   Every morning a different learner should get the opportunity to observe the weather and choose the most suitable pictures.

Figure 3.3 – The daily weather chart

Monday	Tuesday	Wednesday	Thursday	Friday

■ Use symbols to make recipes for baking activities

Using a recipe together with a baking activity is an excellent Emergent Reading activity and is one which you should try to present once a week.

Example

Figure 3.4 – A recipe chart

Savoury sandwich for refreshment time

Take:

1 slice of bread

1 cube of margarine

1 big spoon of grated cheese

1 teaspoon of finely chopped tomato

Mix it all together in a small bowl.

Spread on bread.

A recipe can be used to show the meaning of symbols

How to use recipes as an introduction to reading

Remember the following when using recipes as an introduction to reading:

- When you present this activity for the first time, leave out the written words.

- As your class starts to understand the concept of reading (i.e. understanding that symbols can convey meaning), the written words can be added.

- Try to use the same terms for each recipe, for example, *big spoon* and *cube*.

Words and letters as Emergent Reading and Writing activities

The young child learns about reading and writing by being in a literate environment, i.e. where people often engage in reading and writing. Just as the young child learns to speak by being surrounded by people who are talking, they learn about reading and writing by being surrounded by people who use written language. We tend to think that we need not use written language in the reception year since most learners cannot read or write. However, it is crucial that you model the use of written language for your group.

You can set up a print-rich class environment by doing the following:

- Provided excellent story and picture books in the book corner.

- Write their names on all their art projects (using the correct lettering, which learners will later be learning in Grade 1). Later have a box with all the learner's names and let them find their names and paste it on their completed artwork.

- Use print that is functional and gives messages to the learners. Use words on the bulletin board and in the play areas.

- Label the shelves in the block area with the shapes of the blocks.

- After learners have built a structure, make a sketch and write down words they use to describe their structure.

- Label objects in the class. Using the correct lettering, make labels of words like **wall, chair, window**.

Sight vocabulary as part of an Emergent Reading Programme

Words like **STOP, Coca Cola,** and **Bank** are examples of words which young learners see often and can read before they realise it. Young learners relate these written words to the activities or objects they represent, for example *stopping at a stop street* or the *cool drink* they enjoy. By means of fantasy play activities such as visiting a bank or café which you set up in the fantasy corner, you can use these words in their play. (All the items for sale in the 'café' should have signs above them, written clearly and in your own handwriting, saying what each item is.) (See Figure 3.4)

Figure 3.5 – A shop in the fantasy area provides an opportunity to display familiar words.

By using writing in their everyday play activities, your learners will not only realise the value of the written word, but learn sight vocabulary as well.

> **Definition**
>
> 'Sight vocabulary' are words that children learn to read and understand by recognising the whole word. They do not need to spell these words aloud.

The value of sight vocabulary

Sight vocabulary is very important for two reasons:

1. It helps learners to start reading with ease.

2. Later it helps with reading fluency.

Children learn sight vocabulary in the reception year by being repeatedly exposed to the same words. You can encourage the development of sight vocabulary by doing the following:

- Have a print-rich class environment.

- Read these words repeatedly to the learners.

- Play games with these words (e.g. Lotto games)

- *Never* force your learners to remember these words and *never* use the drill method to teach them. The main aim of reading at this stage is to have fun. It should never be a boring activity.

- Do not start with too many words – start with five words and add new ones if your class seems able to recognise and learn more.

The whole language approach accepts the idea that it is easier for children to learn to read whole words with which he or she is already familiar, as opposed to the abstract sounds that make up words (the phonetic method).

> **Remember**
> *During the reception year, sight vocabulary is developed in an informal, fun way. It is never taught as an isolated skill.*

Word games suitable for the reception class

There are many games which are suitable for young learners of this age and which promote the learning of emergent reading.

- Make up games where you have about ten to twenty different pairs of identical pictures. Paste them on pieces of cardboard and mix them up. Let the young learners match the pairs.

- As they start to learn to recognise words have one set of pictures and another set with corresponding words. To make this game self-correcting, let the halves fit together like puzzle pieces (see Figure 3.6). If the learner chooses the wrong picture or word, it will not fit.

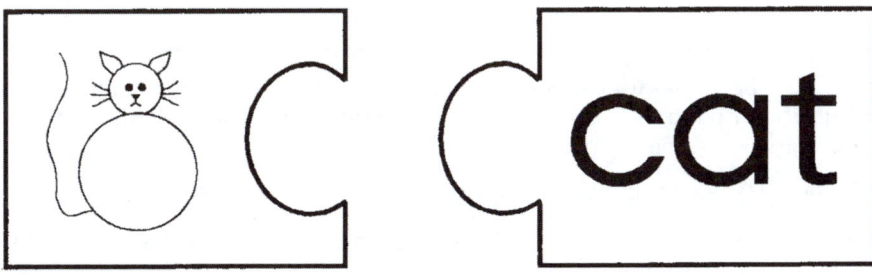

Figure 3.6 – An example of a piece in a word game

Learning letters

Many young learners who cannot yet identify individual letters of the alphabet are able to read words in their environment, and sight vocabulary in books. Young learners eventually will need to learn the sounds which letters represent (the phonetic method) in order to become independent readers. There is, however, no evidence that alphabet identification should be treated as the first skill in an early reading programme. It makes more sense for young learners to learn to identify letters after they have learned a number of sight words.

Activities for introducing your class to the letters of the alphabet

The following is a list of some of the activities you can provide in order to introduce young learners to letters:

- Help the learner to identify the beginning letter of her own name. Find other names and words in the class that start with the letter.

- Provide opportunities such as self-correcting alphabet puzzles. (The learner must find the correct letter to be placed into the correct slot.)

- An alphabet card on the wall with words, letters and pictures.

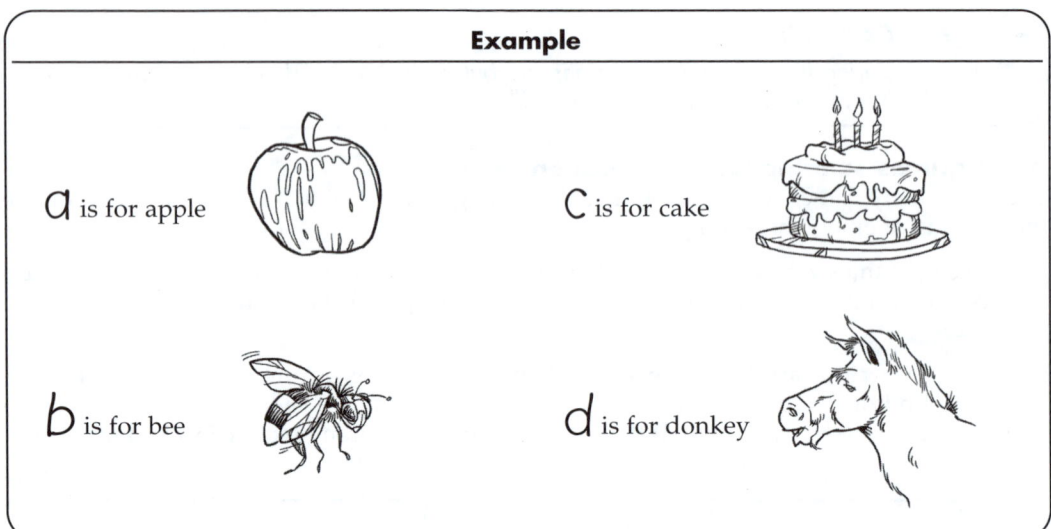

Example

a is for apple

c is for cake

b is for bee

d is for donkey

■ Choose alphabet books for the book area. You can make your own alphabet books using clear full colour pictures from magazines. Write down the capital letter and lower case as well as the word the picture represents.

■ Teach your class songs and rhymes based on letters and words.

■ Provide opportunities in the art area to trace letters using a stencil. Ensure that the correct lettering is used.

Never follow a learn-a-letter-a-week approach. The learners must experience letters and what they represent in a meaningful way; that is, words and letters should always be learnt in context.

Teaching strategies for the learner who would like to learn to read

Although reading is not formally taught in the reception year, you may find there are children in your class who are ready and willing to learn to read during the year. These children may benefit from your individual attention in this regard, as the more formal teaching of reading must be based on individual attention.

The best method of reading instruction: different views

During the last fifty years there has been a lot of controversy about the best way to teach reading and in spite of a vast amount of research, no definitive answer has been reached. The present debate presents two opposing views of how children learn to read:

The phonetic method

The phonetic method maintains that children must learn the subskills first by progressing from letters and the sounds the letters present, to figuring out words from the sounds of the letters, to making sense of these words in sentences. Phonetic rules are taught to learners to help them to figure out words from the sounds of letters. As they learn these subskills, learners are expected to develop comprehension skills.

Phonetic reading programmes include controlled vocabulary and are graded from easy to difficult. New words are used repeatedly so that the learners can get practice and experience in reading these words.

Negative aspects of the phonetic method:

■ The reading materials are usually very boring, and not good literature.

■ All the learners in the same class must be more or less on the same level of competence and the subskills are taught to all learners in the same way.

■ The most important criticism is that more emphasis is placed on decoding (reading words in isolation) than on meaning. Learners learn to read words and sentences but they do not always understand what they are reading. Reading comprehension is therefore poor.

Positive aspects of the phonetic method:

■ Knowing phonetic principles helps learners to learn to read independently.

■ Children learn to spell easily.

The whole language approach

According to the whole language approach, children learn to read and write the same way that they learn to talk, i.e. through natural exposure. According to this method, reading is a constructive process and children get the meaning from symbols in context by using predicting, confirming and correcting strategies. Reading principles are not learned as isolated units but as learners need them to figure out the meaning of any given text. Adults and children, in a print rich environment, provide models and facilitate the process.

Advantages of the whole language approach:

■ This method enhances personalised reading instruction. Skills are taught, as learners need them to figure out the meaning of a written passage.

■ This approach supports the notion that all children can learn to read, even if the rate of progress and the manner in which children learn to read is different

■ Reading is not an isolated skill but is mastered in order to be able to understand an important form of communication – the written word. Meaning and communication is emphasised as being more important than the correct decoding of words.

Disadvantages of the whole language approach:

■ Sight vocabulary is an important feature of this method and some children find it very difficult to 'remember' words.

■ Learners struggle to spell later in school.

The best option

A combination of both the above methods is the best approach when you teach reading. Start with the whole language approach and when learners begin to figure out the principles of reading, use the phonetic approach to encourage independent reading and spelling skills.

Remember

In the reception year, only the whole language approach should be used, even with learners who are ready to learn to read. This method is generally easier for the learners and because they start to read in a very relaxed way, reading remains a fun activity.

When to start formal reading instruction

There are also different views regarding when formal reading instruction should start. It is clear the learners need to be exposed to a great number of activities and opportunities before they are ready for formal reading instruction. However, parents (and often teachers) tend to be very eager for their children to start with formal reading instruction as soon as possible.

Although reading is a very important skill, parents mistakenly believe that early reading is always to the benefit of the learner. Early reading can be harmful if the child is developmentally and environmentally unprepared for reading. The pressure to read before the learner is ready can lead to frustration and fear of reading. These feelings can cause the learner to reject the whole idea of reading, which is exactly the opposite of the intended outcome. It is therefore important to respect the developmental level of each learner, to provide a word- and book-rich environment and to wait until children are individually ready to begin with formal reading instruction.

What can we teach the learner who would like to read?

Although, as said in the above section, the formal teaching of reading has no place in the reception year, you may have learners in your class who are ready and who want to learn to read. Emergent reading instruction for these children must be based on individual attention.

The following is an outline of your role in the beginning of more direct reading instruction:

- If a learner asks the meaning of a specific written word or sentence, read the section while you point to the word as you read.

- Do not spell every word as you read it to the learner. The meaning of words is more important than decoding them.

- Show the learner that a written word can be broken down into sounds. For example, sound out the word c-a-t. Let the learner then find the word 'cat' on the page. (Make sure that the word is used often on the page!)

- One of the best activities to use when teaching reading is the learner's own story. This activity uses the learner's own experiences and level of vocabulary (two of the most important requirements for someone learning to read). The following is a guideline for the teacher:

  – Ask the learner to make up his or her own story. Write down the story using the correct lettering

Go to:

See the example of manuscript writing in Figure 4.11.

- Write down one or two sentences per page.
- Ask the learner to draw suitable pictures on each page.
- Write the learner's name or let the learner write his or her own name on the front page.
- Staple the book together.
- Read the book to the class or help the learner to read his or her own book to the class (if the learner feels comfortable to do so).
- Place this book in the book area for all the young learners to see.

The most important factor of an Emergent Reading Programme

The most important factor in an introduction to reading programme is _fun_. To achieve an enjoyable programme keep the following in mind:

- Never force a child to master a skill before he or she is developmentally ready.
- A love for books and reading is more important than an isolated skill.
- You, the teacher, should always display a positive attitude and love for books and reading.
- Teach your learners that books are special and must be treated with respect.
- _Enjoy_ the activities!

Bibliography

Barchers, SI. 1999. *Teaching reading skills with children's literature.* Englewood: Teacher Idea Press.

Barbour, N & Seefeldt, C. 1993. *Developmental continuity across preschool and primary grades: implications for teachers.* Wheaton: Association for Childhood Education International.

Beaty, J 1996. *Skills for preschool teachers.* Columbus: Merril.

Buchoff, R. 1994. Joyful voices: Facilitating language growth through the rhythmic response to chants. In *Young Children* 49 (4): 26 – 30.

Burke, EM. 1990. *Literature for the young child.* Boston: Allyn & Bacon.

Catron, CE & Allen. 1993. *Early childhood curriculum.* New York: Merril.

Department of Education. 2002a. Foundation phase learning programme policy guidelines: strengthening policy-in-action. Pretoria: Department of Education.

Department of Education. 2002b. *Revised National Curriculum Statements – Grade R – 9 (Schools). Policy. English Home Language.* Pretoria: Department of Education.

Department of Education. 2003. The revised National Curriculum Statements Foundation Phase Learning Programme Policy Guidelines. Pretoria: Department of Education.

Dowling, M. 1988. *Education 3 to 5: A teacher's handbook.* London: Paul Chapman.

Feeney, S, Christensen, D & Moravcik, E. 2001. *Who am I in the lives of children? An introduction to teaching young children.* Columbus: Merill.

Glazer, JI. 1997. *Introduction to children's literature.* London: Prentice-Hall.

Gordon, A & Williams-Browne, K. 2001. *Beginning and beyond.* Albany: Delamr.

Grobler, HM, Faber, RJ, Orr, JP, Calitz, EM & van Staden, CJS. 1996. *The day-care handbook.* Pretoria: Kagiso

Graves, MF Watts, SM & Graves, BB. 1994. *Essentials of classroom teaching. Elementary reading methods.* Boston: Allyn & Bacon.

Lindfors, JW. 1987. *Children's language and learning.* London: Prentice-Hall.

Mallet M. 1992. *Making facts matter. Reading non-fiction 5 – 11.* London: Paul Chapman.

Mayesky M. 1986. *Creative activities for children in the early primary grades.* Albany: Delmar.

Mears, HJ. 1976. *Helping our children talk.* London: Longman.

Morrow LM. 1989. *Literacy development in the early years. Helping children read and write.* Englewood Cliffs: Prentice Hall.

Nikolajeva, M. 2001. *How picture books work.* New York: Garland.

Norton, DE. 1999. *Through the eyes of the child: An introduction to children's literature.* Columbus: Merril.

Raines, S & Isbel, R. 1994. *Stories: Children's literature in early education.* New York: Delmar.

Raum, EA. 2001. *Everyday a holiday: celebrating children's literature throughout the year.* Lanham: Scarecrow.

Soto, LD. 1991.Understanding bilingual/bicultural young children. In *Young Children* 46 (2): 30 – 36.

Chapter

4

Emergent Literacy: The beginnings of writing and spelling

Christie van Staden (revised by Reda Davin)

The purpose of teaching Emergent Writing and Spelling in the reception year is not to teach the learner to write letters and spell isolated words, but to introduce the young learner to the meaning and value of the written word.

OUTCOMES

After you have read this chapter you should be able to:

- explain the importance and relevance of teaching emergent writing and spelling in a developmentally appropriate way within the whole language approach

- understand the difference between writing and handwriting, and the place of each of these skills during the reception year

- explain the importance of early experimentation with 'writing' by the young learner as a prerequisite for future learning of writing and spelling

- understand the relationship between writing and drawing and use this information to present Art as part of Emergent Writing activities

- assess the young learner's Art for the purpose of determining the learner's readiness for the more formal teaching of handwriting and writing in Grade 1

- help the left-handed learner to develop the best writing position

- understand the development of Emergent Spelling in the young learner

- use the knowledge learned in this chapter to plan suitable activities that will enhance the young learner's Emergent Writing and Spelling skills, within a whole language approach

- understand the importance of being a 'writing role model' for your reception year class.

Introduction

As was indicated in Chapter 3, when teaching Emergent Writing and Spelling during the reception year, the focus is not on isolated language or perceptual skills. Your role as a reception year teacher is to introduce the young learner in a purposeful and play-orientated way to the *meaning* and *value* of writing and spelling. The whole language approach also applies to this area – Emergent Reading, Writing and Spelling are not separate language skills, but are part of the young learner's total language development and usage. Your task is to present activities that will help learners to enjoy, understand and experiment with writing and spelling. By doing so you will form the foundation for learners' ability to acquire the formal skills related to these language arts in Grade 1.

During the reception year the Learning Outcomes related to writing are that the learner should be able to:

■ understand the underlying principles of writing within a whole language approach through experiences in a language-rich learning environment

■ discover and experiment with the spelling of words in an informal learning situation

■ develop the necessary perceptual skills needed for writing and spelling through suitable games and activities.

Remember
Remember that during the reception year you will not be teaching children to write and spell. Rather, you will be introducing them to the value and meaning of writing and spelling in a natural, developmentally appropriate way.

In this chapter we will focus on the natural development of writing and spelling as the basis for the teaching of Emergent Writing and Spelling in the reception year.

In order to plan meaningful and developmentally appropriate Emergent Writing activities the first question to be answered is: *What is writing?*

What is writing?

Definition
Writing is the act of communicating by expressing thoughts by means of written symbols. Writing can also be described as the act of putting written symbols, in the form of letters that represent words, on paper with the purpose of retrieving the same meaning at a later stage.

No one understands exactly how we learn to write, but it seems that we learn to write at least as much by *discovery* as by being *taught.*

Before we can discuss the development of writing in the young learner, we have to understand that there is a difference between *handwriting* and *writing*.

What is handwriting?

Definition
Handwriting is made up of the steps and procedures a writer undertakes for producing written language in both manuscript (print) and cursive form.

It is possible for a learner to learn how to produce *handwriting* in the sense of printed letters, as many learners in Grade 1 can, and yet be unable to write meaningful sentences. Learning how to form letters is merely a mechanical act, and can be far removed from any intent to communicate information to others. This will happen in classes (reception year and even in

Grade 1) where young learners learn to form letters without having any understanding of the meaning and, or the use of these letters.

Alternatively, it is quite possible for a young learner to understand *writing* as the ability to use pen and paper to denote ideas or facts in a *symbolic* fashion, and to attempt to communicate information in this way.

The written symbols produced by such a learner are not necessarily presented in the standard and commonly accepted alphabetic letters, as is the case with 'handwriting'. This is however an important milestone in the development of a true understanding of writing as means of communication.

> ### Remember
> *Learning to be an effective writer is not just learning the technical skill of producing letters and words on paper, but is also about developing a true understanding of writing as an expressive skill for communicating information, i.e. a tool capable of **shaping** as well as **sharing** ideas.*

When do young learners learn to write?

In the traditional concept of 'writing (and reading) readiness', reading and writing activities were withheld from many young learners who were eager to know about it but were thought to be too young. The launching of Sputnik by Russia in 1957 left many Americans with the feeling that they were lagging behind. Attitudes began changing due to America's desire to catch up with Russian technology, combined with research pointing to the importance of early learning, and a growing concern about the education of economically disadvantaged young learners. These factors all led to a movement to begin instruction in all academic areas, including reading and writing, at an earlier age.

The trend shifted towards teaching young learners at as early an age as possible, with the same readiness activities and structured instruction of the primary grades presented in the kindergarten/reception year. Unfortunately most young learners were not ready for these 'formal' learning activities. This was potentially more harmful than the earlier delays because initial failure can foster negative attitudes, which can be very difficult to reverse. Unfortunately we still see this practice in reception year classes, nearly fifty years after Sputnik!

Fortunately, a simultaneous downward shift of traditional readiness programmes (with emphasis on motor development and perceptual skills) took place, and a new era of research emerged which would lead to radically different perceptions of readiness and early literacy development. This research focused on early readers who started to read and write outside the traditional approach to readiness. Research found that these young learners, many of whom did not have exceptionally high IQs, had several characteristics in common:

■ they were curious about written language, asking many questions about letters, words and print

■ they showed an early interest in writing and liked to *scribble write* their names, write make-believe letters, notes and so on

■ they had a parent, older sibling, or other adult who answered their questions about written language and who read to them on a regular basis.

The discovery that some young learners of normal intelligence learned to read without formal instruction gave rise to the field of *Emergent Literacy* research. Emergent Literacy (a term coined by Clay, 1972) refers to the process of children learning to read and write naturally, i.e. without formal instruction. Researchers began to use the same procedures used in the study of oral language acquisition to study the natural development of written language. This body of research has revealed that young learners' literacy development begins long before they enter school and receive formal reading and writing instruction.

What does Emergent Literacy research tell us about learning to write?

Traditionally, educators accepted that young learners should be taught to write only when they start their first year of formal schooling. Teachers rarely paid attention to the Emerging Writing skills that young learners often displayed. When young learners scribbled in their porridge, sand or on paper, it was regarded as minimal significance in terms of writing. Researchers no longer dismiss signs of early literacy. When working with learners in the reception year, teachers should be aware of the findings of recent research into how children learn to write, and should allow such findings to influence their approach to the teaching of writing.

> **Research findings**
> - Young learners exposed to literature start reading and writing before formal schooling.
> - Oral language serves as a precursor and later as a companion to reading and writing (this is one of the foundations of the whole language approach).
> - Reading and writing are learned simultaneously, reinforcing one another (this is another basic tenet of the whole language approach).
> - There is a relationship between the way children express themselves in Art and the way they express themselves in language.
> - Young learners are more interested in the *process* of writing than in the end product.
> - Writing should develop in meaningful, functional, real situations.
> - Reading to young learners is an essential part of their learning to read and write.
> - Young learners are curious about print.

What we know about young learners' writing development

Children's first attempts to communicate through writing may look like scribbles. Closer examination reveals that these early writing efforts show a clear distinction between drawing and writing. As time passes, young learners' handwriting progresses through the following stages if they are given frequent opportunities to write:

- progression from drawing to writing
- progression from reliance on copying sight words to sounding out words and the use of invented spelling
- demonstrating knowledge of writing conventions (spaces between words, punctuation, capitalisation, etc)
- elaboration on topics

- awareness of an audience, i.e. someone who will read what they have written.

(Research by Perrotta (1994) indicates that the above stages of development in writing are also valid for young learners who speak English as a second language.)

Researchers therefore conclude that early writing is not merely scribbling, but markings that are intended to signify meaning.

As they mature and gain more experience with 'writing', children 'write' stories and expect adults to be able to read them; i.e. they expect their marks to mean something to the reader. Young learners at this stage reveal an understanding of letter-making and begin to expand their writing skills from scribbles to mock letters and eventually to accurate representations of the alphabet.

Learners then typically progress to the discovery that letters represent phonemes and can be strung together to create words and sentences. They quickly observe that writing is organised differently for specific purposes, and they begin to be aware of their audience.

After young learners have experimented with their own temporary spelling, they usually adopt the standard form in their writing.

Research demonstrates that children's writing skills develop best in the following circumstances:

- when the teacher believes they are capable of expressing their thoughts and opinions on paper

- when they are in a print-rich environment, and

- when they have frequent opportunities to communicate meaningfully in writing.

It is important to be aware of research results demonstrating that young learners begin writing for meaning and communication long before they have mastered oral language or are capable of reading.

This is illustrated in the next figure where Alison (four years old) wrote a letter to her grandmother (see Figure 4.1). It is at this point that the learner's experience of the alphabet system begins.

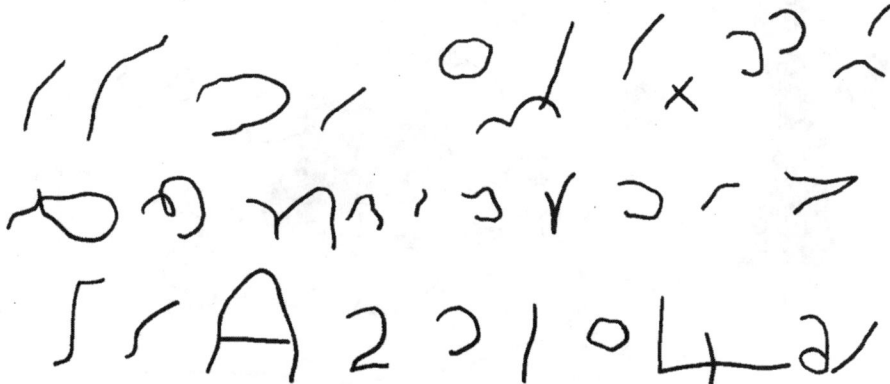

Figure 4.1 – Alison's letter to her grandmother

While still a pre-schooler, the learner is likely to use more and more words amongst the letters and scribbles and these can be understood if the context is explained, or if the learner 'reads' the content to an adult.

The relationship between drawing and writing

Research has revealed that there is a remarkable relationship between the way children express themselves in Art and the way they express themselves in language.

Scribbling is to writing what babbling is to learning to talk. The learner who is scribbling is trying out graphics, whether pictorial or written, and has grasped the notion that marks on paper symbolise things or ideas. Historically, drawing preceded writing. In prehistoric times pictures were painted on the walls of caves to record information which early humans wanted to remember and retrieve for future use. Later, drawings became more abstract, and developed into pictorial symbols that made it easier to communicate information to larger, more distant, more diverse groups of people. Consider the following indications of the relationship between drawing and writing:

■ *Historically*, alphabetic symbols developed from pictorial symbols.

▣ *Developmentally*, young learners also progress from scribbling to *pictorial* and then to *written* symbols. By the time young learners reach the form and shape (preschematic) stage of artistic development, they have begun to master and refine perceptual and motor skills required for handwriting. When they arrive at the pictorial (schematic) stage, they have had extensive experience with graphic materials and frequently include alphabetic symbols as an integral part of their drawings and paintings.

In the illustration below you can see that Karlien has written her own name in her drawing.

Figure 4.2 – Alphabetical symbols are often used as an integral part of a child's drawing

■ Both (drawing and writing) are expressive and both are used for communication.

Art is an important means of expression for young learners and it also provides the teacher with the means of understanding learners' thoughts, feelings and perceptions. Consider the following example of a learner's drawing. When the teacher said, 'Tell me about your drawing', the child answered: 'I've got measles and it's catching'.

Figure 4.3 – Feelings and thoughts are expressed in children's art

Implications for teachers

1. *The use of art materials*

   Teachers must be aware that young learners should be allowed many opportunities to use art materials freely. Bear in mind that transforming and elaborating upon experiences through symbol-making is one of the major ways that a child learns about his or her world and about other people. Young learners are not *copying* the world but *examining* it and, through imaginative creations, *manipulating* it to express their ideas and feelings about it.

2. *Noting when a learner writes his or her name*

   The learner who is able to symbolise objects in her (or his) drawings also grasps the fact that the lines and forms written on her paper by the teacher could be *what her name looks like*. Young learners who have made this discovery are now able to understand that written words can convey meaning.

   Figure 4.4 – Young learners know that little words convey meaning

   Lucinda (3 years old) was in pre-school for only two days when she scribbled her 'name' at the top of her drawing. (According to her mother, she had not done this before.) She had already decided to use certain marks as *writing* and certain marks as *drawing* (see Figure 4.4).

The first piece of writing most young learners produce is their own name. Their teacher prints their names on all their drawings at the top left hand corner. This often means that the learner's name is the first meaningful print he (or she) sees in his surroundings. It is certainly the message most young learners first attempt to write. (See Figure 4.5. These pictures reflect Alta and Heloïse's experiments with writing their names.)

Figure 4.5 – Alta and Heloïse begin writing by experimenting with their names

Writing their own names might achieve several outcomes:

- ■ The young learners learn the use of space on the page (the location of the name).
- ■ They learn the size of the letters on paper.
- ■ The name becomes a collection of known letters.
- ■ They learn to write *other* words of their own choice.

An experiment by Hildreth (1936), on the spontaneous writing by young learners of their names after a drawing session, showed that the learner's ability to write his or her name improved steadily from age three to six without any direct instruction in writing. Consider the drawing in Figure 4.6 where Lucinda, mentioned above, wrote her own name by copying the teacher's example.

Figure 4.6 – Writing by following the teacher's example

3. *The development of drawing skills parallels the development of writing skills*

Scribbling represents motor activity with graphic tools. Although adults seldom consider scribbling to be of value, it should be respected and encouraged as the first stage in the development of drawing skills. Initial scribbles are made accidentally. However, once young children discover that they can create scribbles, they make them deliberately. They need to handle a variety of materials and apparatus that will enhance small muscle control and support fine motor development.

The pre-schooler goes through two main phases in his use of materials and apparatus.

a) The manipulator exploratory stage

This is a process stage in which the learner experiments to discover what can or cannot be done with materials and apparatus. The learner's objective is to gain some control over materials and apparatus. Young children's drawing at this stage is referred to as scribbling. They do not name what they make, but merely experiment to find out what can be done.

b) The communicative stage

This follows when children name and label their drawings. At this stage they know what can be done with the material and look for configurations that they can name.

When is a learner ready to learn to write?

We have already established that young learners start writing before they go to school and therefore ample opportunities should be given to experiment with writing in the reception year. Now we will turn to the question of when the learner will be ready for handwriting instruction. Children should not be pressurised into handwriting instruction before they are ready or have the necessary skills. Lamme (1979) identifies six skill areas which are prerequisites for handwriting:

- small muscle development
- hand – eye coordination
- the ability to hold a writing tool
- the ability to make basic strokes
- letter perception
- orientation to printed language.

The first four skill areas involve fine motor development and the ability to coordinate the workings of the hand and the eye. Before young learners can use a writing tool, they must have control of their small muscles, i.e. they must be able to control their wrists and finger muscles. If the teacher follows an integrated, well-balanced, developmentally appropriate programme in the reception year, there will be ample opportunity for such development to take place.

Children gain this control by, amongst others:

- manipulating art media and apparatus
- manipulating table toys such as Lego, Stickle Bricks, Construct-a-Straw and puzzles.

By observing the learner's drawings and writings, the teacher can determine whether or not the learner is able to form the basic strokes needed for writing.

$$\mathsf{J\,\Gamma\,O\,\Lambda\,-\,I^\supset}$$

Figure 4.7 – Basic writing strokes

A teacher should look out for the following two features in young learners' spontaneous drawings:

1. Straight lines, circles and curved lines.

2. Lines joining each other when houses, cars, people, or other figures are drawn.

These indicate a readiness to begin learning to write.

> **Remember**
> These strokes should not be taught during art activities; they should be allowed to occur naturally by exposing the child to a variety of art activities.

Handwriting involves not only small muscle coordination, but also *perception*. The learner must perceive similarities and differences with regard to shape, size and direction of objects. These perceptions, combined with small muscle control, indicate an ability to write.

Features of young learners' early writing

When young learners produce early _pseudo writing,_ they appear to be trying to discover and manipulate the following principles that can make their productions look like writing (Temple, 1988):

1. The recurring principle
2. The generative principle
3. The sign concept
4. The flexibility principle
5. Linear principles and principles of page arrangement
6. Space between words.

Young learners must understand all of these principles before it can be said that they _write._ Many of these principles are seen emerging in young learners' scribbles and free expressive writing in the reception year.

1. The recurring principle

This refers to the idea that writing consists of the same patterns repeated over and over again (Clay, 1975:27). Young learners derive a great deal of satisfaction from filling whole lines by repeating the same patterns. (See Figure 4.8.)

Figure 4.8 – Carlene and Helnrich's writing illustrates the recurring principle

2. The generative principle

This is the principle that writing consists of a limited number of signs in varied combinations. Children learn from a young age that the same character repeated over and over again is not writing. Writing requires a variety in the arrangement of marks. (See Figure 4.9.)

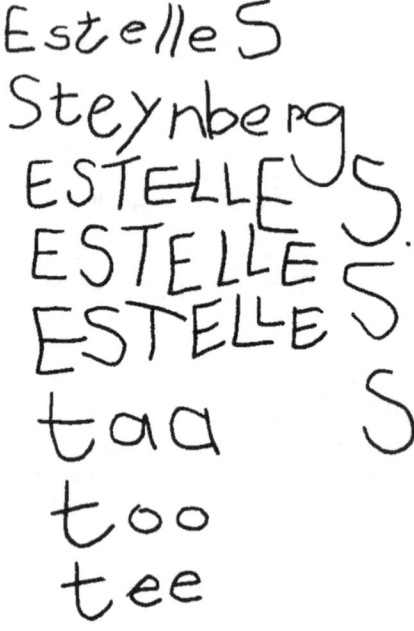

Figure 4.9 – Estelle's writing illustrates the generative principle

3. The sign concept

This refers to the concept that print stands for something beside itself. In Figure 4.10, (i) is a picture of a car and not a *sign*; (ii) contains three signs: a, r, and c while (iii) contains the three signs c, a, and r which collectively make up the sign *car*, which itself looks nothing like a car!

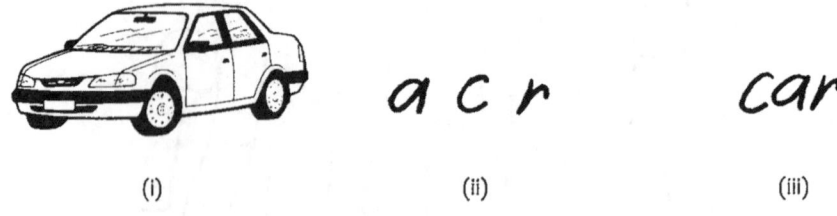

(i)   (ii)   (iii)

Figure 4.10 – The sign concept

4. The flexibility principle

This refers to the idea that there are a limited number of written *signs* and a limit to the number of ways we can make them. Once young learners begin to experiment with writing, it will take a while before they know all the letter forms. Children may also invent letters which do not exist – these are not acceptable *signs*, in that they don't communicate a message to the reader. Harste and Carey's research (1979:7) revealed that the scribbles of 4-year-olds who were instructed to write resembled that of the writing style to which they were exposed (see Figure 4.11). This phenomenon is proof that young learners are influenced by the writing style of their culture.

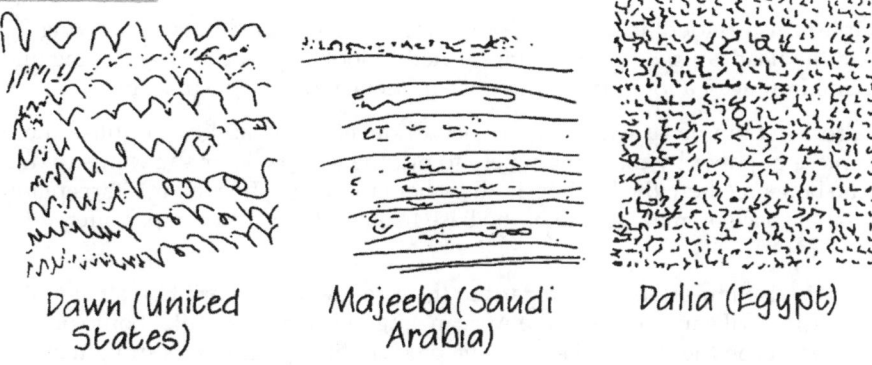

Dawn (United States)   Majeeba (Saudi Arabia)   Dalia (Egypt)

Children's concepts of writing after being exposed to certain writing styles.

Figure 4.11 – Young learners are influenced by exposure to the writing style of their culture

5. Linear principle and principles of page arrangement

Perhaps one of the most difficult things for young learners to grasp in early writing is the fact that the *direction* in which the characters face is significant. Everything else in the child's world retains its identity regardless of direction, e.g. the young learner can look at a table from the top, from the bottom or from any side and know he or she is looking at a table, regardless of perspective. When the learner begins to write, however, this rule changes. Now the visual differences brought on by shifts in perspective change the very *identity* of the object! For example, the same combination of circle and stick can be the letter **b, p, d or q** depending on their arrangement in space.

Writing is one of the very few areas of our experience where identity changes with direction. The identification of letters in this area can be problematic to children for some time. We know from the drawings of young children that they cannot yet draw with the correct perspective because they do not yet have the ability to visualise objects from perspectives other than their own (projective space).

Figure 4.12 – Young learners have an egocentric view and see only from one perspective

This egocentric view is illustrated by the figures who are throwing the ball at each other, but are looking towards the artist drawing the picture. Young learners acquire the ability to reflect perspective in their drawing gradually between the ages of six and seven.

This principle is also evident in a learner's drawings when he or she starts drawing figures in profile, with the heads of the figures being turned to look at what they are doing and not at the artist. Children need a lot of free drawing experience to develop this ability.

Children also need ample drawing experience to develop the ability to utilise the existing space on a piece of paper by planning where to put the objects he or she wants to draw. This principle can be seen where the learner (in the schematic stage of drawing) starts planning his or her available space by making use of the base lines of the piece of paper offered to him or her.

Directionality is also important with regard to the arrangement of print on a page. When one writes in English, Afrikaans or one of the African languages (Xhosa, Zulu, Sotho or Sepedi, for example) one starts on the left hand side of the page at the top, proceeds straight across to the right side, returns to the left, drops down a line and proceeds to the right again – a fairly complicated directional pattern. (This pattern does not extend to all writing systems. Chinese text, for example, is arranged top to bottom and right to left.) Learners take a long time to achieve complete understanding of all the directional principles involved in writing.

Young learners' habits of directionality are remarkably fluid. Adults cannot easily write their names backwards, but many emergent writers appear to do this with little trouble. Consider the ease with which Patricia writes her name backwards in Figure 4.13.

Figure 4.13 – Like Patricia, many beginning writers can write their name backwards

Implications for the teacher

- Teachers of young learners should model writing from left to right by writing the young child's name and the date on the left hand side of the page while the learner is watching. (The date should be written out in full so that the learner also sees how the name of the month and numbers are written.)

- While the young learner's concept of directionality is still fluid, i.e. they haven't grasped that writing should always occur from left to right, top to bottom, the teacher should avoid writing exercises that violate this principle.

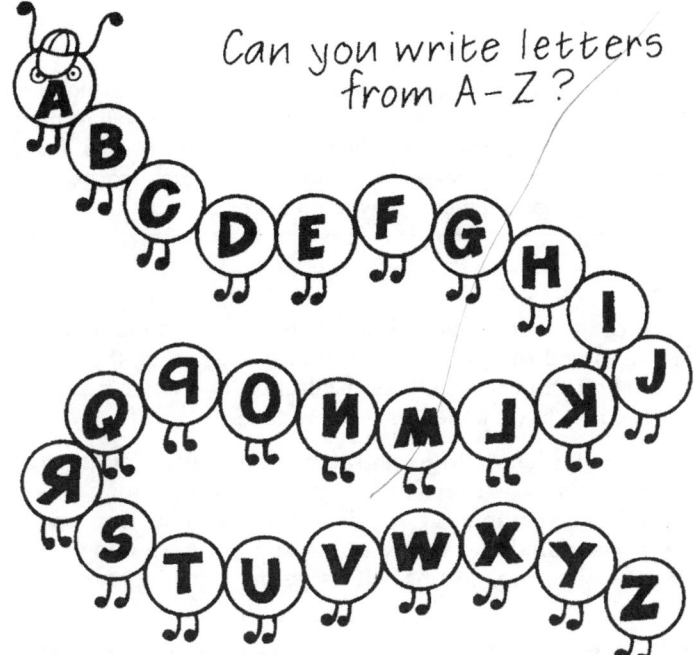

Figure 4.14 – Educators should not encourage writing moving In the wrong direction

Space between words

Our writing system routinely indicates word boundaries by leaving spaces between word units in print. Beginning writers often fail to insert these spaces, possibly because inserting spaces is a highly abstract procedure for young learners to manage. Temple (1988) explains that young learners tend to use positive space (space that you fill in) rather than negative space (space that you leave out) (see Figure 4.15). Nicola (four years old) made a drawing for her mother and wrote **toomaama,** leaving out the usual space conventions, as in: **to mamma.**

Figure 4.15 – An example of a learner using positive space

> **Remember**
> *Young learners must understand all of the principles discussed in this chapter before it can be said that they write. Many of these principles may be seen to be emerging in young learners' scribbles before anyone notices that they are trying to produce writing. It is therefore important that young learners be provided with enough regular opportunities to write and draw.*

Handedness

When handwriting is considered, concerns about whether a child is right or left handed usually surface. This is based on fears that children who favour their right hand have an advantage over those who favour their left hand. Teachers and parents also worry about those children who do not seem to have settled on a preference.

In order to learn more about handedness and its relationship to motor competence in pre-schoolers, Tan (1987) isolated two groups of four year olds. One group was identified as left-handed and one group as having no hand preference. His test, the PHI (Pre-school Handedness Inventory) required learners to do tasks such as, among others, opening and closing a packet of pens, drawing, cutting with scissors, catching and throwing a bean bag with one hand.

The left-handed children were not found to be weak in motor development. They did equally as well as the right-handed children on the motor assessment tasks. (Tan found that left-handed learners are often judged as lacking proper motor development because they look different when they are engaged in motor activity.) On the other hand, the young learners with no preference had below average motor skills. Most of these young learners were boys.

Implications for the teacher

- It is important that the teacher identifies these young learners (i.e. those with no preference regarding handedness) and helps them to strengthen their motor skills through developmental activities in an integrated programme.

- The teacher should also give attention to young learners' posture and ensure that the relative height of the writing surface to the chair is comfortable. Ensure that the learner's writing arm rests lightly on the table, with his elbow just off the edge. The writer's head should be kept centred. (See Figure 4.16.)

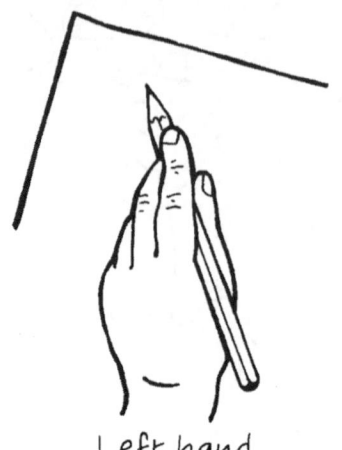

Left hand

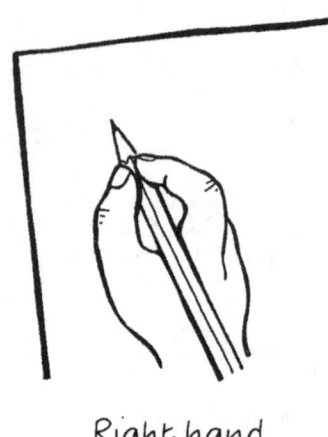

Right hand

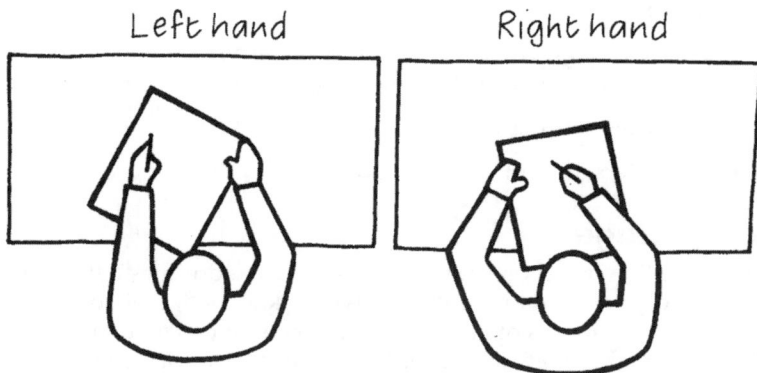

Figure 4.16 – Correct writing positions for right- and left-handed young learners

Spelling

Learning to spell is part of a learner's development in literacy. Emergent Writing, including spelling, will occur naturally when rich language experiences are presented in the reception year. Young learners spell words based on their knowledge of language. Young learners possess this knowledge without knowing that they do, and this permits them to *invent* the spelling of words. The inventive speller moves through stages, which eventually results in traditional spelling.

The development of spelling in the young learner can be divided into five stages (Mcgee and Richgels 1990):

Non-spelling stage

The learner demonstrates only alphabet knowledge, strings letters together randomly and is probably unaware of the concept of creating words by correctly arranging letters.

Early invented spelling stage

The learner knows almost all the letters of the alphabet and knows that sounds and letters can be associated. The learner now invents spellings, usually starting with consonants and omitting vowels, for example writing *hpe* for *happy*. This could develop as follows (Daily 1991):

- using the *initial consonant* to represent an entire word – **m** for **monster,** followed by
- using *initial and final consonants* as boundaries – **mr** for **monster,** followed by
- inclusion of *medial consonant* – **mstr** for **monster,** followed by
- adding *vowels* which may be incorrect – **mestr,** followed by
- starting to use the *correct vowels* and *consonants.*

Purely phonetic spelling stage

At this stage, the learner:

- bases words on letter–sound relationships only

- represents all parts of words
- has developed names for long vowels as a way of identifying these for spelling purposes and seems to articulate all short vowels in the same way
- omits silent vowels when writing words
- segments strings of letters at most word boundaries.

Mixed spelling stage

The learner invents spelling based on sounds and symbols and writes letters for each sound in a word. He or she writes words without displaying knowledge of some conventions of spelling but displays an awareness of basic (English) spelling conventions such as putting a vowel in every syllable, e.g.: *he shard some then he toek owt some frush sosigis*

Fully conventional spelling stage

At this stage, the learner displays an understanding of the basic rules of the spelling system, can detect his or her own misspellings, and can write many words correctly. Teachers must encourage young learners to write initially without concern for correct spelling. Lots of free writing, teacher guidance, and directed teaching lead to traditional spelling.

Guidelines for the teacher assisting with Emergent Writing and Spelling

Remember that
- *the process of learning to read and write begins before the learner enters the reception year*
- *learners come to the reception year with different experiences concerning literacy.*

As a reception year teacher you need to find out, by means of assessment, what each learner already knows, and build on that (this is also called *pre-existing knowledge*). In the reception year, teachers must provide opportunities for young learners to develop:

- the necessary fine motor skills necessary to control a pencil or pen for the purposes of writing
- perceptual abilities to recognise differences in print
- an understanding that we can communicate using writing
- a desire to write.

Your goal should not be that young learners 'practise' letters and words, but rather to expose them to meaningful print and give them many opportunities to experiment with writing in an integrated, developmentally appropriate programme. Teachers can do much to foster Emergent Literacy by providing enjoyable experiences aimed at the eventual development of writing.

The following guidelines are suggested:

- Provide a variety of art materials daily so that young learners experiment with the different possibilities of the art materials. These will not only provide opportunities for the development of fine motor skills but will also encourage the learners to be creative and develop a creative attitude towards 'writing'.

■ Provide your class with opportunities to plan and play in a fantasy area with different themes – such as 'shop'; the 'post office', a 'bank' and the 'hair salon'. Provide a make-believe bank, shop or post office with real forms. The young learners then have the chance to fill in forms, to draw money, to buy goods or perform other transactions which provide writing experiences in context.

■ Provide opportunities for free drawing and painting by having a constant supply of blank sheets of paper, paint, crayons and markers.

Research findings

Jenkins (1980:22) states that free drawing, as opposed to colouring within lines, has been found to require and develop the skills needed for lettering and cursive writing. Kellogg (1970) stresses the important role that art plays in developing the writing abilities of the pre-school learner by suggesting that even the Grade 1 school learner should be allowed to draw freely for at least 30 minutes each day, as this enhances and refines his or her writing abilities.

■ Write down the stories and incidents related by the young learners.

■ Provide opportunities to gain control of small arm and finger muscles by encouraging the young learners to play with:

- puzzles
- pegboards
- small blocks
- construction toys
- (blunt-nosed) scissors.

■ Ensure that your classroom is full of print in clear view of the learner, including words, letters and numbers in order to show writing in context and to indicate that it has meaning.

■ Put labels on artwork, lockers and storage areas, common objects in the room, objects of interest and science tables.

■ Provide recipes when baking as a class.

■ Write down the outcomes of science experiments, and record the state of the weather on weather charts.

■ Write down songs and rhymes that the children know and place them where they can see them.

■ Provide captions for young learners' work, current interest displays and science table displays.

■ Provide a writing corner with writing utensils so that the young learners can play at make-believe writing – e.g. writing a thank you note to Mum, a letter to Granny, making a grocery list for the doll house, etc. Supply the following:

- pens

- pencils
- unlined paper
- writing pad paper
- cartons to make greeting cards
- discarded typewriters
- a post box.

■ Young learners' spontaneous efforts at writing should be displayed in the same way as their art is displayed. This sends the important message to the learner that writing is a valued activity.

■ Be a 'public' writer. Announce to the children when and what you are writing as this will focus their attention on the writing process. The announcement should include the purpose of the message (e.g. a letter to the young learners' parents about an outing or a request for something for the classroom), and a discussion about what is being written. The young learners can help the teacher to decide the content of the letter. While explaining what you are writing, use terms such as *word, sentence* and *letter.* When the young learners are used to doing this later in the year, you could occasionally spell some common words aloud and describe how to form some of the letters.

What about computers?

Computers (if available) can be added as an activity to choose from in an interest corner. Through this, young learners will be exposed to the letters on the keyboard and see what happens on the screen when randomly using the keys.

If you are able and would like to use a computer programme to introduce the learners to letters of the alphabet, ensure that the programme provides the following:

■ the entire alphabet in upper and lower case letters

■ integration of skills such as letter recognition and letter matching

■ an enjoyable experience for learners in which they have direct control over what happens and in which something happens every time they operate the programme.

Create an integrated and interactive experience by adding alphabet books, alphabet blocks and alphabet magnet letters to the corner, giving opportunities for hands-on three-dimensional experiences.

The teacher's own handwriting skills

Manuscript (i.e. print) should be used for labelling purposes by the teacher in the reception year because it is the script used in the first story books and basal readers to which young learners will be exposed. Make use of lowercase symbols when labelling and writing for young learners. Uppercase symbols are used only where they are necessary, such as for the first letters of children's names. You have an important responsibility as a model for good manuscript writing. Much of what the young learners write (e.g. their names, labels and the date) will be copied from something you, as the teacher has written. Consider the following example of manuscript writing for you to follow:

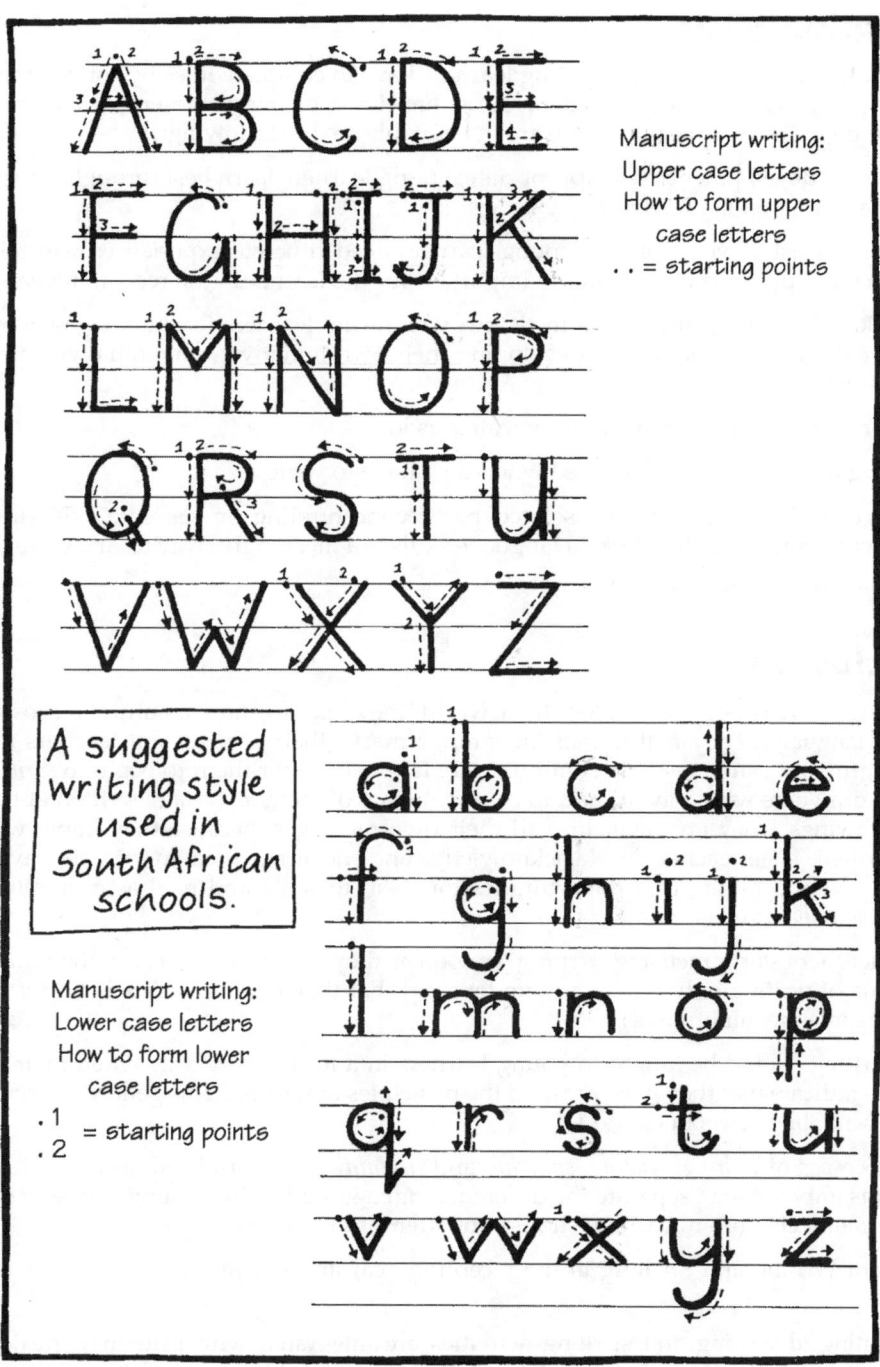

Manuscript writing:
Upper case letters
How to form upper
case letters
.. = starting points

A suggested
writing style
used in
South African
schools.

Manuscript writing:
Lower case letters
How to form lower
case letters
.1
.2 = starting points

Figure 4.17 – A suggested writing style commonly used in South African schools

Criticism of workbooks and ditto activities in the reception year

Workbooks and activities where young learners have to complete lines by connecting dots or other copying activities are not suitable for enhancing the young learner's Emergent Writing and Spelling. The reasons why these are not suitable are the following:

- They are developmentally inappropriate; young learners learn best through direct hands-on participation in meaningful activities.

- Until at least 11 years of age, young learners need concrete experiences with objects to form concepts. This is particularly important for the learner in the reception year.

- Workbook writing directs the focus away from the learner. Teachers using workbooks prevent young learners from developing their own initiative – the initiative comes from the teacher.

- The concept of writing for communication is lost.

- Young learners become inhibited when they have to write.

- Language is broken up into isolated parts, concentrating on separate skills instead of presenting activities that link all language skills in a meaningful way for the young learner.

- Writing objectives aren't achieved.

Conclusion

As young learners begin to explore their world, they tend to show a natural curiosity about written language. They realise that the strange marks their parents and teachers make are meaningful and can be used to communicate. It is natural for them to begin to *scribble* write in their drawings with crayons and to be very aware of their *own names* written at the top of their drawings. They are eager to read their own messages, because they know what they have written. Their teacher should acknowledge and encourage them in their endeavours and provide many activities and opportunities for them to write and read as naturally as they learned to speak.

Young learners start practising 'writing' as soon as they start to scribble, but they understand the value of writing only when they understand that they can use symbols to portray their thoughts in a meaningful way.

Handwriting should be taught to young learners in a formal way only when their 'writing' samples indicate that they have grasped the principles of writing. This generally occurs when formal schooling starts in Grade 1.

The processes of *writing, reading, speaking* and *listening* are interrelated and interdependent. Since it is impossible to separate the different language skills in the young learner's everyday environment, classroom teaching should not attempt to separate them.

Emergent Writing and Spelling in the reception year are best promoted in an environment where:

- meaningful writing and spelling activities are integrated with listening, speaking, and reading activities in an integrated daily programme, and in a print-rich environment

- young learners have frequent opportunities to take risks with writing

- writing is treated as an act of communication, rather than as a practice or drill activity
- young learners write for their own purposes about themes that are of interest to them
- children talk about and reflect on their writing which focuses primarily on *content*
- teachers model good writing habits in meaningful situations
- teachers believe young learners are capable of writing.

Bibliography

Beaty JJ. 1992. Preschool: *Appropriate practices*. Orlando: Harcourt Brace Javanovich.

Beaty, J. 1996. *Skills for preschool teachers. 5th edition*. Englewood Cliffs, NJ: Merrill.

Brewer, JA. 2001. *Introduction to early childhood education: preschool through to the primary grades. 4th edition*. Boston: Allyn & Bacon.

Brittain WL. 1979. *Creativity, art and the young child*. New York: Macmillan.

Calkins L. 1983. *Lessons from a child*. Exeter, NH: Heinemann.

Cole, M & Cole, SR. 1993. *The development of children*. 2nd edition. New York: Scientific American Books.

Clay M. 1975. *Concepts about print*. Portsmouth, NH: Heinemann.

Cohen EP & Gainer RS. 1984. *Art: Another language for learning*. New York: Schocken Books.

Dailey KA. 1991. Writing in kindergarten. *Childhood Education* Spring: 170 – 175.

Department of Education. 2002a. *Foundation phase learning programme policy guidelines: strengthening policy-in-action*. Pretoria: Department of Education.

Department of Education. 2002b. *Revised National Curriculum Statements – Grade R – 9 (Schools). Policy. English Home Language*. Pretoria: Department of Education.

Department of Education. 2003. *The revised National Curriculum Statements Foundation Phase Learning Programme Policy Guidelines*. Pretoria: Department of Education.

Dyson AH. 1990. Symbol makers symbol weavers: how children link play pictures and print. *Young Children* 45 (2): 50 – 57.

Eddowes, EA & Ralph, KS. 1998. *Interactions for development and learning: birth through eight years*. Upper Saddle River, NJ: Merrill.

Essa, EL. 1999. *Introduction to early childhood education. 3rd edition*. Albany: Delmar.

Feeney, S, Christensen, D & Moravick, E. 2001. *Who am I in the lives of children?* Columbus: Merrill.

Fischer, J. 1996. Reflecting on the principles of early years practice. *Journal of Teacher Development*. Vol 5 No. 1 pp 17 – 26.

Gardner H. 1980. *Artful scribbles: The significance of children's drawings*. London: Jill Norman.

Glazer SM & Burke EM. 1994. *An integrated approach to early literacy*. Boston: Allyn & Bacon.

Gordon, A & Williams-Brown, K. 2001. *Beginning and beyond*. Albany: Delmar.

Graves D. 1983. *Writing, teachers and children- at work*. Exeter NH: Heinemann.

Herberholz B & Hanson L. 1990. *Early childhood art*. Dubuque: WMC Brown.

Hildreth G. 1936. Developmental sequences in name writing. *Child development* 7 : 291 – 303.

Hubbard R. 1987. Transferring images: not just glued on the page. *Young Children* 42 (2) : 67.

Jackson M. 1993. *Literacy*. London: David Fulton Publishers.

Jenkins PD. 1980. *Art for the fun of it*. Englewood Cliffs: Prentice-Hall.

Kane F. 1982. Thinking drawing – writing reading. *Childhood Education* 58 (5) : 292 – 297.

Kamovski L. 1986. How young writers communicate. *Educational leadership* 44 (3) : 58 – 60.

Kellogg R. 1970. *Analyzing children's art*. Palo Alto:

Mayfield. Klein ML. 1985. *The development of writing in children*. Englewood Cliffs New Jersey: Prentice-Hall.

Kuball YE. 1995. Goodbye dittos: a journey from skill-based teaching to developmentally appropriate language education in a bilingual kindergarten. *Young Children* 50 (2) : 6 – 14.

Lamme LL. 1979. Handwriting in early childhood curriculum. *Young Children* 35 : 20 – 27.

Machado JM. 1985. *Early experiences in language arts*. Albany NY: Delmar.

Mcgee IM & Richgels DJ. 1990. *Literacy's beginnings: Supporting young readers and writers*. Boston: Allyn & Bacon.

Norton DE. 1989. *The effective teaching of language arts*. Columbus: Merrill.

Mills H & Clyde JA. 1991. Children's success as readers and writers: It's the teacher's beliefs that make the difference. *Young Children* 46 (2) : 54 – 59.

Perrotta B. 1994. Writing development and second language acquisition in young children. *Childhood Education* 70 (4) : 237 – 241.

Peyton J. 1990. Beginning at the beginning: First grade ESL students learn to write. In Padilla AM, Fairchild H & Valades C (eds) *Bilingual education issues and strategies*. Newbury Park Ca: Sage Publications.

Pinsent P. 1984. *Some current perspectives on the writing of young children. Early Child Development and Care*. 14 (1&2) : 125 – 140.

Schickedanz JA. 1991. Young children can learn some important things when they write. In Lauter-Klatell N (ed) *Readings in Child Development*. Mountain View California: Mayfield.

Stewart E. 1993. Language. In Yule RM (ed) *Aspects of Junior Primary Teaching*. Johannesburg: Lexicon.

Tasher, DM. 1995. *From talking to handwriting. Key stages 1 & 2*. London: John Murray

Temple C, Nathan R, Bums N & Temple F. 1988. *The beginnings of writing led*. Boston: Allyn & Bacon Inc.

Van Staden CJS. 1993. The importance of art as a prewriting activity. *Kleuterklanke SA Journal for Preschool Education*. 18 (2) : 33 – 39.

Van Staden CJS. 1987. *Die aard en struktuur van kleuterkuns: 'n Didaktiese perspektief. Unpublished MEd thesis*. Pretoria: University of South Africa.

Chapter

5

Emergent Numeracy:
The learner's world of Mathematics

Christie van Staden

OUTCOMES:

After working through this chapter you should be able to:

- choose Learning Outcomes to develop mathematical activities for the Numeracy Learning Programme for learners in the reception year
- appreciate and understand the importance of exposing young children to Mathematics
- facilitate mathematical activities
- implement the Learning Outcomes for Mathematics to develop activities for the three Learning Programmes
- integrate mathematical activities with the other learning areas
- develop a learning unit for Mathematics.

Young learners are mathematicians

Experience in Mathematics is just another way in which young children try to make sense of their surroundings. They are actively involved in the physical world around them and are naturally curious about numbers, shapes, position and size. They discover basic mathematical concepts in everyday experiences: playing with blocks; playing in the sandpit; 'shopping' and 'banking' in the fantasy corner; making a graph to see who is the tallest in the class or measuring how fast beans grow. They usually have positive feelings about numbers and their uses, and do not see them as work. Mathematical concepts therefore develop naturally as young learners move, touch, manipulate real objects, solve problems, and hear and use new words about these experiences. Basic ideas upon which all future mathematical skills are built are formed in this way. Keeping this in mind, Mathematics is not a sit-at-your-desk-with-paper-and-pencil ditto and workbook activity, but an active, hands-on part of life, rooted in concrete experiences that children have on a daily basis.

The young child's attitude toward Mathematics is formed largely in the early childhood years. This is the reason why the teacher's approach to Mathematics needs to be positive and enthusiastic. Mathematics can be fun for both young children and their teachers.

Teaching strategies for Mathematics in the reception year

Various strategies can be adopted when teaching Mathematics in the reception year. We will consider each strategy individually.

Mathematics as part of the whole curriculum

Because Mathematics is about thinking, calculating and communicating, it is relevant to all things children consider, measure and count. Applications can be found in many Learning Areas. When planning your activities/lessons, think of ways that Mathematics can be used in other subject areas, e.g.:

- freeplay outdoors
- movement activities
- role play in the fantasy area
- creative art
- books and stories
- games, puzzles, educational toys, blocks
- songs, rhymes and science activities.

Examples are given later in this chapter of activities which can be used to develop the various mathematical concepts.

Mathematics linked to the learner's life and world

Mathematics for children is about making sense of their world, not about absorbing facts far removed from real life.

> ### Example
>
> **Teacher:** We must buy food for the bunnies. What do you think they will want to eat?
>
> **Marieta:** Carrots!
>
> **Teacher:** How will we know how many carrots to buy?
>
> **Raymond:** Ask my mom.
>
> **Teacher:** Yes, we could do that, but she isn't here now.
>
> **Nadeep:** Count the bunnies!
>
> **Teacher:** Let's count the bunnies.
>
> **Mpo:** Teacher, I see six bunnies.
>
> **Teacher:** Who else counted six bunnies? Good, we know we have six bunnies, so how many carrots will we need if we want to give each bunny a carrot?
>
> **Sipho:** Six carrots!
>
> This conversation can be continued provided the children show an interest. The cost of carrots can also be explored.

Constructivism

Two major trends have emerged from the research that has been undertaken in Mathematics education over the last ten years. The first is that children (and students) actively construct their own knowledge, i.e. their own ways of knowing things mathematically. (This was explicitly formulated by Von Glasersfeld, a renowned philosopher in Mathematics.) This view embodies the well-known theory of constructivism in Mathematics teaching and learning.

The second trend recognises the role of social and cultural aspects involved in the learning of Mathematics. Teachers should not alienate mathematical teaching and activities from their social and cultural origin and relatedness.

Research

It is believed that children:

■ are capable of building their own understanding of mathematical ideas

■ this understanding is strongly influenced by the social and cultural nature of the group in which the children find themselves while doing Mathematics. The teacher is a major role player in this group.

This view of teaching and learning Mathematics has serious implications regarding the role of the teacher, as well as the social setting in the classroom.

The problem-orientated approach

The role of the teacher
As the facilitator, the teacher should:

■ continuously ask questions and challenge the children to think creatively;

■ allow adequate time for children to engage in mathematical activities;

■ allow children to think aloud while solving problems;

■ remember that incorrect attempts are not worthless – it is the process which is important and there are several of ways to solve any problem;

■ allow children to solve problems in small groups.

Keep in mind that mathematical content should be communicated by:

■ allowing the child to experience it with his body (kinaesthetically) – e.g. counting while climbing the steps of the slide;

■ making use of real (3-dimensional) objects which children can touch – e.g. counting blocks, shells, stones;

■ allowing the children to start working with mathematical concepts using pictures and making marks on paper (2-dimensional) only once they have had extensive experience of the above two methods.

The role of the child
The problem-solving approach allows children to:

■ gain knowledge of Mathematics through solving problems;

■ think about how they have solved a problem;

■ take note of how others have solved the same problem;

■ be aware that there is more than one way to solve a problem.

■ when formulating mathematical problems the teacher should bear in mind that reception year children are confronted with problems in their day-to-day lives. Mathematics can be used to make sense of such problems.

How can children solve problems?
Children can:

■ use real objects to represent a problem;

■ act out problems;

■ draw pictures;

■ use trial and error (guessing and then checking solutions);

■ find missing information in a book, or ask someone;

■ co-operate with other children to solve a problem.

Example

acting out

Limiting the number in a group

The problem is that too many children want to use the reading corner.

Teacher: What can we do so that not too many children use this corner?

Tom: We must take turns.

Elsie: We all want a turn!

Mponyani: How many can take a turn?

Teacher: Let's decide how many can take a turn.

Bennie: Let's see how many can fit in.

The children physically arrange themselves in the book corner until they feel comfortable.

Teacher: Is this how many can fit into the corner?

Gladys: Let's count the children – five can fit into the reading corner.

It is decided that five children can use the corner at a time and they constantly check to see when a child leaves and they can take a turn.

Taking attendance

Teacher: How many children do you think are absent today? How can we find out?

Children discuss this among themselves.

John: There are four children absent.

Teacher: How do you know that?

John: I guessed.

Amy: There are five children absent.

Teacher: How did you find that out?

Amy: I counted the empty lockers.

trial & error

Nkopodi: I counted on one hand that two of the girls are not here and on the other hand that three of the boys are not here. I counted (added) together the fingers of both hands (which represent the absent children) and also got five.

Mpo: There are five empty chairs.

The children decide that there are five children absent.

Feeding the pet rabbits

Teacher: How many carrots do we need to feed the rabbits? (A bunch of carrots has been provided)

Jenny counts the rabbits and draws six rabbits. She draws a carrot·in every rabbit's mouth.

Jenny: We need six carrots.

Neels counts the rabbits, finds six and then counts off six carrots.

Piet: We need eight carrots.

Teacher: How did you arrive at that answer, Piet?

Piet: Two of the rabbits are daddies because they are bigger than the others. They are each going to eat two carrots and four rabbits are going to eat one carrot each.

The children now decide that more than one answer could be right, because the baby might only want half a carrot and the daddies might eat more.

Remember
Worksheets are not recommended in Mathematics. By doing worksheets, children seem to persist in thoughtless counting-all and counting-on strategies instead of thinking, and they also miss out on the exchange of different points of view. Worksheets tend to reduce autonomy: teachers decide on the problems, how many are to be tackled and when, and whether the answers are right or wrong.

The steps in the child's understanding of numbers

A list explaining the gradual development of children's understanding of numbers is provided below. This list will assist you in your observation, enabling you to recognise zones of development in children. This, in turn, will assist your planning of appropriate mathematical experiences for the children in your class.

Over time, children develop the ability to:

■ use invented signs as if they were numerals, along with invented letters, with little or no awareness of their correct numeral meaning;

■ engage in counting-like behaviour;

■ know number names and recite them, first randomly, then in order;

■ count items but not in order, and possibly not touching or dealing with all the items;

■ impose order, mentally, on all items being counted;

■ match each item to a number name, in systematic order;

- count in an ordered fashion and understand that the last number name that is mentioned signifies the quantity in a set of items (i.e. cardinal number);

- use counting as a dependable tool for assessing quantity;

- understand 'more than', 'less than', 'all', 'no more', and so on, with respect to quantity (number of objects), distance, volume and mass (weight), even before the relevant language is known;

- use language for these concepts;

- place uniform items, such as blocks, in increasingly exact relationship to each other, in vertical or horizontal building;

- establish order and pattern in using materials, starting with apparently random placement;

- organise objects into groups, not necessarily according to criteria by which the objects may be considered similar;

- sort and classify objects according to criteria chosen by the child, and later, according to criteria suggested by someone else;

- re-sort objects by changing the criteria by which they may be grouped;

- recognise that some objects may qualify for inclusion in more than one group or set;

- recognise that there are degrees of membership in sets, using 'fuzzy' logic;

- recognise that the groups, when sorted, may include small or large numbers of items. That is, show awareness of the different sizes of sets, numerically;

- compare the groups of objects:

  - in terms of the characteristics of the items in the set, such as green, cars, animals, broken things;

  - in terms of the numerical size of the group, such as the number of items (many, lots, just a few), and number names and symbols;

- visually compare two sets of items and estimate which is the larger set (the number of items increases: for example, four-year-old children can quickly label 1, 2, 3, 4 and 5 spots on cards);

- realise that counting can be used to verify the number that is estimated (early counting will not be accurately ordered);

- realise that one-to-one checking can be used to verify the equality of sets;

- use formal numerals for representing number in an intentional way (cardinal, ordinal and nominal);

- use numbers for labelling things;

- say which numbers come before and after a given number;

- know the ordinal number names (first, second, third etc);

- use numbers for identifying where one thing is in relation to other things, and for putting things in (serial) order;

- know that, on a number line, the numbers are always in the same order;

- know that the number symbols (numerals) are used to mark positions on the line;
- 'move', i.e. count backwards and forwards, along the number line;
- know that each position on a number line indicates a value or amount, and that the value changes as we move backwards and forwards;
- count on the number line proceeding through the zero position;
- know that moving below zero involves numbers less than zero, that is, negative numbers;
- know that the 'distance' between numbers on the line is a cardinal number;
- know that positions between the numbers on the line also have meaning, such as 'half way between 0 and 1' and 'almost as far as 6';
- construct and remember relationships between numbers, i.e. number combinations;
- do the following in counting games:
  - move a marker along spaces using one-to-one correspondence counting from the place where the marker is resting as the first move;
  - count on to the space *next to* the one where the marker is resting.

Using the child's stages of development when presenting Mathematics

When presenting Mathematics the reception year teacher must bear in mind, that when a child learns, he or she progresses from the kinaesthetic to three-dimensional, and finally to the two-dimensional way of representing knowledge. This means that when starting to count, the child should first encounter a number by means of experiencing it with his or her body: e.g. counting the number of mouthfuls it takes to eat a sandwich (kinaesthetic), and touching and counting real, concrete objects such as blocks (three-dimensional). After many experiences with mathematical concepts using the first two types of encounters, children can work with mathematical concepts by means of pictures and marks on paper (two-dimensional).

The language of Mathematics

Mathematics has its own language and from the outset we should use words that mathematicians use. It is better to expose children to the correct terms *as they learn the mathematical concepts* than to *later* explain why the words that have been used previously are incorrect and why others should be used.

What does this tell us about the role of the teacher?

The teacher has an active role in implementing the above strategies. The teacher makes it possible for the children to discover and construct mathematical concepts. She achieves this by:

- planning a rich mathematical environment
- providing mathematical experiences in an integrated programme
- sequencing these experiences so that there is a progression from simple to more difficult concepts, facilitating a growing understanding of these concepts
- selecting materials with which to explore and discover mathematical concepts

■ adding verbal labels to the children's explorations and discoveries

■ asking thought-provoking, open-ended questions

■ continually assessing children's progress on an individual basis and adapting learning experiences in accordance with her findings.

Learning Outcomes for Mathematics

The five Learning Outcomes for Mathematics indicated for the reception year in the Revised National Curriculum Statement 2005 should be used when:

1. choosing mathematical content, and

2. assessing a child's mathematical ability in the reception year, the first year of the Foundation Phase.

The Learning Outcomes and Assessment Standards for Mathematics are as follows:

Learning Outcomes	Assessment Standards	Learning Outcome focus (Find more examples in the text)
Learning Outcome 1 – Numbers, operations and relationships The learner will be able to recognise, describe and represent numbers and their relationships, and to count, estimate, calculate and check with competence and confidence in solving problems.	**We know this when the learner:** 1. Counts at least 10 everyday objects reliably. 2. Says and uses number names in familiar contexts. 3. Knows the number names and symbols for 1 to 10. 4. Orders and compares collections of objects using the words 'more', 'less' and 'equal'. 5. Solves and explains solutions to practical problems that involve equal sharing and grouping with whole numbers of at least 10 and with solutions that include remainders.	Learning Outcome 1 builds on the learner's number sense, which is the foundation of further study in mathematics. Contexts should be chosen in which the learner needs to count, estimate, and calculate in a way that builds awareness of other learning areas, as well as issues experienced in South Africa (e.g. human rights, social, cultural, environmental, political, economic justice). For example, the learners should be able to: ■ compare counting in *different African languages* ■ interpret climatic conditions (e.g. keep a weather chart)

6. Solves verbally stated addition and subtraction problems with single-digit numbers and with solutions to at least 10.

7. Uses the following techniques:

   - building up and breaking down numbers to at least 10

   - doubling and halving to at least 10

   - using concrete apparatus (counters).

8. Explains own solutions to problems.

- calculate within financial contexts found in the Economic and Management Sciences learning area (e.g. *costing objects in their environment – simple buying and selling transactions in context.*)

In the Foundation Phase, the number concept of the learner is developed through working with physical (concrete) objects, because young children learn best with concrete apparatus. Collect a variety of concrete (real) objects to teach number concepts, such as:

(a) **Natural materials**: stones, peach seeds, mealie pips (5y), shells.

(b) **Found materials**: corks, beads (5y), washers, paper clips, buttons, beans, bottle tops, ice cream sticks.

(c) **Commercial materials**: linking cubes, Cuisenaire rods, pattern blocks; and **teacher-made aids**.

Learning Outcome 2 – Patterns, functions and algebra The learner will be able to recognise, describe and represent patterns and relationships as well as to solve problems using algebraic language and skills.	**We know this when the learner:** 1. Copies and extends simple patterns using physical objects and drawings (e.g. using colours and shapes). 2. Creates own patterns.	Provide opportunities for learners to use physical objects to: - copy, extend, create and describe geometric patterns (e.g. geoboards); - create numeric patterns (e.g. counting in two's, skip counting, etc.)

Learning Outcome 3 – Space and shape (geometry)

The learner will be able to describe and represent characteristics and relationships between two-dimensional shapes and three-dimensional objects in a variety of orientations and positions.

We know this when the learner:

1. Recognises, identifies and names three-dimensional objects in the classroom and in pictures, including:

   a) boxes (prisms)

   b) balls (spheres).

2. Describes, sorts, and compares physical three-dimensional objects according to:

   a) size

   b) objects that roll

   c) objects that slide.

3. Builds three-dimensional objects using concrete materials (e.g. building blocks).

4. Recognises symmetry in self and own environment (with focus on front and back).

5. Describes one three-dimensional object in relation to another (e.g. 'in front of' or 'behind').

6. Follows directions (alone and/or as a member of a group or team) to move or place self within the classroom (e.g. 'at the front' or 'at the back').

The study of space and shape is very practical and hands-on:

■ The learner begins by recognising and describing objects and shapes in the environment that resemble mathematical objects and shapes (e.g. squares, circles, rectangles, etc). The learner should handle these objects and shapes, cut out and draw sketches, and describe them with appropriate and expanding vocabulary.

■ Learners should be given opportunities to follow and give directions as well as to describe his or her own position and the position of objects in space using appropriate vocabulary.

Learning Outcome 4 – Measurement	**We know this when the learner:**	In the Foundation Phase the learner's concept of measurement is developed by working practically with different concrete objects and shapes.

The learner will be able to use appropriate measuring units, instruments and formulae in a variety of contexts.	1. Describes the time of day in terms of day or night.
	2. Orders recurring events in own daily life.
	3. Sequences events within one day.
	4. Works concretely comparing and ordering objects using appropriate vocabulary to describe:
	
	  a) mass (e.g. light, heavy, heavier)
	
	  b) capacity (e.g. empty, full, less than, more than)
	
	  c) length (e.g. longer, shorter, wider, tall, short).
		■ These investigations should happen through making direct comparisons and using non-standardised measuring units (e.g. parts of the body, toys, crayons, straws, boxes, blocks, pieces of string, wool). The learner should develop appropriate vocabulary to describe these comparisons (e.g. five hands long, shorter than, longer than).
		
		■ Gradually make available standardised measures by the last term of the reception year.
		
		Activities related to time should be structured with the awareness that the learner's understanding of the passing of time should take place before he or she reads the time.

Learning Outcome 5 – Data handling	**We know this when the learner:**	**Through data handling:** The learner develops the skills to collect, organise, display, analyse and interpret information.
The learner will be able to collect, summarise, display and critically analyse data in order to draw conclusions and make predictions, and to interpret and determine chance variation.	1. Collects physical objects (alone and/or as a group or team) in the environment according to stated features (e.g. collects 10 dead flowers).	

2. Sorts physical objects according to one attribute (property) e.g. red shapes.

3. Draws a picture as a record of collected objects.

4. Answers questions (e.g. 'Which has the most …?') based on own picture or own sorted objects.

In the Foundation Phase, of which the reception year is the first year, the focus in teaching and learning data handling is on sorting objects and data in different ways, based on the different features of the objects or data.

The learner should be able to represent data in different forms that involve a one-to-one correspondence between items in the data and their representation. For example, get learners to find out which fruit the reception year group likes the most. Each child places a counter (something that represents the fruit, such as a bottle placed on a sheet on the ground, under real examples of fruit) on a graph. The counters can be counted and certain deductions made – e.g. which fruit is least or most popular; which fruit is runner-up, etc. The learner should develop an awareness that the selection of attributes used for sorting data will influence:

- how the data is represented

- how conclusions or predictions are made.

How children experience Mathematics

Number (LO 1)

Children initially learn about numbers by counting by rote. The counting skill requires children to do two different things:

- say the number names by rote in the proper order
- apply the number names to objects in the correct order to find out how many there are.

To perform the first skill, children need to know the names and order of numbers. Children love to count, and many four-year-olds enjoy counting by rote to twenty and beyond – although they often omit a number here and there.

Counting objects, the second skill, is altogether a different matter. In addition to knowing the names of the numbers and the order of the numbers, children also need to apply one number to one object when they count. This is more difficult for the young child than simply reciting a series of numbers. Counting the number of objects is based on the concept that each successive number is one more than the previous number and that the final number they say represents the total number of objects.

Because young children frequently omit a number when they count, their totals are often not accurate. Even when they touch or point to each object that they are counting, they often skip one. This is no cause for concern – they will learn to do this correctly eventually. A child's knowledge of number is neither complete nor meaningful unless they have direct experiences with concrete materials and objects.

Research: Age trends in counting ability

Research indicates that:

- by the age of three, children usually know the first four or five of the conventional counting words.

- by the age of four and a half to five, they might know the first 18 to 20 counting words. Counting accuracy (tagging every item and not counting items more than once) is quite rare in children under three.

- by the time they approach their fifth birthday they are usually rather accurate in counting up to five, and some children can even count up to twenty objects.

It is important to keep in mind that any child's counting performance should be evaluated in terms of that child's previous experience. One would expect different performances from a child who has been to preschool where activities prompting informal counting were provided, or who comes from a family where parents interacted to a considerable degree with their children, compared with a child who does not have a background that includes such experiences.

(Fuson, 1988)

Activities to help children grasp the mathematical concept of counting (LO 1)

The following are guidelines to follow when helping children to grasp the concept of counting:

■ Counting activities should begin by having the child touch each object.

■ Teach the children to count from left to right. If left on their own they will sometimes start counting from the right (as they often do when they start writing their own names). They may then move to the left, and then count those in the middle, often losing count of the number during this process.

■ Encourage children to count objects in the following progression:

1. Body parts (e.g. eyes, legs, fingers on hands and toes on feet) and experiences involving their bodies (e.g. jumping three times). Consider Figure 5.1 – a drawing by a child who is very aware that she has five fingers on each hand and five toes on each foot.

2. Real, concrete objects such as bottle caps, cotton reels, wooden beads, shells, buttons, stones, fruit pips (peach), plastic animals, plastic counters.

3. Do not always arrange the objects to be counted in the same way, as children need to realise that *three* is always *three* no matter how the objects are arranged (see Figure 5.2).

Figure 5.1 – A drawing by a child who is aware of the numbers of her fingers and toes

Figure 5.2 – The number remains the same Irrespective of the arrangement

4. Use pictures.

Figure 5.3 – The use of pictures in Mathematics

5. Use dominoes.

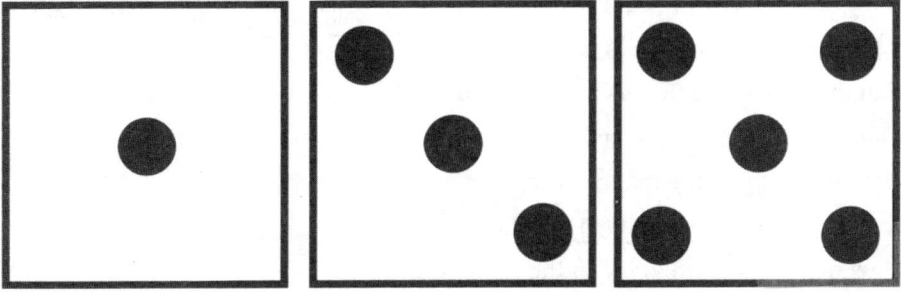

Figure 5.4 – The use of dominoes in Mathematics

6. Use number symbols.

1 2 3 4 5

Figure 5.5 – The use of number symbols in Mathematics

7. Use word signs.

one two three

Figure 5.6 – The use of word signs in Mathematics

8. Use ordinal number word signs.

first second third

Figure 5.7 – The use of ordinal number word signs in Mathematics

Mathematics: games and everyday experiences

These opportunities are preferable to worksheet exercises. The following are some activities which can be used by the teacher to introduce children to number concepts:

1. **Number games**

    Make numbers personal. Children associate themselves with numbers when they tell their age by showing the appropriate number of fingers to indicate their age. Once children have become familiar with rote counting to ten, they may be ready to count objects. Such counting should always begin with concrete (real) objects first. Make it personal:

    ■ Can they count the fingers on one hand?

    ■ Can they count the fingers on two hands?

    ■ Can they count the toes on their feet?

    ■ How many shoes are they wearing?

    ■ Can they count the objects in the classroom?

    ■ How many tables are there in the classroom?

    ■ How many chairs are there around each table?

2. **Finger rhymes**

TEN FINGERS

I have ten little fingers,	(hold up hands)
I can make them jump high,	(reach above head)
I can make them jump low,	(touch floor)
And they all belong to me.	(point to self)
I can make them do things:	
I can fold them up quietly,	(fold fingers together)
Would you like to see?	(point to eyes)
I can shut them up tight	(make a fist)
Or open them wide.	(spread fingers)
I can put them together,	(fold fingers together)
Or make them all hide.	(put behind back)

3. **Songs**

(a) *Concept:* Counting, experiencing and recognising cardinal numbers by singing.

THE NUMERAL SONG

(Adapted from Charlesworth and Radeloff (1978) and sung to the tune of *Here we go round the mulberry bush.*)

The children sit in a circle. The teacher keeps a set of numerals from 1 to 5 (and later from 1 to 10) on her lap and lays a matching set out on the floor in the centre of the circle. These must be large enough for all to see. One child is chosen or volunteers to stand in the centre of the circle. The teacher holds up the first numeral (e.g. one) and everybody sings:

> Do you know the numeral one?
> The numeral, the numeral one?
> Oh, do you know the numeral one?
> It looks just like this.

The child in the centre picks up the matching numeral from the group on the floor and everybody sings:

> Yes, I know the numeral one
> The numeral, the numeral one.
> Oh, yes, I know the numeral one.
> It looks just like this.
> The teacher and children clap the numeral and sing:
> Can you clap the numeral one
> The numeral, the numeral one?
> Oh, can you clap the numeral one?
> It sounds just like this.

The teacher and children stamp with their feet, click with their fingers, or whatever they choose to do, the number of the numeral at the end of the verse.

> I can click the numeral one
> The numeral, the numeral one.
> Oh, I can click the numeral one.
> It sounds just like this.

Another child is chosen or volunteers to go to the centre and the game is repeated with two, three, and so on.

(b) *Concept:*

Counting in twos.

ONE, TWO, BUCKLE MY SHOE

One, two,
Buckle my shoe;
Three, four,
Open the door;
Five, six,
Pick up sticks;
Seven, eight,
Lay them straight;
Nine, ten,
A good fat hen.

(c) *Concept:*

Subtraction and names of cardinal numbers and the concept of none. Show the children a picture of the Hoopoe bird before singing this song.

FIVE LITTLE HOOPOES

(Hoopoes: *Intleki'Bafazi* or *laughing women* – Xhosa)

Five little Hoopoes peeping at the door,
One flew away and then there were four.
Four little Hoopoes sitting in a tree,
One flew away and then there were three.
Three little Hoopoes looking at you,
One flew away and then there were two.
Two little Hoopoes sitting in the sun,
One flew away and then there was one.
One little Hoopoe sitting all alone,
He flew away and the there were none.
Hoopoe, Hoopoe, happy and gay,
Hoopoe, Hoopoe, fly away.

FIVE LITTLE KITTENS

Five little kittens sitting on the floor,
One ran away and then there were four.
Four little kittens playing round a tree,
One went to sleep and then there were three.
Three little kittens begin to 'mew,'
One climbed the tree and the there were two.
Two little kittens played in the sun,
One went home and then there was one.
One little kitten left all alone.
He chased a mouse and then there were none.

(d) *Concept:* Use of ordinal numbers.

LITTLE DOGS

The first little dog barked very loud.
The second little dog ran after a crowd.
The third little dog said, 'Let's eat!'
The fourth little dog said, 'Let's have meat!'
The fifth little dog said, 'I think I will stay,
In my own backyard and sleep all day!'

4. **Teaching subtraction and addition through everyday experiences.**

Keep the following four aspects of subtraction and addition in mind when providing this experience to the child.

The idea of subtraction and addition can be taught to children utilising everyday situations. The situations can be classified under four different categories:

(a) Change

Thandi had 4 sweets. Thuli gave her 2 more. How many sweets does Thandi have altogether? (Addition)

Thandi had 5 sweets She gave 3 to Thuli. How many sweets does she have?

(Subtraction)

(b) Combine

Jim has 3 red marbles and 2 blue ones. How many marbles does he have? How many blue marbles does he have?

Jim has 6 marbles: 3 are red and the rest are blue. How many blue marbles does he have?

(c) Compare

Thandi has 7 sweets. Thuli has 4. How many more sweets does Thandi have than Thuli?

Thandi has 6 sweets. Thuli has 3. How many fewer sweets does Thuli have than Thandi?

(d) Equalise

John has 6 marbles. Jim has 4. How many marbles does Jim have to buy to have as many marbles as John?

John has 5 marbles. Jim has 3. How many marbles does John have to give away to have the same number of marbles as Jim?

5. **Board games**

Start off with simple, homemade board games. Mark a sheet of cardboard with pathways for early practice in learning number names, ordering and counting. (See example in Figure 5.8.) The same type of game can be used later to practise different skills such as adding and subtracting. More complicated games can have longer paths with problem steps to land on, which might say, e.g. 'Go back 3 steps'.

Figure 5.8 – How to make a simple board game

6. **Counting books**

As has already been mentioned, progression with counting should be from concrete objects to pictures and, if available, computers. After a child has engaged in many manipulative experiences with numbers, counting books can confirm the accuracy of these direct experiences by offering children pictorial proof in imaginative ways. Counting books are participatory – both the child and the teacher should be involved in reading them.

The following are some examples:

■ The simplest and clearest counting books are of those in the style of Dick Bruna books such as *I can count* which introduce the mathematical concept of number as sequence – with one numeral and a matching object on each page.

■ In *Ten, nine, eight,* Molly Bang uses a countdown backwards from ten to one as she pictures a small child being put to bed by a loving father.

■ Eric Carle's *The very hungry caterpillar* can reinforce counting skills and the concept of sets.

■ John Rowe's *How many monkeys?* (Human & Rousseau) is a counting book in English, Afrikaans, Zulu and Xhosa.

■ Mitzi Margoles' book *Ten are too many!* (Human & Rousseau) is a delightful, humorous counting book about a mother and baby who encounter nine other characters, one by one on a walk, and all of whom they invite to tea. For various reasons, these characters leave the tea party by ones and twos and threes until only the mother and baby remain once more.

7. **Number symbols**

Although number symbols are abstract, just as letters are, young children can learn:

■ their personal age number, apartment or house number and telephone number, by choosing the correct number from sets of three dimensional numbers which can be kept for them to handle;

■ various number symbols by playing board games such as 'Snakes and Ladders' with a homemade die. Prepare a toy block with the symbol of the number as well as the number of dots that make up the symbol on the sides. When the child can handle this die, he or she can graduate to the normal sized, smaller die.

8. Matching experiences (LO 5)

Matching, or one-to-one correspondence, is the most basic component of number. It is the understanding that one group belongs to, has the same number of things or characteristics as another. For example, each cup has a saucer, each foot has a shoe, each dog has a house. The teacher should look out for examples in the everyday activities of young children where matching could take place: things are passed out during the day such as food, apparatus or notes to take home. Matching is *preliminary to counting* and *basic to the understanding of equivalence* and the concept of *conservation*. Without this concept, the act of counting becomes meaningless. When this is grasped, however, saying the numbers one, two, three, four, five, can be matched with objects and *counting becomes reliable.*

There are five characteristics of matching activities, which we consider individually.

(a) Perceptual characteristics

The way the matching materials look, feel and sound, will determine how easy or difficult it will be for the child to match them. To match a hand with a mitten is easier to match than two flowers of the same type, with only minor differences between them. To make tasks more difficult, objects to be matched could be chosen that look very much the same.

(b) Number of items to be matched

The more objects there are in a group to be matched, the more difficult it is to match them. Groups with fewer than five objects are easier to match than groups of five or more. Start with groups of fewer than five and gradually work up to groups of nine.

(c) Concreteness

The more closely the objects resemble the things they represent, the more concrete they are. The teacher should keep in mind that the less real (concrete) the object is, the more difficult it is to match. Real objects such as small toys, crayons, household objects, fruit, leaves, stones, flowers, shells and buttons should be used in early matching tasks. Later, cut out shapes such as circles and triangles, sucker sticks, tongue depressors and plastic forms can be used. These can be followed by pictures of real objects and pictures of shapes. Use the least concrete objects last of all – e.g. dots and symbols.

(d) Physically joined or not joined

It is easier for the child to decide whether objects match if he or she can join the objects. Initially, the objects may be joined by a line or string so that the child can see that there is a match.

The following simple demonstration will help a child to understand that the number in a set of objects remains the same whether the objects are near to each other or whether they have been spread further apart:

The teacher places five objects in front of herself and the child matches this set by putting five of the same objects in front of him or her. When the teacher moves her objects apart, many young children will believe that they have fewer objects than the teacher has. By joining these objects with string, the child will come to understand that the number in a set remains the same if no objects have been added or taken away.

Read the story of Goldilocks and the three bears to the children. Make cut-outs of the Daddy, Mummy and Baby bears, as well as three bowls, three chairs and three beds (a large bed, a middle-sized bed and a tiny bed.) These cut-outs can be pinned to a bulletin board. The children can connect each bear with a bowl, chair or bed by means of string or a length of wool (see Figure 5.9). The same may be done with cut outs of the three pigs and their houses of straw, sticks and bricks.

Figure 5.9 – An illustration of matching items, using the story of Goldilocks and the three bears

(e) Groups of equal or unequal numbers

Matching unequal groups is more difficult than matching equal groups. When the groups have the same number, the child can check to be sure that he or she has used all the items. This can be done in the same way as the previous example. With this example, it is easy to show that one group has more items than the other: take away one of the bowls and one bear is left without a bowl. Another example is: Match six ping-pong balls, stones or wooden beads to five plastic egg cups. There is one left over; in other words, there is one too many (see Figure 5.10).

Figure 5.10 – *The matching of unequal groups*

(f) Grouping together according to science concepts

Select two sets of objects: one set should float and another set should sink. Allow the children to place all of these simultaneously into a bowl of water, and to see which remain on the surface and which go to the bottom (see Figure 5.11).

Figure 5.11 – *Grouping together according to Science concepts*

Some more examples of matching activities:

◾ Prepare a series of carton strips or paper plates with a certain number of dots, starting with one and ending with ten (or to make this activity easier, end with five dots). Children can then match the same amount of washing pegs or paper clips by attaching them around the rim of the carton.

■ Prepare a set of tins with the numbers 1–5 written on them, as well as the corresponding number of dots. Provide sticks, straws or any other concrete objects – children then put the correct amount of these objects in the tins, according to the number written on the tin. The numbers can be enlarged to 10 if the children are managing to do this acivity correctly.

Think of other matching activities that you may prepare in a similar way with other apparatus. The outcome for these activities is that children in the reception year will be able to recognise number names and learn to count by corresponding the objects they put in the containers to the amount written on the container. Start off with only the first three numbers and gradually work up to 10.

Classification (LO 5)

Classification involves the ability to recognise the similarities and differences between objects and to group them accordingly. It is one of the cognitive abilities that a child needs in order to form a precise concept of number.

Classification involves sorting (separating) and grouping (joining). While they sort, group and regroup, children find out how things are classified by special properties such as, amongst others, size, shape, colour, texture, length and weight. Figure 5.12 shows how a teacher and children identify the shapes, sizes and colours of squares and circles cut out of two colours of cardboard. The teacher then tells the children to 'put together the ones that are the same'. In this way the children decide to classify according to colour, size or shape.

*Large square and large circle\
small square and small circle*

*Large square and small square\
large circle and small circle*

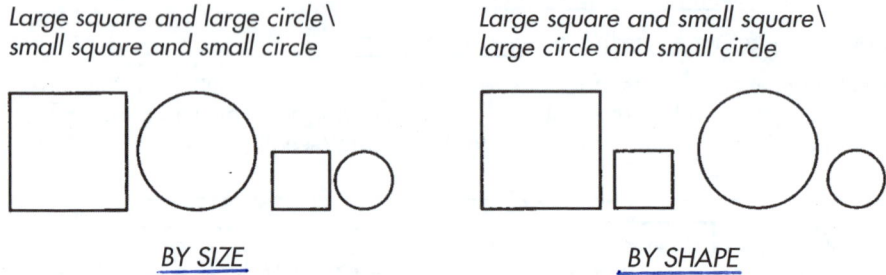

BY SIZE

BY SHAPE

Figure 5.12 – Grouping by size and by shape

The teacher then asks the children to explain why they decided to group the shapes in certain ways.

Children can practise sorting by kind by sorting miniature play figures and animals, e.g. sorting doll's house furniture into appropriate rooms; or animals into those that belong in a barn and those that belong in the fields.

By sorting things, children experience the concept of a set in a very simple way: a collection of objects having at least one characteristic in common. They can, for example, sort through a mixture of cardboard or plastic shapes to find five circles that may form a set. This set of five circles can also be divided into two sub-sets, for example, a subset of three red circles and a subset of two blue circles. Before doing any formal addition and subtraction, children need to learn about sets and how they can be joined and separated.

Seriation (LO 4)

Seriation means ordering according to a property and requires that objects be arranged in some clearly discernible way. It involves placing objects in a sequence from first to last. For example, objects could be ordered from smallest to largest, shortest to tallest, lightest to heaviest. A child gets the idea of ordering when working with 'nesting' toys where items of the same shape, but of varying sizes, fit into each other.

Example

To demonstrate the concept of ordering, the teacher could begin by showing the children a set of concrete objects (e.g. shells, stones, corks, empty cotton and wool reels) and then say, 'Let's play a game with the shells. I'll start the game by putting the smallest shell here. Now let's see if you can find the next biggest shell. Good, now it's my turn again. My shell is just a little bit bigger than yours. Your turn again ...' Continue until about five or six shells are seriated (or placed into the correct order). The shells could then be mixed up again and the child could play alone with the shells. Encourage the children to work from left to right, as this is the direction in which they will later write sums.

Seriation activities

The following is a list of suggested activities to demonstrate seriation to the children:

■ The children can arrange themselves in a row from the shortest to the tallest.

■ The children can pack away the blocks, starting with the largest and ending with the smallest. The next time they do this, they can do it the other way round.

■ Collect nesting materials such as tins, a set of measuring spoons and cups. After the children have nested the objects, they can set the objects in the right order on the table.

■ The children can make balls of various sizes from clay or play dough. They can then seriate these balls according to size.

■ The children can paint lines from the longest to the shortest or from the thickest to the thinnest.

■ Fill tins with stones, mealies, seed and sand. The children can arrange these tins from the one that makes the loudest sound to the one that makes the softest sound.

Patterning (LO 2)

Patterning is another form of ordering based on repetition. When children create bead necklaces with alternating colours; make a row of circles, a row of crosses and a row of triangles when printing with sponges; or sing the same chorus line after each song, they are experiencing patterns. There is a particular logic involved in patterning – in order to create or follow a pattern, a rule must be discovered. As a designer, the child can set his or her own pattern or find out what the rule is in somebody else's pattern. The teacher must take care not to confuse the sequencing of patterns with seriation. Seriation builds on a property of an object, such as ordering from the widest to the narrowest ribbon, whereas sequencing builds on the continuation of a pattern such as red, blue, green, red, blue, etc.

Mathematics is the study of patterns

Creating, constructing, and describing patterns make up an important part of Mathematics learning as they require problem-solving skills. Patterns can be based on:

- Geometric attributes (*shapes*, e.g. circle, triangle, oval, oblong, square);
- Relational attributes (*sequence*, e.g. first there is a red bead, then a blue bead and then a yellow bead in the necklace; now repeat this pattern with the other beads; *function*, e.g. the ball will roll because it is round; what else will roll or will not roll?).

Compare the following places where patterns are found:

- Natural patterns as found in nature: the inside of an orange cut horizontally; petals are arranged in patterns in different flowers.
- Manmade patterns as found in art and construction.
- Cyclical patterns as found in life cycles, the water cycle, the cycle of seasons and time.

Patterns help children develop *number sense, ordering, counting and sequencing*. Therefore it is important that children experience at an early age finding, completing, and creating patterns. There are several different types of pattern activities that children should experience on a regular basis. The following are four different ways that patterns might be used in developing mathematical ideas:

1. Finding a pattern in their environment

    Help children to find patterns in their immediate surroundings:

    - look at the patterns on their sweaters, dresses and shirts, animals (camouflage)
    - look for patterns on crockery, vases, clay pots, walls of houses, basket work, bead work

    After having done this for a certain period, young children will have a good idea of how a pattern works.

2. Copying a pattern

    Children are shown a pattern and then asked to make one 'just like it', for example, pack out a pattern with coloured blocks:

    RED, RED, YELLOW, RED, RED, YELLOW and get your learners to continue the pattern. Patterns could also be laid out for children to copy, using pegs in a pegboard or making patterns with rubber bands on a geoboard.

3. Finding the next one

    Ask children to find the next object needed in the pattern.

    - Make use of buttons, blocks or beads – arrange buttons in the following pattern: red, blue, green, red, blue, . . . And ask the child: What comes next?
    - Complete the pattern around the border.
    - Show learners the following pattern: _◊__◊__◊__◊ - _◊__◊_ And ask: What has been left out?

4. Creating their own patterns

    Children need opportunities to create their own patterns and are usually eager to do so.

Example

For art activities, you can cut sponges into shapes or cut patterns from halved potatoes. Children then dip these into poster paints poured into shallow tins. Patterns can be printed on computer paper, or any other kind of paper readily available. Language and communication are important during these activities. Encourage children to say what they are thinking as they create their patterns: Why did they choose a certain piece and decide on this particular pattern? Show the children how the shapes can be repeated to make patterns.

Activities for patterning

There are many activities you can facilitate in order to make children aware of patterning:

- The children can play *Follow my leader*. One child can stand in front of a group and do three different actions in sequence, with the rest of the group trying to follow the child's directions.

- The teacher can jump in a sequence according to a plan, then children can take turns to make their own jumping sequence (see Figure 5.13).

Figure 5.13 – A jumping sequence to show patterning

- Invent a pattern for a necklace with waste material: e.g. polystyrene chips, milk bottle tops, plastic straws cut in lengths, cotton reels.

- Copy a pattern to arrange dishes on a placemat.

- Clap hands and do body percussion according to a pattern. The children can then take turns to invent their own clapping and body percussion patterns for the other to follow.

- Children can invent a pattern to form a border for their painting or drawing.

Shape (LO 3)

Everything we see around us has its own shape. Young children see and feel shape differences long before they can describe these differences in words. Shape is often used as the basis for matching and classifying objects.

Young children can learn the names of basic (geometric) shapes. First they learn to label *circles*, *squares* and *triangles*. Then they can learn about the *rectangle, diamond* and *oval*. Shapes should be introduced to the young child directly in various ways during his daily activities, in the same way as any other new idea is introduced. Call attention to shapes within the immediate environment of the child and use words describing shapes whenever referring to them. For example, ask the child to put the paper on the *round* table and the puzzle in the *square* box. When introducing shapes, start with one at a time. Once one shape is understood and recognised, the next one can be introduced. Remember to review a familiar shape before a new one is introduced. Encourage the child to discriminate between familiar and unfamiliar shapes, by asking questions such as 'How are the shapes alike?' and 'How are the shapes different?'.

Activities with shapes (LO 3)

■ Children can form shapes with their hands or with their whole bodies. They can jump into shapes formed with cardboard or outlined with rope.

■ Children can paste different geometric and freeform shapes onto paper, using shapes from nature such as leaves or seeds.

■ Post shape forms in various ways into corresponding forms.

■ Play shape games (see Figure 5.14). This game is played in groups of five or six.

■ Create a die using shapes instead of 'numbers'. Allocate one shape per learner. One child rolls the die. The learner moves forward when the die represents his/her allocated shape.

Figure 5.14 – A shape game where children can act as counters

■ Parquetry blocks are blocks of different shapes and colours which can be organised into patterns.

■ 'What's in a square?' and 'What's in a line?' are two games which become progressively more demanding and which provide experience with shape.

■ Collect empty grocery boxes of different sizes, lengths and shapes. Tape the lids down to strengthen them. Allow the children to play with these as they would with blocks, and then use them for box construction.

■ Collect sets of differently sized shoe boxes. Tape the lids firmly to the boxes and cover these with shelf paper or paint with a non-toxic paint. **Please note: Do not use any paint containing lead on children's apparatus.**

If possible, each reception year classroom should have its own set of unit blocks. Unit blocks are recommended because they come in proportional sizes that allow children to learn mathematical concepts as they become involved in using them. (See Figure 5.15.)

Name	Preschool	Reception year
Square	40	80
Unit	96	192
Double unit	48	96
Quadruple unit	16	32
Pillar	24	48
Half Pillar	24	48
Small triangle	24	48
Large triangle	24	48
Small column	16	32
Large column	8	16
Ramp	16	32
Ellipse		8
Curve	8	16
Quarter circle		8
Large switch & Gothic door		4
Large buttress		4
Small switch		4
Small buttress & half arch		4
Arch & half circle		4
Roofboard		24
Number of shapes	12	23
Number of pieces	344	760

Figure 5.15 – The suggested numbers and types of unit blocks

One of the most important teaching techniques for making children aware of Mathematical concepts in block play is to *talk* to them while they are playing.

The key to talking to children about their block play is to use statements that describe what the child has done, or to ask open-ended questions that encourage children to talk about their work. Look at the following example for some ideas:

Example

When the teacher uses the correct names for the block shapes, children will automatically mimic the correct terms to express learned concepts of shapes.

- *What blocks have been used:* 'You found out that two of these blocks make one long block.'

- *Where the blocks have been placed:* 'You used four small squares to make a big square.'

- *How many blocks have been used:* 'You used six long oblong blocks to make the road. Will other blocks also do the job?'

- *Whether the blocks are all the same size/shape:* 'Are all the blocks in your building the same size/shape?'

- *What is noteworthy about the design:* 'Which blocks could you use to make your building as tall as the shelf?'

- *How the blocks are connected:* 'Are all your blocks touching?'

- *How the blocks are balanced:* 'Those long blocks are holding up the short ones. Could it also work the other way around?'

Spatial awareness

Children develop the concept of spatial relationships from a very young age. Even small babies track the objects they see in the space surrounding them, trying to reach and grasp them. Space involves the way one object or set of objects relates to others based on *position, direction* and *distance.*

Children develop concepts about space as they notice the relationship between their bodies and other people and objects:

- The concept of *position* may be developed in day-to-day activities such as putting away blocks, with the long ones on the bottom shelf and the short ones on the top shelf.

- The concept of *direction* may be developed as the child first drives a tricycle forwards and then backwards.

- The concept of *distance* is explored, for example, when a child throws a ball or bean bag to another child or into a basket – the child will need to throw with more or less effort depending on what distance the other child or basket is from him.

Through increasing knowledge of their own bodies, young children learn different ways of fitting and moving in space – steering themselves around tables; sitting down on chairs and moving through doorways; climbing onto, over, into and down from outside large apparatus, boxes or trees. As the child has opportunities to move around in different spaces, to handle different objects of different shapes and sizes and to fit them into spaces, arranging and rearranging things, he or she learns about distance and position in space.

In so doing the child builds up some understanding of terms such as *near* and *far*, *in between* and *next to, on top of* and *underneath, in front of* and *behind.*

Suggested activities to enhance spatial awareness

As the reception year teacher, you might like to make use of the following activities to encourage learners to have a greater awareness of space.

1. **Board games**

   Pegboards and geoboards are used to organise patterns in space. Pegboards can be used by arranging pegs into different figures in evenly spaced holes. Geoboards are square boards with attached pegs or nails. Rubber bands of different colours can be stretched between the pegs to form patterns and shapes.

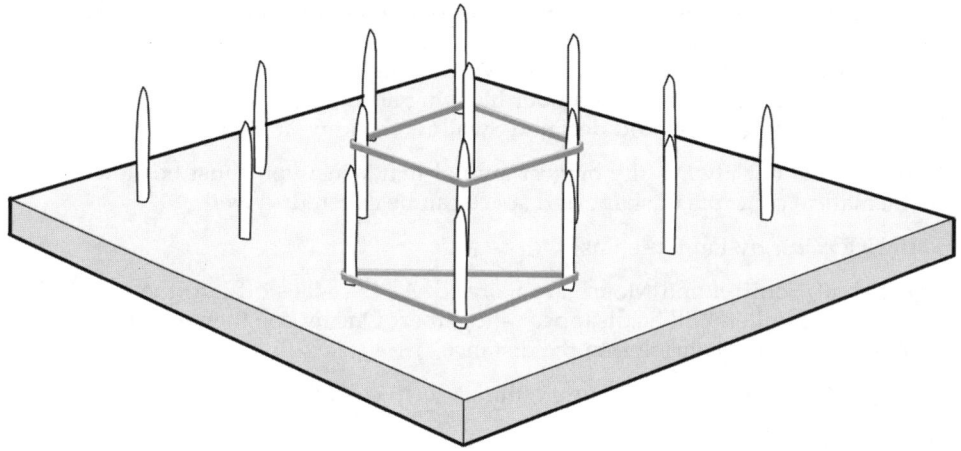

Figure 5.16 – An example of a geoboard

2. **Block play**

   The children can:

   - arrange and rearrange blocks in flat, enclosed spaces, as well as make towering structures in space;

   - arrange and rearrange small scale figures (e.g. dolls, animals, cars) in different layouts involving blocks.

   In so doing, the child can build up some understanding of such terms as *near, next to, on top of, underneath* and *in front of* (see Figure 5.17).

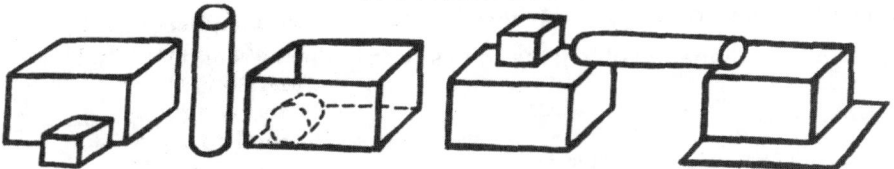

Figure 5.17 – Suggested activities to enhance spatial awareness

3. **Stories and rhymes**

The following stories and rhymes can be used to enhance spatial awareness:

■ *The wolf who wanted to fly* (Indigenous story)

Wolf wants to fly like Vulture to see how things look from high up above. Clever fox pastes some feathers on wolf's tail and vulture agrees that he can hold onto her tail feathers until he is high enough to let go. Of course the honeycomb sticking the feathers to wolf's tail melts and he falls to the ground as he lets go.

Concept: The higher above ground one is, the smaller things look below.

■ *King of the birds* (Indigenous story)

The birds decide that the bird who can fly the highest will become king of the birds. Eagle knows that it has to be him and starts to fly high up in the sky. He looks up and sees Swallow just above his head. He flies even higher but every time he looks Swallow is above his head. What he did not know was the Swallow was flying just under his wing and Eagle had to do all the hard work flying against the wind – and as soon as he looked up Swallow flew out under his wing and quickly flew just above his head. In the end Eagle gave up and declared Swallow the king of the birds.

Concept: It is not always the biggest animal that wins; you must be clever too. The mathematical concepts of shape and space can be covered as well.

■ *Shrinking mouse* by Pat Hutchins

Fox, Rabbit, Squirrel and Mouse are worried. As Owl flies off into the wood, he gets smaller and smaller. Will he disappear altogether? One by one they set off to rescue him and one by one they shrink into the distance.

Concept: As you move further away, things seem smaller in space.

4. **Creative Art activities**

Art activities provide plenty of scope for developing a perception of space:

■ through the use of free drawing and painting with a variety of drawing and painting media on backgrounds of different sizes and shapes;

■ through developing children's ability to use space on a background while:

■ drawing on and not off the boundaries of a background;

■ drawing egocentric drawings of themselves in the middle and other objects floating around them.

■ through planning the use of space by using base lines as a point of departure; (see Figure 2.8, which shows a child arranging objects on a baseline.

■ through collage activities and box construction – arranging and pasting three-dimensional materials in a design on a background;

■ through art activities involving the child's perception of his or her body.

● **Go to:**

Schematic stage – Chapter 2.

Refer to the section entitled *Preschematic stage* in children's drawings – Chapter 2.

Measurement (LO 4)

Measuring should be experienced as part of the daily activities of learners in the reception year.

Measurement is the process of comparing size, volume, weight, time or quantity to a standard. Adults use numerically expressed standards such as metres, litres or the rand. Children discover the concept of measurement when they experiment to find out how many unit blocks or pieces of string (or any other measuring tool, such as their hands or feet) equal the width of the table; or when they count the number of tablespoons of flour for the recipe for cup cakes or compare their height with the heights of their friends.

The early development of measuring skills is thus based on the idea of comparison. Early experiences should be informal, using concrete materials, and should deal with arbitrary comparative measurements, which might emerge during water or sand play: e.g. the biggest or smallest pail; or the longest or shortest handle (of a spade). From here, measurement could proceed to informal measurements with meaningful, *non-standard* units: the book is two straws, two pieces of string, two hands or four crayons long.

One toy car may weigh the same as two blocks, five wooden beads or one cup of water. It may take four cups of sand to fill the small pail and six cups of sand to fill the large pail. By making these simple comparisons between objects through linear measurements, estimating volumes and weighing objects, the child will form a sound foundation on which formal measurement with standard units can be introduced in the primary grades.

FIRST ...

Take the longest rope.

Arbitrary measurements

NEXT ...

This book is two straws long.

Experiences in measuring non-standard units.

EVENTUALLY ...

The samp weighs 60 grams.

The child will progress to standard measures.

Figure 5.18 – Various measuring experiences

Suggested activities for the beginning of measurement

Three aspects of measurement will be considered in the following paragraphs:

1. Linear measurement

2. Measurement of volume

3. Measurement of weight.

1. Linear measurement

The following activities can assist in developing the learners' understanding of linear measurement:

- Compare the height of the children. Have them compare their hands and feet with their classmates' to see who has the longest and the shortest. Compare the length of different objects in the room. Have them guess which would be the longer – two straws laid end to end or five paper clips. Their guess can be verified by doing the measuring.

- Have children guess which pieces of apparatus on the playground are furthest from each other. They can then walk heel to toe to each piece of apparatus and so pace off the distance to see if they were correct.

- Children can use the width of their index fingers or the width of their hands to measure the length of smaller objects, e.g. crayons or books. They can measure larger objects (e.g. a table or bookcase) with the length of their arms – from the elbow to the middle finger.

- Learners can make and use non-standard measurements such as painted footprints. They will later realise that not all our footprints are the same length and that this is the reason that we need *standardised* measuring objects.

2. Volume measurement

Here are some examples of the type of activity a teacher can arrange in order to expose the child to measuring volume:

- Give the child a tablespoon and a pail of sand. Ask the child to spoon sand into a cup, a plastic glass and a small jar. The child counts how many spoons of sand he needs to fill each.

✳ Example

Materials: paper, crayon, and a pair of scissors

Instructions: Children trace the shape of their own feet on paper and cut out the shapes. Continue doing this until they have made many feet outlines. Show them how to use the shapes as a pattern, and how to put the shapes end-to-end to measure a particular distance.

Ask them, for example, 'How many of your feet does it take to measure the distance from the door to the table?'

Figure 5.19 – Measuring with non-standard units, e.g. footprints

---

- Children can 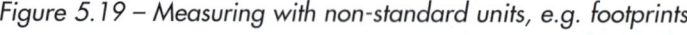 try to arrange four different containers in order of capacity. They can test their guess by pouring cups of water into the containers and counting the cups.

- Learners can use the same cup as a measure and find out how many cups of rice, mealies, samp or beans it would take to fill the same container. A tally can be kept of the counting by making use of graphs.
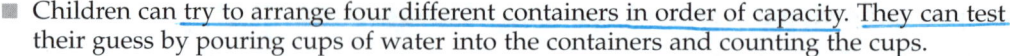

How much does each container hold?

Figure 5.20 – Using everyday measuring items to determine capacity

3. Weight measurement

Children usually judge the larger object to be heavier when asked to guess the weight of two objects. They believe that the bigger the object, the heavier it will be. Have the children use a scale to compare the weight of a larger rubber ball with that of the smaller cricket ball. They will come to understand that weight cannot always be determined by the appearance of an object.

■ Fill five cans with varying amounts of sand or stones. The children can arrange the cans in order from lightest to heaviest by feeling their weight. Afterwards, use a scale to determine whether or not they were correct.

■ Have children experiment to see how many metal washers or nails can balance various other single objects such as a block, a cup, or anything that is at hand.

Understanding time

Time is a complicated concept for the young child, since time is made up of at least three dimensions: time as the present, time as a continuum, and time as a sequence of events. Children should understand all three of these fully before they can be said to have grasped the concept of time.

■ Children learn that certain activities start at a certain time by a given signal (e.g. when the teacher strikes a chord on the piano; the bell rings or a tambourine is struck).

■ They become aware that clocks and calendars are used to mark the passage of time. Children come to know the sequencing of events in time: i.e. which events occur first, next and last. Having an order of events through a consistent daily programme (schedule) helps children learn this aspect of time. When the child wants to know when he or she is going to eat lunch or when he or she is going home, it is better initially to refer to events than simply to the time. Tell the child that everyone will be going home at 12:00 and this is after we have painted, played outside, had our sandwiches, been to the bathroom and listened to a story.

■ Children also benefit from anticipating future events and making the appropriate arrangements. When a grandmother is coming to visit, they may count the sleeps until she comes and may help to prepare for her arrival.

Activities for time concepts

The following is a list of suggested activities that will help learners in the reception year to understand the concept of time:

■ Read books which convey an idea of time. Here are some suggestions:

■ Daly, N. *Not so fast Songololo*. Bantam.

■ Hoban, R. *A birthday for Frances*. Harper & Row.

■ Hoban, R. *Bedtime for Frances*. Harper & Row.

■ King, C. *The birds from Africa*. Macdonald Education. (Seasons)

■ Kraus, R. *Leo the late bloomer*. Windmill.

■ Martin, J. *Fast and slow*. Platt.

■ Schlein, M. *Fast is not a ladybug*. Scribners.

■ Arranging pictures in sequence

■ Have children look at a series of pictures of incidents and decide which incident follows which. They arrange the pictures in sequence and say why they think this sequence is correct.

Figure 5.21 –
A sequence showing a child's life in pictures

■ After you have told a story with flashcards, leave the flashcards out for the children to play with. Ensure that the flashcards are shuffled, so that the sequence is incorrect. The children retell the story but need to arrange the flashcards themselves.

Go to:

Chapter 3, where this is discussed in more detail.

■ The children can arrive at an understanding of how time passes in a week (as well as the concept of *yesterday, today* and *tomorrow*) by making a weekly calendar depicting something outstanding that happened each day of that week.

■ This can be followed with a monthly calendar. After drawing pictures for each day, the children can also make a set of numbers to put in each block in order to number each day of that month.

■ Later still, a calendar can be made with the months of the year indicating in which month the children have their birthdays.

Data handling (LO 5)

Graphs

Graphs are used to show a comparison of information *visually*. When children make graphs, they use the basic skills of classifying, comparing, counting, and measuring to make a picture reflecting information. Children go through different stages in the type of graphs they can make and understand.

Stage 1

At this stage, real objects are used to make a graph, such as blocks, stacking cubes, Lego or Duplo blocks. At this stage only two things are compared.

For example, the children could reflect in a graph which colour play dough they want to play with the following week: yellow or blue. The basis for comparison is one-to-one correspondence, i.e. each child selects one block to represent his or her colour of choice. If the blue stack is higher (more) than the yellow stack, the preference is for blue clay.

Stage 2

During this stage, children are able to compare more than two items.

Example

The class might consider the months of the year in which each child in the class has a birthday.

Mark off twelve columns on a large piece of construction paper, each column representing a month of the year. Give each child a cardboard circle on which to draw, paint or construct his or her face. The children stick their faces on the graph in the appropriate month. They then compare the months to see which month has the most birthdays and which month has the fewest.

Jan	Feb	Mar	Apr	May	Jun	Jul	Aug	Sept	Oct	Nov	Dec

April has the most birthdays. There are five.
February and October have no birthdays.
Three months have three birthdays.
Two months have two birthdays.
Four months have one birthday.

Figure 5.22 – A birthday graph

Once they grasp how a graph works, children often think of their own problems to solve. For example, the children might want to make some of the following comparisons with their graphs:

- hair colour
- eye colour
- colours of clothing
- kinds of pets children have
- favourite foods

- how many claps it takes to reach different places – e.g. from the swings to the verandah, the slide, the tyres, the cement tunnel.

Materials for making graphs

Many materials can be used for making graphs in the first stage:

- unifix interlocking cubes
- pop beads
- dowels and cotton reels
- buttons or squares
- circles of carton glued to cardboard.

Assessment of young mathematicians in the reception year

The information that is gathered about children's concepts of Mathematics over a period of time enables the teacher to become aware of children's progress. This information should also influence her planning of further learning experiences. There are many ways of collecting information for the purpose of assessment – this is discussed in great detail in Chapter 7. The checklist which follows is only one of the methods you can use, and should be used in conjunction with other methods.

MATHEMATICS					
Name...					
Category	**No evidence**	**Beginning**	**Developing**	**Secure**	**Comments**
DEVELOPMENT					
Becoming autonomous: thinking and making own decisions					
Unafraid to make estimates					
Becoming an independent learner					
Curious about mathematics					
Using mathematics intentionally					
Sharing and conferring ideas in problem-solving					
Able to explain thinking to teacher					

Category	No evidence	Beginning	Developing	Secure	Comments
Volunteers information about how answers were found					
ACQUIRING MATHEMATICAL CONCEPTS					
Displays counting-like behaviour					
Knows number names and recites them randomly, then in order					
Counts items but not in order; may not touch ordeal with all the items					
Impose order, mentally on all the items counted					
Says which number comes before and after a given number					
Uses number for identifying position (serial-order)					
Can count forwards and backwards in a number game					
Knows that on a number line the numbers are always in the same order					
Can conserve number					
Understands patterning					
Can match equal and unequal groups					
Can classify according to one property					
Understand sets and subsets					
Understands space concepts: position, direction, distance					

Makes use of informal measurements – non-standard units: linear, volume, weight, time					
Keeps a tally using graphs					

The above checklist can be adapted to fit each teacher's specific needs.

Numeracy learning unit for the reception year

Concept Web

Theme: We all need a hat   **Duration:** 10 days   **Date:** …………………………..

What do we use hats for?

Hats and jobs

We all need a hat

When do we use which hats?

What are hats made of?

Learning Outcome	Assessment Standard	Integration	SKVAs	Learning Activities	Resources	Assessment
Maths LO 5: Data handling	Collects everyday objects (hats); Sorts hats according to one property: e.g. colour, material the hat is made of, use.	Home language LO1: Listening to teacher reading a story	Skills: Data sorting and classifying hats; Space and shape – constructing hats; Number – using money to sell hats.	1. Reading the book 2. Classifying hats 3. We all need a hat 4. Table with hats brought by children 5. Discussion of different hats 6. Making hats 6. Hat parade 7. Making a simple graph of hats according to different shapes – which shape are most hats made in?	A copy of book *Happy Hats* by Peter Curry (A hat shop sells hats for every occasion; from party hats to parade hats – hats of all colours, shapes and sizes). Hats children bring from home. Hats and head coverings, including examples of head coverings worn by different cultural groups in South Africa.	Method: Educator assessment; Peer assessment – learner to learner. Tools: Observation. Forms: Question and answer; drawings, collages and models.
Maths LO 4: Measurement	Describes the time of day certain hats are worn; Measures circumference of head to make sure hats will fit	Home language LO3: Reading and viewing a book and picture	Knowledge: Language concepts regarding different kinds of occupations, materials.			
		Home language LO2: Discuss different indigenous head gear				
		Arts and Culture LO1: Dramatise a story; Talk about and share stories about the hats they have made.	Values: Respect for different occupations.			
Maths LO 3: Space and shape	Recognises, identifies and names shapes of hats in pictures and three-dimensional shapes in basic forms hats are made from: squares, cones and cylinders					
Maths LO 1: Numbers and operations	Reliably counts everyday objects (e.g. caps and monkeys) up to 10 and later 12;	Home language LO 1: Listening to teacher reading a story	Skills: Orientation to the story, sequencing. Space: Where are the monkeys in the tree?	1. Reading the book 2. Counting the caps	A copy of the book *Caps for sale* by Esphyr Slobodkina. (A traditional story of a hawker selling hats. One day	Method: Educator assessment;

Learning outcome	Assessment Standard	Integration	SKVA's	Learning Activities	Resources	Assessment
Maths LO 5: Data handling	Sorts hats according to one property: colour.	Home language LO 3: Reading and viewing a book	Number: Counting, addition, multiplication; Posing and solving problems with money; Chance and data handling: Number – identifying ways of arranging items	3. Working out how much money is needed for the caps 4. Classifying caps according to colour 5. Drawing a picture of what they liked most in the story	he wakes up where he is sleeping under a tree to find the monkeys in the tree have stolen all his hats. How will he get them back?) Pictures for flannel board based on story to use as more concrete apparatus – Hawker, large tree, twelve monkeys, twelve caps: four grey, four red, four blue and four yellow caps.	Peer assessment – learner to learner. Tools: Observation. Forms: Question and answer; drawings.
Maths LO 1: Numbers and operations Maths LO 3: Space and shape	Counting monkeys forwards and backwards – in ones and twos. Identify coins and their values. Solve simple money problems up to 10 cents.	Home language LO 2: Speaking: Memorises and performs action rhyme: *Monkeys swinging from a tree.* Home language LO 3: Reading and viewing the rhyme.	Skills: Counting backwards in one's and two's. Developing fine finger muscles. Knowledge: Recognises and knows the names of coins up to 50 cents. Values: Valuing other peoples' property	1. Saying the rhyme with finger actions. 2. Number: Counting backwards in ones, then in twos. 3. Posing and solving problems, e.g. How much do the caps cost? Start off with caps only costing 1c each.	*Monkeys swinging from a tree* (finger rhyme) Eight little monkeys (hold up eight fingers) Hanging from a tree (wiggle fingers) Teasing Mr Hawker, 'You can't catch me.' Along came Mr Hawker as quiet as can be (walk fingers like tiptoes), Quiet as can be, And snatched one monkey	Method: Educator assessment. Tools: Observation. Forms: Question and answer; Reciting and miming finger rhyme.

Learning outcome	Assessment Standard	Integration	SKVA's	Learning Activities	Resources	Assessment
	Describe one tree (three-dimensional object) surrounded by many monkeys: monkeys in relationship to another object (branch of tree) with regard to position (in, under, in front, behind, etc.)			4. How much will the hawker get if he sells 1, 2, 3, 4, 5, 6, 7, 8, 9, 10 caps?	Right out the tree. (Clap hands on 'snatched') (Continue counting backwards by one) Seven little monkeys … Five little monkeys … Four little monkeys … Three little monkeys … Two little monkeys … One little monkey … No little monkeys hanging from a tree, Teasing Mr Hawker 'You can't catch me' Along comes Mr Hawker, Quiet as can be, 'I've got all the monkeys,' said he! Counters; Unifix blocks (the same colours of the caps); Money – sets of South African coins up to fifty cents.	

Context: The learners become aware of Numeracy concepts by means of clothing.

Conclusion

We should approach mathematics as a natural part of everyday life, helping children to make sense of and cope with the world they live in. In this chapter we have illustrated that young children learn mathematical concepts best when they have fun with and discover concepts themselves while playing, manipulating and exploring concrete objects that are of interest to them. This does not mean that the teacher has no role to play. In fact, the teacher's role is very active. She chooses mathematical content by ensuring that a balance of mathematical activities is chosen for covering the Learning Outcomes. It is the teacher who makes it possible for the learners to discover and construct mathematical concepts by planning the mathematical environment and providing the materials for mathematical experiences.

Bibliography

Apelbaum M and King J. 1993. *Exploring everyday math.* Portsmouth, NH: Heinemann.

Athey C. 1990. *Extending thought in young children.* London: Paul Chapman Publishing Ltd.

Bames K. 1992. *The maths buddies explore 0-10.* Rustenburg: Karet communication.

Barnes K. 1992. *The maths buddies explore 0-20.* Rustenburg: Karet communication.

Beaty JJ. 1992. *Preschool: Appropriate practices.* Orlando, Florida: Holt, Rinehart & Winston.

Charlesworth R & Radeloff DJ. 1978. *Experiences in math for young children.* Albany, New York: Delmar.

Cobb P. 1994. *Where is the mind? Constructivist and sociocultural perspectives on mathematics development.* Paper presented at the annual meeting of the American Educational Research Association, New Orleans. April 1 – 28.

Curry, P. 1991. *Happy Hats.* London: Hippo Books.

DOE. 2002. *Revised National Curriculum Statement.* Pretoria.

Dodge DT. 1988. *The creative curriculum.* Washington, DC: Teaching Strategies.

Dowling M. 1992. *Education 3 – 5.* London: Paul Chapman.

Feeney S, Christensen D & Moravcik E. *Who am I in the lives of children? An introduction to teaching young children.* Columbus, Ohio: Merrill.

Fuson KC. 1988. *Children's counting and number concepts.* New York: Springer-Verlag.

Greenberg P. 1994. How and why to teach all aspects of preschool and kindergarten Math naturally, democratically and effectively. *Young Children* 49 (2) : 12 – 18, 88.

Griffiths, R and Clyne, M. 1996. *Read your way to maths.* Melbourne, Australia: Longman

Hirch ES (ed). 1974. *The block book.* Washington, DC: NAEYC.

Hutchins, P 1997. *Shrinking Mouse.* London: Red Fox

Lemlech JK. 1994. *Curriculum and instructional methods for the elementary and middle school.* New York: Macmillan.

Mannigel D. 1992. *Young children as mathematicians.* Wentworth Falls, NSW: Social Science Press.

Maree K. 1994. *Kry wiskunde klein.* Pretoria: Van Schaik.

Margoles M. 1990. *Ten are too many.* Cape Town: Human & Rousseau.

Mayesky M. 1986. *Creative activities for children in the early primary grades.* Albany, New York: Delmar.

Maxim GW. 1993. *The very young.* Columbus, Ohio: Merrill.

Moomaw, S and Hieronomous , B. 2000. *More than counting: Whole Math Activities.* Beltsville MN: Redleaf Press.

Murray H, Olivier A and Human P. 1993. Learning through problem solving and social interaction. In *Proceedings of the 17th international conference for the Psychology of Mathematics Education.* Tsukuba, Japan. July 193 – 203.

Overholt, JL, White-Holz, J and Dickson, S. 1999. *Big math activities for young children.* Chico, California: Delmar.

Rudolph M and Cohen DH. 1984. *Kindergarten and early schooling.* Englewood Cliffs, New Jersey: Prentice Hall.

Saxe GB, Gubermaan SR and Gearhart M. 1987. *Social processes in early number development. Monographs of the society for research in child development* 52 (2).

Schickedanz JA, York ME, Stewart IS and White DA. 1990. *Strategies for teaching young children.* Englewood Cliffs, New Jersey: Prentice Hall.

Spodek B, Saracho ON and Davis MD. 1991. *Foundations of early childhood education.* Englewood Cliffs, New Jersey: Prentice-Hall.

Chapter

6

Life Skills and exploring Science and Technology

Christie van Staden

OUTCOMES:

After working through this chapter you should be able to:

- choose Learning Outcomes to develop activities for the Life Skills Learning Programmes for learners in the Reception Year

- value the importance of Life Skills for young children

- facilitate Life Skills activities (know how to present these activities)

- implement the LOs of the Learning areas covered in this chapter to develop activities for the three Learning Programmes

- integrate activities with the other learning areas

- develop a learning unit for Life Skills

- choose content and provide activities for the learning areas Natural Sciences and Technology.

Life Skills Learning Programme synopsis

(Cain & Evans 1984, Charlesworth & Lind 1995, Harlan 1995.)

Children discover the content of Science by applying the processes of Science; therefore teachers should emphasise the following science processes, for they are also lifelong skills that will enable children to learn independently.

Life Skills Learning Programme

Many life skills are developed before learners enter the reception year, such as developing their own, positive identity, washing themselves, toilet training, brushing their teeth and putting away their possessions. They now need to develop some more life skills that will help them to organise and manage their affairs and to deal effectively with people and things in a variety of situations in their environment.

The prescribed Learning Programmes: Literacy, Numeracy and Life Skills do not have prescribed Learning Outcomes, as they draw their Learning Outcomes from all eight of the Learning Areas. There are, however, Learning Programme Statements available to guide the design of these programmes. The Life Skills Statement is stated below(GID Training Manual Modules 8-9):

Life Skills Statement

This Learning Programme deals with the full range of life skills to empower learners:

- to develop their full potential physically, emotionally, socially and intellectually
- to participate effectively within their environment and develop scientific and technological skills
- to be empowered citizens and to prepare them for the world of work
- to be creative learners.

> **Remember**
> The Life Skills Learning Programme *is a Learning Programme in its own right. However, it should be integrated into all other learning areas prescribed by the National Curriculum.*
>
> Life Skills should be part of everything we teach.
>
> The **focus outcomes** for Life Skills are derived from the **Life Orientation** Learning Outcomes, covering the following aspects:
>
> - Health
> - Physical
> - Emotional
> - Spiritual
> - Intellectual
> - Creative
>
> Figure 6.1 illustrates this.

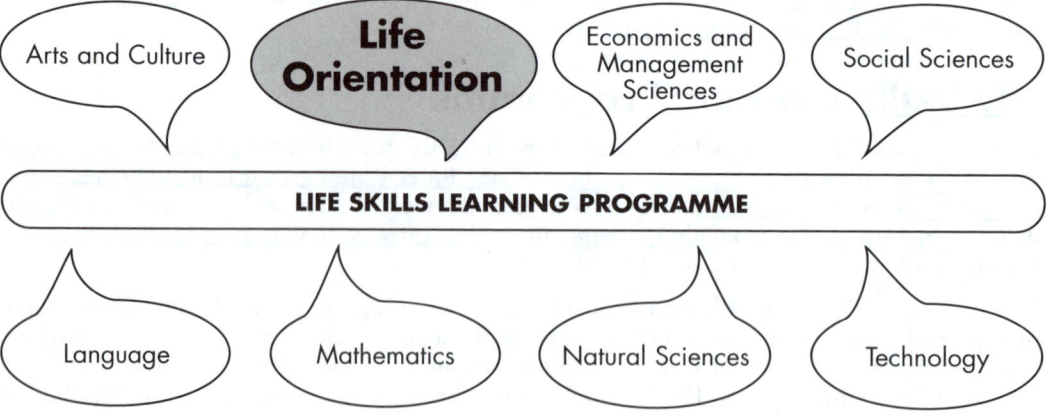

Fig 6.1 A diagram of the Life Skills Learning Programme

Main outcomes for the Life Orientation Learning Area

The **purpose** of the **Life Orientation Learning Area** is to empower learners to use their talents to achieve their full physical, intellectual, personal, emotional and social potential. They will develop the skills to:

■ relate positively to others

■ make constructive contributions to family, community and society (while practising the values imbedded in the constitution)

■ respect the rights of others

■ show tolerance for cultural and religious diversity in order to build a democratic society.

The following **four Learning Outcomes** have been set aside for Life Orientation in the Foundation Phase. We focus on the Assessment Standards for the reception year:

Learning Outcomes	Assessment Standards	Learning Outcome focus (Find more examples in the text)
Learning Outcome 1 – Health Promotion The learner will be able to make informed decisions regarding personal, community and environmental health.	**We know this when the learner:** 1. explains the importance of drinking clean water and eating fresh food. 2. describes steps that can be taken to ensure personal hygiene. 3. demonstrates precautions against the spread of communicable diseases. 4. explains safety in the home and at school. 5. explains the right of children to say no to sexual abuse, and describes ways in which to do so.	The learner in the Foundation Phase is exposed to communicable childhood diseases. Therefore, the learner should have knowledge of these diseases, as well as HIV/AIDS. Sound health practices, and an understanding of the relationship between health and the environment, can improve the quality of life and wellbeing of the learners. At this age, the learner is vulnerable to abuse. Safety measures particularly relevant to the learner in this phase should be addressed.
Learning Outcome 2 – Social Development The learner will be able to understand and demonstrate an understanding of, and commitment to, constitutional rights and responsibilities, and to show an	**We know this when the learner:** 1. identifies basic rights and responsibilities in the classroom. 2. recognises the South African flag. 3. knows members of own family, peers and caregivers.	The Foundation Phase learner should know and exercise rights and responsibilities as guaranteed in the South-African Constitution. The learner should be encouraged to recognise and oppose unfair discrimination.

understanding of diverse cultures and religions.	4. listens to and retells a story with a moral value from own culture. 5. identifies and names symbols linked to own religion.	Knowledge of diverse religions will contribute to non-discriminatory attitudes to counter and prevent prejudices.
Learning Outcome 3 – Personal Development The learner will be able to use acquired life skills to achieve and extend personal potential to respond effectively to challenges in his or her world.	**We know this when the learner:** 1. says his own name and address. 2. describes what own body can do. 3. expresses emotions without harming self, others or property. 4. adjusts to classroom routine and follows instructions.	The self concept of the Foundation Phase learner is at an early stage of development. The learner already has some attitudes and feelings regarding personal worth; these are dependent on the learner's experiences. It is important to give the learner opportunities for positive self-concept formation, as well as to explore and express feelings. The learner needs to be assisted to adjust to the learning environment.
Learning Outcome 4 – Physical Development and Movement The learner will be able to demonstrate an understanding of, and participate in, activities that promote movement and physical development.	**We know this when the learner:** 1. plays running, chasing and dodging games using space safely. 2. explore different ways to locomote, rotate, elevate and balance. 3. performs expressive movements using different parts of the body. 4. participates in free play activities.	The learner in the Foundation Phase enters school with many emerging motor control, body awareness and perceptual motor abilities which need further development. The learner's affective and social responses are usually egocentric. Through discovery, the learner needs to develop the necessary skills for each of the developmental aspects. Using a variety of new functional movements, the learner develops an awareness of the body and how to move in challenging, exploratory and problem-solving ways.

Life Orientation Learning Outcome 1 – Health Promotion

The learner will be able to make informed decisions regarding personal, community and environmental health.

Content can be planned in contexts to cover the following concepts:

- We need to take care of our bodies
- Our bodies need rest
- Brushing teeth, washing hair and bathing are ways to keep our bodies clean
- Nutritious food keeps our bodies healthy
- We need a balanced diet
- Medical checkups ensure that we stay healthy
- Clothing protects our bodies
- Poisonous plants are harmful.

A healthy balanced diet

Recognising and appreciating nourishing foods

We eat food for three reasons:

- Food gives you energy and keeps you warm
- Food gives you substances that your body needs to be healthy
- Food gives you the building blocks for health and repair

Food contains the following substances:

- Fat – to store and provide energy
- Protein – to grow new tissue, repair damage and provide energy
- Carbohydrate – to provide a supply of energy. The two main forms are sugar and starch
- Water – to carry things around the body and replace lost water
- Minerals – to make healthy blood, bones and other tissues
- Vitamins – to take part in important chemical reactions in the body
- Fibre – to keep the digestive system healthy.

A balanced diet contains the correct amount of all food types. A simple rule is to eat something every day from each of the food groups. Malnutrition is caused by having a diet that is not balanced.

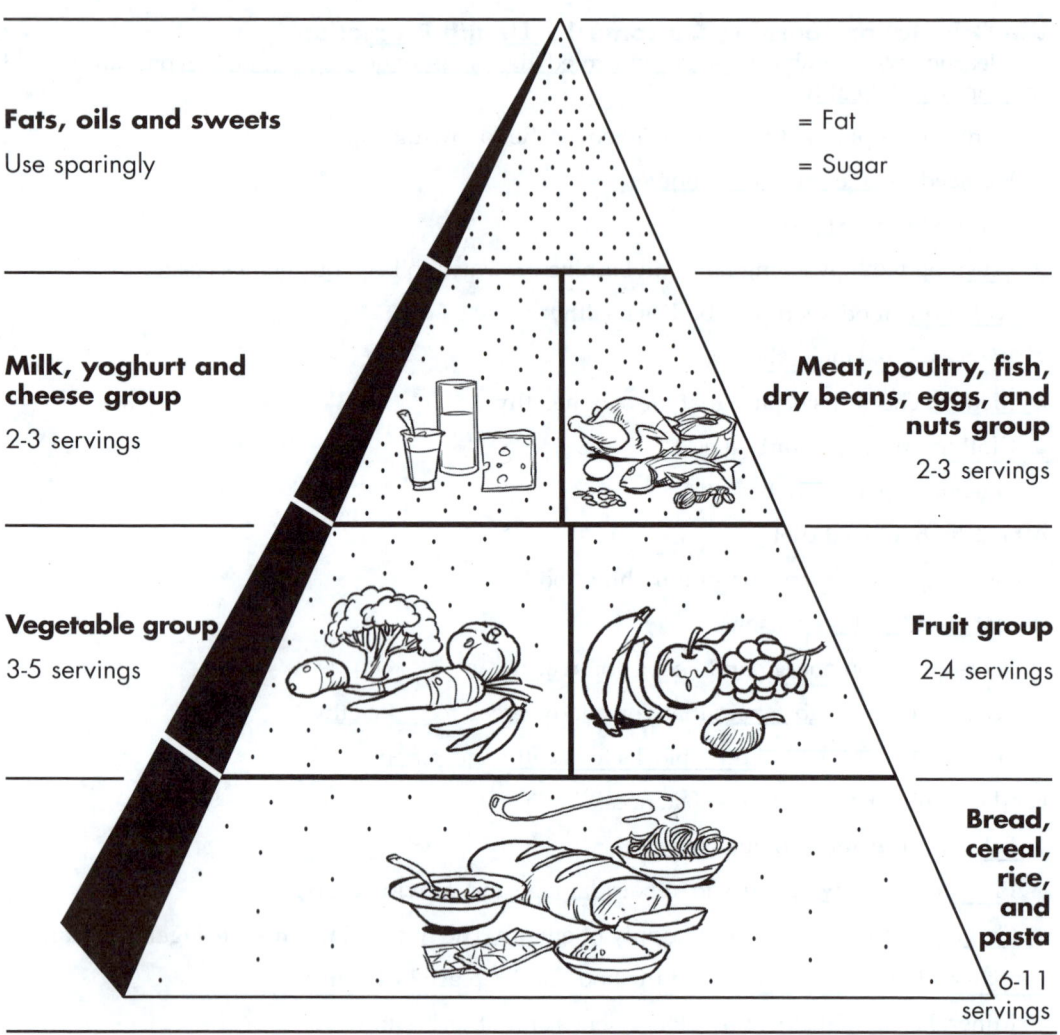

Fig 6.2 A food guide pyramid

Maintain a safe and healthy physical environment

Hygiene

- An Early Childhood site catering for reception year learners should have adequate washing and toilet facilities for both children and adults.

- The number and size of toilets and wash basins are usually prescribed by the local health or other regulatory bodies.

- There should be a rule in place about the non-sharing of personal items.

- Staff and children should not be allowed to share personal items like towels, face-cloths, toothbrushes or linen. Each person must have his/her own personal items which are clearly marked and regularly cleaned.

Hand washing

We need to keep in mind that most diseases are spread if hands are not washed. To prevent the spreading of diseases there must be a "hand washing policy" in place at your site that the staff and children must wash their hands.

Staff, volunteers and children must wash their hands:

- when arriving at the beginning of the day
- before preparing, eating or touching food
- before feeding a child
- after visiting the toilet or helping a child with toileting
- after touching any body fluids such as mucous, blood, vomit, urine or faeces, or handling items contaminated with body fluids
- after wiping noses, faces or buttocks
- before and after cleaning any injuries or sores
- before and after giving any medicines
- after touching pets or any other animals
- after doing any cleaning
- after removing gloves
- after handling any plant material.

Wash your hands in the following way:

- use liquid soap and clean water (do not wash hands in water that has been used by someone else)
- Rub your hands vigorously for at least 15 seconds and wash all areas including backs of hands, wrists, between fingers and under fingernails (use nailbrush).
- Rinse hands well under running water.
- Dry your hands on a paper disposable towel or other clean towel.
- Turn off the tap using the same paper towel.
- Do not wash hands in water that has been used by someone else.
- Do not dry hands on a wet or dirty towel but rather dry hands in the air.
- Where water is scarce, fill a clean, empty, plastic 2 litre milk/juice bottle with water. Make some holes in the lid of the bottle and replace. Now tilt the bottle so that a little water sprinkles out onto hands.

Cleanliness

> **Remember**
>
> Water for drinking and food preparation
>
> *Any water which does not come from a municipal supply should be made safe before it is used for drinking, preparing food or washing eating utensils (this includes water from boreholes, rivers, wells or dams). To do this, either boil the water for 10 minutes or disinfect the water with household bleach to kill any germs.*

Making water safe for use with household bleach:

Add 5 m*l* (1 teaspoonful) unscented household bleach to 25*l* water.

Allow this to stand for two hours before using.

- The classroom/playroom should be cleaned daily, and equipment that is used regularly should be sanitised on a regular basis.
- Nontoxic paint must be used in all circumstances, including on outdoor equipment, toys and as art materials.
- Playroom dress-up clothing, pillows, nap blankets and cuddle toys all need regular laundering, either at the site or at home.

Guarding children from environmental hazards

The first golden rule about safety is that young children should be supervised by a responsible person at all times. Children should never be left alone, whether in the playroom/classroom or outdoors.

Everything is planned with the children's safety in mind. Walk around the playroom, school and yard and identify potential safety problems. Deal with these problems by removing them or making them safe.

Inside the facility

The following are suggestions of where safety hazards may occur:

- Are there any sharp corners at children's height?
- Are rug edges snagged or loose?
- Are absorbent surfaces used (so that the surface is not slippery) wherever there is water? Are mops available for water spillage?
- Are hot water, pots and primus stoves out of the children's reach?
- Are children allowed to run inside?
- Are there rules regarding the children's use of woodwork apparatus [hammers, saws, scissors (these should be blunt nosed), knives (provide only plastic knives for children's use)].
- Are safety rules explained to children and upheld by adults?
- Are all walls and furniture painted with nontoxic paints (paint should not contain lead)?
- Are all electric outlets covered when not in use?

- Do open stairwells have gates?

- Are medicines and household cleaning agents stored away and out of children's reach?

- Are there any ropes, cords or string hanging around loosely (cords from blinds) which might ensnare a child's neck or other body parts?

- Does traffic flow easily?

- Are the toys safe for children's use? Are they developmentally appropriate? Young children should not be playing with toys that have small parts which could become loose, or beads and seeds which could be swallowed, placed in ears or nostrils. Children of this age still put everything in their mouths. Are the toys nontoxic and clean?

- Are pest control procedures carried out when children are not present (over weekends or holidays)?

- Smoking should not be allowed on the premises.

Hazards outside:

- Is broken equipment removed or fixed promptly?

- Are fences high enough to protect and safe to touch (electric and razor wire should not be accessible)?

- Are there areas where wheel toys can move freely without fear of collision?

- Are swings placed away from traffic areas and set apart by bushes or fences?

- Are children warned not to run in front of swings and to keep a safe distance away from swings when they are being used by other children?

- Can a child's foot or ankle be caught on equipment or under a chain-link fence?

- Are any plastic bags lying around? Knot these and put them away where children cannot reach them. Children can suffocate if they pull plastic bags over their heads.

- Are poisonous plants removed from the garden? Consult a book from the library about toxic plants, or get the advice of an expert from a plant nursery. Children should not put any parts of a plant in their mouths.

- Are outdoor play areas shaded? Do children wear hats during outside play to protect them from the sun? All skinned children should wear sun protection cream (sun protection factor of at least 15.

Emergency procedures

Example

Injuries

Injuries to children do happen. Every school should establish procedures for dealing with children who are injured on the property. First aid instructions should be made available to all practitioners as part of their in-service training. Each school should be equipped with a first aid kit.

Emergency numbers must be posted near the telephone and include those of:

- the ambulance

- fire department
- police
- nearest hospital
- consulting doctor (if possible)
- nearest clinic.

Health policy

Every Early Childhood Centre should have a clear health policy and make it known to the parents. A child should be observed every day by adults, who will help teachers to identify nasal discharge, inflamed eyes and throat and skin conditions of a questionable nature. This daily check screens out more serious cases of children too ill to remain at school. Educating parents about the warning signs of illness will encourage sick children to be cared for at home.

It is important to inform parents about what happens when children are refused admittance because of illness or those who become ill during the school day.

Handling emergencies

Every school site should have a school policy regarding the handling of emergencies. All families enrolled at the school should be aware of the school policy regarding injuries at school and provide the school with *emergency information* which could be kept in the child's file. Emergency information for each child should include:

- the name of their physician
- any allergies of the child, for example, for bee stings
- any medicines the child needs to be given, with the times and proper dosage to be given
- how to locate the parents (telephone number and other information)
- who else might be responsible if parents cannot be reached.

> **Remember**
>
> *Journal or incident book*
>
> *To ensure proper care and safety, even minor injuries such as superficial cuts and bruises must be reported to the parents.*

It is always difficult to remember exactly what happened exactly when an injury took place, so it is better to put it down in writing.

All injuries and the circumstances surrounding it need to be written down in *a journal or incident book:* State:

- the child's name
- the date
- the name of the supervising person
- the place/location where child was injured
- the time of the injury
- the manner of the injury

 what procedures were taken by the responsible, supervising person.

First Aid for minor injuries

<u>Always wear surgical glove</u>s when handling blood or body fluids as protection from HIV/AIDS.

Exposure to blood and body fluids: If a blood spill occurs, children should be removed from the area which should then be cleaned.

If an area or surface is soiled by body fluids or any other potentially infectious material, the area needs to be cleaned with soap and water to remove any organic or solid matter. It should then be disinfected with bleach sanitising solution.

For any exposure to blood, blood-stained clothing or other infected body fluids the following Universal Precautions should be used:

> **Universal Precautions for use in schools/ECD sites:**
> - All blood, blood products and blood-stained body fluids must be regarded as potentially infectious.
> - Everybody must use every possible method to prevent direct contact with blood or blood-contaminated fluids (e.g. use waterproof gloves or plastic bags to protect hands).
> - Injuries to hands should be covered with waterproof plasters.
> - Nonporous gloves should also be worn when cleaning up blood spills.
> - Thorough hand washing must be done after the gloves are removed or after any accidental blood contact.

<u>Fire safety</u>

Most local fire regulations stipulate that <u>fire extinguishers must be in working order and placed in each playroom and in the kitchen area</u>. Fire exits, fire alarms and fire escapes should be well marked and should function properly.

Children and teachers/practitioners should take part in <u>regular fire drills</u>.

> **Procedure in the case of fire**
> - Sound the alarm to evacuate the building. This should be a signal that you have discussed and practised with the staff and the children beforehand.
> - Notify the fire station.
> - Evacuate the building quickly, in an orderly way. Do not use lifts.
> - Have someone check that all areas of the building have been evacuated and that the doors of every room have been closed.
> - In the case of a bomb threat, the doors and windows should be left open and strange objects should not be touched. Notify the police.
> - If possible, switch off the main electricity supply.
> - Close windows and doors behind you.
> - Do not allow anyone to re-enter the building to fetch personal belongings.
> - Gather at an area decided on beforehand.
> - Have an alternative plan if you cannot reach this area.

Activities for Health Promotion

Fantasy play

Create dramatic play areas:

For example, *a doctor's office* can be created by placing white clothing, stethoscopes, thermometers, magazines, bandages, a small bed or mattress and plastic syringes without needles in a corner.

A *Restaurant* can be created by placing table and chairs, menus with pictures of healthy food, writing material for taking "orders", a collection of boxes, tins and clay examples of food and vegetables, a stove and pots to prepare food into a designated space. You can make a sign for the area (For example, "Eating healthy food").

Literacy

Brushing Teeth
I jiggle the toothbrush again and again
(pretend to brush teeth)
I scrub all my teeth for a while.
I swish the water to rinse them and then
(puff out cheeks to swish)
I look at myself and I smile.
(smile at one another)

The naughty soap
Just when I'm ready to start
on my ears,
That is the time that my soap disappears.
It jumps from my fingers, and
slithers and slides,
down to the end of the tub
where it hides,
and acts in a most disobedient way,
and that's why my soap's
growing thinner each day.

Bath time
I've been playing all day
and I'm covered in dirt
So I head for my bathroom
and pull off my shirt.
With all these things to use,
I'll be clean as can be.
My toys will enjoy my bath time with me.
My whale squirts water
up to the sky
while hundreds of bubbles go floating by.
With lots of shampoo, I lather my head.
Goodnight everybody, I'm off to my bed!

Arts and Culture

■ Paper plate meals. Provide magazines and scissors for learners to find healthy food to cut out and paste on a round background or paper plate.

■ Paint with discarded tooth brushes for paint brushes.

■ Do spatter painting with tooth brushes.

Mathematics

■ Food group sorting

Children bring empty food containers to school. The food containers can be sorted into the different food groups.

- Measuring

   Weigh and measure each child throughout the year. Record the data on a chart.

   Cooking encourages the use of measurement.

Making soda pop

Ingredients:
lemons or oranges cut in half (two halves for each child)
baking soda
bowl of cold water
ice cubes
honey
teaspoons
$^1/_2$ measuring cup
$^1/_4$ measuring cup
large clear plastic cups or yoghurt glasses
ice cream sticks
orange squeezer

RECIPE CHART

Juice of 1 lemon

$^1/_2$ cup of cold water

3 Teaspoons of honey

$^1/_2$ teaspoon of baking soda

Stir everything with your ice-cream stick

Natural Sciences

■ Making toothpaste

Learners can mix their own toothpaste. Place 4 teaspoons of baking soda, 1 teaspoon salt and 1 teaspoon of water into individual plastic bags. Add a drop of food extract such as peppermint, mint, orange or strawberry as flavouring.

Life Orientation Learning Outcome 2 – Social Development

The learner will be able to understand and demonstrate an understanding of, and a commitment to, constitutional rights and responsibilities, and to show an understanding of diverse cultures and religions.

Concepts for Reception year learners to grasp:

■ A friend is someone I like and who likes me

■ Everybody can be my friend

■ We share and learn with friends

■ We help friends and they help us

■ Friends talk and listen to us.

Activities for Social Development

Language

■ Reading *The Bad-Tempered Ladybird* by Eric Carle

Synopsis: The bad-tempered ladybird does not want to share the aphids on a plant with another friendly ladybird. He picks a fight with every animal he meets, but soon learns the importance of friends and sharing.

■ Choose religious stories demonstrating good morals from your learners' religious background.

Field trips/Life Orientation

■ Learners can visit an old age home/ children's hospital. They can take flowers and talk/sing to elderly people and ill children.

■ Resource people from the community.

Invite the following community helpers into the classroom for discussions with the learners:

■ doctor, nurse, dentist

■ police officer

■ fire fighter

■ garbage collector

■ milkman

■ postman

■ baker

■ parents from all cultures to demonstrate cooking of various dishes

Mathematics/Life Orientation (movement)

■ Numeracy game

Prepare a game based on the principle of Snakes and Ladders (counting on and counting back). Vegetables that grow above the ground (ladders move along) and vegetables that grow below the ground (snakes move backwards).

FIVE LITTLE FRIENDS
(Hold up five fingers and: subtract one with each action)

Five little friends playing on the floor,
One hurt his foot and then there were four.
Four little friends climbing in a tree,
One jumped down and then there were three.
Three little friends skipping to the zoo,
One rolled over and then there were two.
Two little friends swimming in the dam,
One got a cramp and away he ran.
One little friend took a nap after his run,
And then, of all the little friends, there was none.

Life Orientation Learning Outcome 3 – Personal Development
The learner will be able to use acquired life skills to achieve and extend personal potential to respond effectively to challenges in his or her world.

> ### Remember
> *Children's social and emotional development have already received attention in Chapter 2, Know the Child. Read through this section again before giving attention to the notes which will follow.*

Nurturing a positive self-concept in learners

Self-concept includes all the feelings and perceptions that children have about them. Children aren't born with a self-concept; it develops from the way people talk to them and treat them. In addition to parents, teachers/practitioners have an important influence on what type of self-concept a child will develop, whether it is a positive (feeling good about themselves) or a negative (feeling bad about themselves) self-concept.

Sometimes a practitioner may, by means of what is being done or said, make young children feel bad about themselves. This will happen when children are expected to do activities in which they will not be successful because it is too difficult for them, or too easy for them. Stereotyping children by calling them names, using put-downs, comparisons, criticisms, and overprotection: ("you are always lazy", "you act like a baby", "you are a troublemaker", "you are not as clever or good as your sister") can handicap children.

Each child should be made to feel important, respected and valued. This will help the child to develop a positive self-concept.

Each person is important, respected and valued

Following are some simple strategies to support the reception year learners you are responsible for with their personal development, to feel good about themselves and develop a positive self-concept:

■ Accept children for who they are and what they are. Your acceptance will lead to feelings of self-acceptance in the child.

- Set clear, reasonable rules and expectations of behaviour. When children are set boundaries and know what behaviour is expected of them, they tend to develop higher self-esteem.

- Encourage autonomy (allow children to do things themselves) and independence in children.

- Allow children to make decisions and accept responsibility.

- Provide a secure environment where children can feel safe and express their feelings and opinions freely.

- Show respect for and value all children in your care. Embrace their difference in racial, gender, religious and cultural backgrounds.

- Try to provide many experiences that the learners are developmentally capable of completing (for their intellectual, social, emotional, physical, language and creative development).

- Have realistic expectations; replace discouraging remarks and criticism with encouragement and praise.

- Help the children you teach to see that they are unique and special. Find something they do well as a starting point to encourage them in areas where they might be weak. (For example, "You can climb on the apparatus to the top; let's still practise your cutting.")

- Don't expect children to be perfect. Show them that it is fine to fail and help them learn how to deal with their mistakes and to learn from failure. (For example, "It doesn't matter that your paint dribbled down the page; you can paint over the dribble and change it into something you would like to paint. Try to take less paint on your brush by wiping the brush inside the container before you paint and then there won't be any more dribbles.")

- Do not make insulting or negative remarks about children in their presence, or to anyone else. Don't allow learners to degrade themselves or others.

- Be enthusiastic and positive. Think positive thoughts about yourself, your learners, and your situation.

- Praise and reinforce children to let them know that you recognise their worth. Use words such as, "A good try, all right, much better, thank you for…, I'm proud of …, a great effort …, that's right, you really tried hard, you're doing better, I knew you could…, etc.

- Give children lots of smiles and positive reinforcement.

Activities for personal development to encourage a positive self-esteem

Language

- Have a child star each week. The child brings objects from home which belong to him/her and tell the other children something about the object so that the children can get to know and appreciate that child. Everybody in the group thinks about something kind to say about this child. Make a poster about this child with their picture, or one they've drawn, their favourite activities, pets, some positive comments about why the other children like this child, etc.

- Encourage children to draw pictures and to dictate stories about their feelings.

- Ask learners to look in a mirror and to say one thing that they like about themselves. Make "I can" posters. Let children draw pictures or dictate sentences about all the things they can do.

Arts & Culture

▪ Do <u>finger painting</u> with happy/sad music (creative expression)

Finger paint recipe
1 cup of cornstarch
4 cups water
^{1}/2 cup of sugar
food colouring if desired

Method:

Cook water, cornstarch, and sugar until thick. Mixture will be clear and glossy. Add food colouring for desired colour.

▪ Feelings – <u>dramatise and sing to the tune</u> of "Twinkle twinkle little star".

> *I have feelings.* (point to self)
> *You do, too.* (point to someone else)
> *Let's all sing about a few.*
> *I am happy.* (smile)
> *I am sad.* (frown)
> *I get scared.* (wrap arms around self)
> *I get mad.* (stomp feet)
> *I am proud of being me.* (hands on hips)
> *That's a feeling too you see.*
> *I have feelings.* (point to self)
> *You do, too.* (point to someone else)
> *We just sang about a few*

▪ Let each child make an "<u>All About Me</u>" book. They can draw pictures of themselves and their family, home(s), school, likes, dislikes.

▪ Ask children to <u>complete this sentence: "I'm special because</u> ..."

▪ Learners can each make a <u>happy and sad face</u> on different sides of a paper plate stuck onto a rod to make a <u>puppet.</u> They can <u>show how they feel by e</u>ither showing the sad or happy face. They can then <u>explain why</u> they feel happy or sad and what will make them feel better.

▪ <u>Modelling</u> – Playing with <u>play dough</u> provides <u>sensory experie</u>nces, which are pleasing and have a calming effect on learners.

Play dough recipe 1

2 cups of flour
1 cup of salt
1cup of hot water
2 table spoons cooking oil
4 teaspoons cream of tartar
food colouring.

Method:

Mix well. Knead until smooth. Keep in a plastic bag or covered container and use again. If it gets sticky, add more flour.

Play dough recipe 2

2 cups of cornstarch
4 cups of baking soda
2 $^1/_2$ cups water
food colouring if desired.

Method:

In a pan, combine the baking soda, cornstarch and water. Cook over medium heat, while stirring constantly. When mixture thickens and forms a ball, remove from the heat. Knead until cool and add food colouring if desired.

Goop

Mix together food colouring, 1 cup of cornstarch and 1 cup of water. If larger quantities are required, double or triple recipe.

■ Self portraits (getting to know what their bodies look like and accepting themselves). Learners draw around each other and colour themselves in with any drawing, painting or collage materials.

Self portraits build self-image

Life Orientation Learning Outcome 4 – Physical Development and Movement
The learner will be able to demonstrate an understanding of, and participate in, activities that promote movement and physical development.

Movement Education

Movement education teaches young children physical skills related to moving. Different movement skills may include the following:

Type of Skill	Details of Skill
1. Locomotory skills	Provide a wide variety of motor challenges: walking, running, skipping, hopping, galloping.
2. Climbing skills	Offer experiences of climbing over low, inclined planks, packing boxes, on jungle gyms, stairs, ladders.
3. Balancing skills	Offer activities involving simple balancing – scooters, walking on a low plank, walking on a rope, balancing a bean bag on the head while walking.
4. Throwing and catching skills	Allow for hand-eye experiences with balls of different sizes, bean bags, throwing and catching balloons, beach balls.
5. Strength and agility in movement	Throwing balls at skittles, offer hurdles to jump, mini obstacle courses, practise starting and stopping, dodging, changing direction.

Movement and use of space during free play outside

Children will begin to experience and explore space within their own movement. They can also experiment with their own body shape to find out whether it will fit into a box or not.

Teachers/practitioners can provide a wide variety of challenging experiences that are inherent in the equipment they put out or make available for children to play with:

Large apparatus:

- Climbing frames provide experience in space for children by their moving in and out as well as up, down, over and on top of. There is also the experience of being enclosed by a three-dimensional shape. If climbing frames aren't available; trees will work just as well. You can look around in the environment and find substitutes for apparatus you may not have. Crates, wooden/cardboard boxes, discarded telephone cable spools of different sizes, discarded tyres and planks will come in handy to construct your own apparatus.

- Scrambling nets need more awareness and control of body weight in space than fixed frames. Homemade scrambling apparatus can be made by fixing tyres together in a mat.

- Slides: certain body control is required. Body position can also be varied by, say, sitting or lying face down going down.

- Swings: where children need to transfer their body weight as they go forwards, backwards, up and down.

- Seesaws lead to estimation of weight as children look for a comfortable partner, so as not to sit in the air all the time. They also learn to balance their weight by sitting in different positions.

■ Tunnels made from barrels or large pipes can either lie flat on the ground or be raised on frames, so that steps or sloping planks are needed to get into them. Children learn to change their own shapes as they move from one tunnel to another. They also gain experience of spatial order, as overtaking is impossible and "first in, first out" becomes the rule.

Keep in mind that *improvised apparatus* can be made from cardboard cartons, discarded milk crates, planks, bricks, old tyres and tree stumps. Children can also arrange these themselves to gain confidence.

Obstacle course

Provide an obstacle course including the large apparatus on the playground with different activities covering as many of the physical skills as possible.

Organising outdoor space for movement

Learning takes place outdoors as well as indoors. Outdoors is the perfect place for children to run, jump, swing, climb, and use all the large muscles in their bodies. They can enjoy nature, plants and take care of a garden.

The outdoors should also be planned with certain areas in mind. There should be shaded and sunny areas. Make provision for:

■ permanent equipment, such as swings, and large climbing apparatus

■ a place for a water tray and a sandpit for sand play

■ wheel toys and a paved or other hard surface for their proper use (such toys must not be used near swings or climbing apparatus)

■ an area for running and playing with balls (out of the way of swings)

■ creative arts and woodwork

✳ A Life Skills Learning Unit ✳

A Life Skills Learning Unit

Theme: Caring for my body   **Duration:** 10 days   **Date:** ....

Context: The learners become aware that their bodies have physical needs which they should pay attention to. Focus on Nutrition.

Learning Outcome	Assessment Standard	Integration	SKVAs	Learning Activities	Resources	Assessment
LO 1 Health Promotion LO 3 LO 4 Movement	The learner can: differentiate between healthy and junk food and make good choices of food in the different food groups. Prepare simple healthy dishes.	HL LO 1 Listening to story told about: *The Boy who wanted eat upside down.* Read story. HL LO 3 Reading and viewing: Food chart, labels on interest table. HL LO 2 Discuss: Food chart, different indigenous dishes. HL 4 Children make drawings of healthy food and dictate labels for teacher to print for them. Place on interest table. FAL LO1 Provide names of fruit and vegetables in first additional language M LO 4 Measurement: measure ingredients for cooking dishes, following a recipe.	Skills ■ Classifying different food groups ■ data sorting and classifying between healthy and junk food – preparing healthy food (cooking) ■ Number, money – saving money by growing own vegetables.	1. Listening to story 2. Classifying different food groups/ healthy and junk food. 3. Creating a table with real, or pictures of, health and junk food brought by children. Discussion of different types of food. 4. Cooking: Making a fruit salad; vegetable soup; lemon soda pop, making a grilled cheese sandwich, sprouting alfalfa seeds. 5. A caregiver prepares an indigenous SA dish.	■ Large chart of the Food Guide. Pyramid. ■ Story: *The boy who wanted to eat upside down* [Synopsis: Grandmother shows boy the food guide pyramid on cereal box which shows us how to eat a balanced diet. Boy looks at upside down triangle on box and decides that he must be a bat so that he can eat upside down. ■ Fruit and vegetables children bring from home for interest table (Show and tell)	■ Method: Educator assessment, Peer assessment – learner to learner. ■ Tools: Observation ■ Forms: Question and answer, drawings, paintings, collages and models.

Learning Outcome	Assessment Standard	Integration	SKVAs	Learning Activities	Resources	Assessment
		M LO 3 Space and shapes. Recognising, identifying and naming shapes of shadows of fruit and vegetables. How many cherries and oranges will fit into the same container? Why will more cherries fit in than oranges? M LO Data handling: create a fruit graph. A&C LO 1.Draw, paint and model vegetables and fruit. NS LO 1 Become aware of the different cooking processes and how food changes.	**Knowledge** ■ Strong growing bodies need healthy food. ■ Which food belongs to different food groups? ■ An idea of a balanced diet. **Values** Choose healthy food above junk food	6. Making simple graphs of preference of fruit/vegetables by learners. 7. Religious story – parable of the sower. 8. Playing game (Hot potato).		

Making sense of the world through Science

Science does not consist of isolated pockets of information which children are taught and which they 'soak up like sponges'. Science is about children getting to know things about themselves and the real world through self-discovery, through hands-on experience. For example, children learn that grass turns yellow when covered up and that plants die when they aren't watered. Science is more than knowledge about the living and non-living things in our environment; it is also a process – a way of finding out about the world by:

- noticing (becoming aware of a problem)
- wondering why (hypothesising – proposing an explanation)
- finding out (experimenting)
- sharing results with others.

Children younger than seven do not find out about things by reading or being told about them; they actively participate through physical interaction with their surroundings and have concrete experiences. Reception year children acquire scientific information through the process approach, which is more important than committing scientific facts to memory. The teacher serves as a guide and resource person. This approach fosters development in all areas of learning, not just in memorising facts.

The Natural Sciences Learning Area

Purpose

The Natural Sciences Learning Area deals with the promotion of scientific literacy. It does this through:

- the development and use of science process skills in a variety of settings
- the development and application of scientific knowledge and understanding
- the appreciation of the relationships and responsibilities between science, society and the environment.

Go to:

Read the Introduction to departmental documentation for more background.

Development of Science process skills

The teaching and learning of Science involves the development of a range of process skills that may be used in everyday life, in the community and in the workplace. Learners can gain these skills in an environment that supports creativity, responsibility and growing confidence. Learners develop the ability to think objectively and use a variety of forms of reasoning while they use process skills to investigate, reflect, synthesize and communicate.

Development of scientific knowledge and understanding

Scientific knowledge and understanding is a cultural heritage that can be used to:

- answer questions about the nature of the physical world
- prepare learners for economic activity and self-expression
- lay the basis for further studies in science

■ prepare learners for active participation in a democratic society that values human rights and promotes environmental responsibility.

The four main content areas or knowledge strands to be covered in Science

While there are similarities in the ways scientists work, it is not possible to put all scientific knowledge and activities together under a single umbrella heading. In the Revised National Curriculum Statement, the fields which scientists study have been grouped into four main content areas or knowledge strands. These are:

1. **Life and Living** which focuses on life processes and healthy living, on understanding balance and change in environments, and on the importance of biodiversity.

Core knowledge and concepts in Life and Living for the Foundation Phase

Life processes and healthy living	Interactions in environments	Biodiversity, change and continuity
■ Many of our body parts correspond to parts of animals, such as limbs, heads, eyes, ears, feet, and in many cases animals use them for the same purposes we do. ■ Animals and plants have needs similar to ours, for food, water and air.	■ We depend on plants and animals for food, and we breed certain animals and grow certain plants as crops. ■ We see cultural diversity in the kinds of food people like to eat. ■ Some animals, like flies and ticks, carry germs which can make people sick.	■ There is a large variety of plants and animals, which have interesting visible differences and similarities. They can be grouped by their similarities. ■ Plants and animals change as they grow, and as the years pass, and as the seasons change.

2. **Energy and Change** focuses on how energy is transferred in physical and biological systems, and on the consequences that human needs and wants have for energy resources.

Core knowledge and concepts in Energy and Change for the Foundation Phase

Energy transfers and systems	Energy and development in South Africa
When we say we feel "full of energy", we mean that we feel ready to move fast or to do a lot of work.	People who do not have enough food or the right kind of food to eat, feel tired and lack energy.

3. **Planet Earth and Beyond** focuses on the structure of the planet and how the Earth changes over time. It focuses on understanding why and how the weather changes, and on the Earth as a small planet in a vast universe.

Core knowledge and concepts in the Planet Earth and Beyond for the Foundation Phase

Our place in space	Atmosphere and weather	The changing earth
Many different objects can be observed in the sky. Examples are birds, clouds, airplanes, the sun, stars, the moon, planets and satellites. All these objects have properties, locations and movements that can be investigated with a view to determining patterns, relationships and trends.	Weather changes from day to day in ways that can be recorded and sometimes predicted. There are occasional unusual weather events like storms, floods and tornados which impact on people's lives.	Soil and rocks vary in appearance and texture from place to place. By investigation, learners can find out that some soils erode more easily than others do, while some soil types support plant life better than others. Learners could investigate what some of the factors involved might be.

4. **Matter and Materials** focuses on the <u>properties and uses of materials,</u> and on understanding their structure, changes and reactions in order to promote desired changes.

Core knowledge and concepts in Matter and Materials for the Foundation Phase

Properties and uses of materials	Structure, reactions and changes of materials
Materials have different properties such as texture, colour, strength and heaviness, and can be classified by these properties. We make things with materials which have the properties we want.	Substances can be mixed and sometimes changes can be seen, such as the dissolving of a solid, or the creation of new colours when food colourings/paints are mixed.

The following <u>Learning Outcomes and Assessment Standard</u>s are relevant for the Foundation Phase. Reception year teachers will focus on those relevant for the reception year.

Learning Outcome 1: <u>Scientific Investigations</u>

The learner will be able to <u>act confidentl</u>y on curiosity about natural phenomena, and to investigate relationships and solve problems in scientific, technological and environmental contexts.

Assessment Standards in the Foundation Phase

Assessment Standards Grade R	Assessment Standards Grade 1	Assessment Standards Grade 2	Assessment Standards Grade 3
We know this when the learner: **Plans** - Contributes towards planning an investigative activity. - Asks and answers questions about the investigation, using show and tell; or stories to say what action is planned. **Does** - Follows simple instructions with assistance - Explains what is being done or played (e.g. Games according to the rules). **Reviews** - Thinks and talks about what has been done. - Uses simple words, pictures or other items with assistance to explain what has been done.	**We know this when the learner:** **Plans** - Plans an investigation independently. - Shows how plans are used to find out about things which rouse learners' curiosity. - Uses pictures, drawings or other markings of choice to explain what is going to be done. **Does** - Participates independently in planned activity, carries out instructions independently and shows or tells what is being done. **Reviews** - Thinks about what has been done and says what has been found out individually or with assistance.	**We know this when the learner:** **Plans** - Plans an investigation as part of a group. - Discusses and plans with others. - Negotiates joint understanding of who does what. - Decides on what materials or models will be used to communicate the plan. **Does** - Participates in a planned activity independently or as part of a group. - Plays a role in a group and carries out instructions independently. - Explains what is being done, and answers the question, "What are you trying to find out?"	**We know this when the learner:** **Plans** - Uses materials selected by the group in order to communicate the group's plan. - Lays out the materials the group intends to use. - Tells who will use the materials and the purpose of each. **Does** - Participates constructively in the activity with understanding of its purpose. - Explains the purpose of the activity. - Answers the questions, "Why are you doing this?", "How are you trying to find that out?" and "Is your plan working?" - Agrees or disagrees with other opinions, giving reasons.

Assessment Standards Grade R	Assessment Standards Grade 1	Assessment Standards Grade 2	Assessment Standards Grade 3
	Shows and tells what was done using own ideas and objects to explain what roused curiosity	**Reviews** ▪ Explains and reflects on what action was intended and whether it was possible to carry out the plan. ▪ Reviews how actions of members in the group contributed to the purpose. ▪ Reviews what is needed to do better next time. ▪ Uses a number of different ways of presenting information. ▪ Reflects on what other topics might be investigated.	**Reviews** ▪ Shows and explains what was intended and how it was done. ▪ Explains own contribution to the investigation. ▪ Uses several different ways to communicate own ideas. ▪ Is curious about what might happen if the situation was changed in some way.

Life and Living Strand

As children use the processes of Science (such as observing and classifying) they are developing concepts of living things such as plants and animals. Concepts to develop are:

Living things:

- can grow (change)
- can move
- need food and water
- can react to what is around it
- need air (change)
- can reproduce
- can get rid of waste.

Different types of living things (diversity and unity). These can be categorised into broad categories:

- Is it a living or a non-living thing?
- Is it a plant or an animal?
- Is it a farm animal or a wild animal?
- Although there are different types of animals – farm and wild animals (diversity), all of them are still animals (unity).

Interdependence between living things:

- planting and maintaining a vegetable garden
- looking after a pet.

All living things have a beginning and an end:

- Life cycles of silk worms, frogs, chickens.

Plants

Children in the reception year may enjoy planting seeds, watering them and observing and measuring them while they grow. They will also be interested in observing seeds spouting.

Seed germination

Position a damp sponge or wad of cotton wool, onto which some radish or bean seeds have been placed, inside a glass jar. Place the jar in a warm place and keep the sponge or cotton wool moist until the seeds sprout. The children can observe that the plants send out roots to absorb the moisture and that they grow downwards.

As they observe the seeds changing, the parts of the plant can be named (roots, leaves, stem) and the changes discussed as the seed grows. Children can bring different seeds into the class. (This demonstrates the concept of *diversity,* in that there are different seeds, and *unity* in that, even though they are different, all of them are seeds.) They can also bring fruit to be displayed on the nature table and/or planted (e.g. orange, sweet potato, apple, mango or avocado).

Experiments can be done to find out what plants need in order to grow.

Plants need light

Plant bean seeds in soil, and water daily. After the seeds have sprouted, a plant can be planted in a pot with an opening cut out on the side. This opening should be the only light source. The children can observe how the plant grows towards the light.

Plants drink water

Stir red food colouring into a glass of water. Slice a piece of celery across the bottom and let the children observe the stalk. Stand the stalk in the tinted water for about an hour. The stalk will change colour. Cut the stalk lengthways and crosswise and observe. Do the same with a white flower and leave overnight.

Ask children to draw their own inferences by asking them questions such as:

Why do you think …?

What happened …?

Do we also need light, food and water?

Animals

Animal life can be observed in the classroom environment in the form of class pets such as hamsters, mice or goldfish. This allows children the opportunity to care for, observe, make inferences and communicate with each other. If this is not possible, a pet may visit the class for a few days. Investigate the possibility of keeping a pet on the playground (doves, rabbits or fowls). Try to attract wild birds to the school garden by planting indigenous varieties and providing wild bird seed.

Children will often bring insects to school which they have captured (snails, worms, locusts etc). Encourage them to bring a part of the plant on which the insect was found. Observe the insect for a day or two and then let it go free again, especially if you do not have enough food, or the right food, to sustain it. Buying a few magnifying glasses, or making some yourself, is a must for observing insects. Turn over a stone or a log on the school grounds and note which insects live there.

Children can observe insects' habits, development and change by keeping insects in small cages (glass jars must be aerated).

Keep them for only a day and then release if you do not have food for them (see figure 6.3).

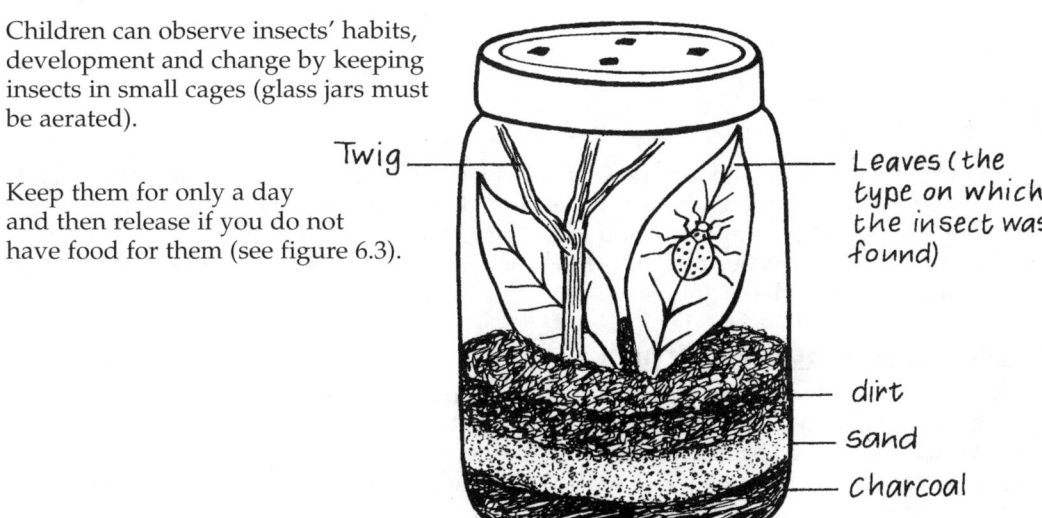

Twig

Leaves (the type on which the insect was found)

dirt

sand

charcoal

Figure 6.3 – An Insect Zoo

How to make a home-made magnifying glass

To make a simple magnifying glass, cut three circles of 4 cm diameter from the sides of a tub-like container. Cover the top with clear plastic and keep in place with a rubber band or string. Slowly pour lukewarm water onto the plastic until it sags and the water forms a round concave lens. Ask the children to place tiny insects inside the magnifier below the lens by putting their fingers through the holes. They can then view the insects through the lens.

Figure 6.4 – A home-made magnifying glass

Birds can be attracted to a school garden or home by means of bird feeders. These can be made by rolling a pine cone in peanut butter and seeds and suspending it from a branch by a string, for example scraps of porridge, rice and bread placed in a bowl are also well liked by birds. Keep a bird bath. This can be any shallow flat round dish filled with water that can be placed next to the feeder or underneath tree.

Energy and Change Strand

Energy and Change focuses on how energy is transferred. It focuses on the consequences that human needs and wants have for energy resources. An initial understanding about forces and motion can be developed by finding out what reception year learners understand about 'what makes things move'. The teacher can write down the ideas of learners in a *concept web* – see the following example of such an exercise:

What makes it move?

Wind blows them (leaves)

They fall down (children)

Someone turns them on (vehicles)

Engines make them go (car)

They slide down a hill (children)

Someone spins them (top)

What makes it move?

Someone winds them up (toys)

They move on their own

Falls into a hole (rabbit)

It has batteries (toy)

Pull them on a string

Moved in a lift (shopping)

Pushes the toy

Concept web

I can move

Learners can:

- be helped to understand the concept of movement by thinking about how they themselves move.

- be encouraged to show movement in a variety of ways: walking, running, rolling, jumping, skipping, sliding, climbing, kneeling, bending, twisting, turning. (Make a list of movement words.)

- describe which part of the body is used when they move. (Are all these body parts used for whatever types of movement, such as rolling?)

- discuss how their bodies feel when they do different movements.

- draw themselves moving.

- look for pictures of people making different movements, cut them out and paste them under the different movement words.

I can make things move

Young learners can be made aware of the fact that objects cannot move on their own without the help of something or someone such as the children themselves. Provide hands-on experiences where the children can experiment by themselves with making things move (thinking about what force they use).

Activities to do with young learners:

■ moving (pushing, pulling) my body to and fro to make the swing go; swing a yo-yo

■ pulling and pushing toys

■ winding up the springs of toys, clocks

■ moving toys to and fro to make them go (friction)

■ letting different objects roll down a ramp

■ turning the handles (gears) of egg beaters

■ activating a battery-driven toy, torch bulb

■ using magnets to pull some things

■ using simple tools to help us to move objects (levers, pulleys, wheels)

■ experimenting with elastic band energy

■ using water/air to move objects: blowing paint through a straw to make a picture

■ setting up a tug of war outside (forces are balanced and unbalanced)

Example

Experiment

Pose the following question:
How do I move these objects?

(Learning Outcomes LA NS LO1):While doing these experiments, the children should be prompted to

■ understand the working of forces

■ practise the skills of observing, predicting, inferring, and experimenting

■ become aware of their own power (force).

What shall we need?

Objects that can be moved: bottles with lids, screw driver, pens or crayons, paper, scissors; golf ball and straw; tray.

How shall we do it?

Put the objects to be moved onto a tray. Put the tray and all the other materials on your Science table. Plan to leave them there for several days.

Conclusion:

The learners will reflect on and explain how they made the objects move.

Movable objects

Look at all the objects in the room that can be moved, and those that cannot. Discuss the reasons why. Sort the objects into those that need:

- a slight touch
- a light push or pull
- one person's weight
- the energy, force or power of a small group
- the energy, force or power of a large group.

Reading and listening.

Read *The Enormous Turnip* and dramatise it.

The wind (air) can make things move (has power)

Go to a window or go outside with the children. Ask them if they can see the air moving anything outside. Even on a day that is not very windy, the tips of the leaves might be moving. Ask, "What do we call moving air?" "Try to spot more clues that air is moving outside."

Example
A good 'attention getter' is to show children an inflated balloon which has not been tied at the base (This is best done inside). Ask children if they know what is inside the balloon. They might know that it is filled with air. Tell them that you want them to feel the air inside the balloon. Gently press the balloon down the children's legs or arms and release a little air onto each child's skin. They can feel the *force* of the wind on their skin. Ask them, "Can you feel how strong the air is? How it is pushing you?" ■ If you do not have access to the above, simple sensory explorations could be provided for children by folding paper to make a fan or making streamers (paper strips attached to a stick) to swing on a breezy day.

- Stories/poems/drama. Tell the story of Umoyana, the little wind by Appleby, Bala, Ciliza and Galant (see Bibliography if you want to acquire it for your school). It is the story of Fatima, who lives in Cape Town, and her adventures with the wind as she walks through the Gardens.

Art activities

- Put blobs of paint on a background with a medicine dropper and blow paint through straws to form different line patterns on the paper.
- Blow air into a small bowl of coloured water to make bubbles and take a bubble print.
- Paint by squeezing an injection needle pump or squeeze bottle filled with thick, coloured, starch paint.

Air in motion/air power

Experiment

Children are given opportunities to experiment with some <u>pump and suction tools in order to find out how they work and to feel and see how much power (force) air (wind) can have</u>. (The children gain confidence in the use of these tools.)

Learning Outcomes

While engaged in these activities, the children:
- practise the skills of observing, predicting, inferring, experimenting and measuring
- become aware of the wind's power (force).

What shall we need?

Medicine droppers; squeeze bottles; bicycle pump; plastic foot pump (for inflating inner tubes) and a few objects to move: feathers; scraps of tissues; paper clips; marble; golf ball; tray.

How shall we do it?

- Put the non-wind making materials onto a tray. Put the tray and all the other materials onto your Science table. Plan to leave them there for several days. The children can also blow air with their mouths.
- Children predict what they think will happen to the objects and then experiment freely.
- They make inferences about what they have seen and later check whether their predictions are true or not.
- Children measure (using any nonstandard measurement: hands/straws/pieces of string) which tool could blow an object the furthest.
- To communicate our findings, make a graph to show which "air tool" will be able to blow an object the furthest.

Natural science

Magnets can make things move

Children can learn about magnets well before attending formal school. There are many examples of magnets about us to explore: automatic can openers have magnets to hold opened can lids; cabinet doors remain closed because of magnets; some toys have magnets which are used in some way in their mechanism; magnets can be used to pick up nails or hairpins.

Magnets attract iron and steel, but do not attract the following metals: brass (an alloy of copper and zinc), aluminium, tin, silver, stainless steel (an alloy of several metals), copper, bronze (an alloy of copper and tin), and gold. The following concepts underlie the use of magnets:

- Magnets pull (attract) some things, but not others.
- Magnets pull through some materials.
- One magnet can be used to make another magnet.
- Magnets are stronger at each end.

■ Each end of a magnet acts differently.

■ Take care of magnets or they lose their power.

Activities with magnets

■ *A scrap-dance box.* To become aware that magnets pull through some materials, we can put together a magnet toy with the children. You will need a small, but strong magnet of any type, a shallow box, some plastic wrap, tape, and a steel wool pad. Shred very small bits of steel from the scrubbing pad. Shred enough fine steel bits to cover the bottom of the box. Stretch the plastic wrap over the top of the box to make a cover, and secure it to the side of the box with tape. The children can enjoy making the scraps dance and creating patterns by pulling the magnet beneath the box.

■ *Temporary magnets.* A temporary magnet can be made from an iron nail by stroking it in *one* direction with one pole of a permanent magnet. Its power increases with the number of strokes you apply (at least 20 strokes). Be sure to lift the magnet clear at the end of each stroke you apply.

■ *A hidden magnet hunt.* Undertake a hidden magnet hunt through the school. Discover useful but unseen magnets in paperclip holders; cupboard door catches; flashlight holders, message holders; magnetic alphabet letters and numbers; the magnetised plastic strip that holds the refrigerator door tightly shut; the magnetised strip on the card that you slide into automatic bank teller machines.

Magnets and what they attract

Experiment

Children have the opportunity to experiment with magnets to find out whether they attract and pull some objects.

Learning Outcomes

While engaged in the experiment, the children:

■ practise the skills of observing, predicting, inferring, classifying and experimenting

■ become aware of a magnet's power (force).

What shall we need?

Various small objects (pins, a pencil, a R2 coin, a screw, chalk, a rubber, a rubber band, scissors, paper clip, marble, etc) a magnet, two cartons with "pulled", "not pulled" labels pasted on-to them, and a plastic tray.

How shall we do it?

Put the objects and magnet onto a tray. Put the tray and the materials on-to your Science table. Plan to leave them there for several days. Change the objects with new ones every two days.

■ Children predict what they think will happen to the objects and then experiment freely.

■ They classify the objects into two boxes marked "pulled" and "not pulled".

■ They make inferences about what they have seen and check whether their predictions are true or not.

Take care of your magnets:

- Never drop or pound them.
- Never heat them.
- Use a keeper.
- Put the north and south parts (poles) together.
- Do not use near a computer.

Planet Earth and Beyond

The Sun, Moon and the Stars (Astronomy)

Children's experiences in this area are limited throughout their early childhood development years. They are able to observe the sky and the heavenly bodies, to compare and describe what they have seen as well as make drawings or paintings of them.

A theme called *Day and Night* could be developed, using the sun and moon as sources of light. The following are some suggestions:

- Have a discussion about what happens during the day and what happens at night.
- Find out which animals do things in daylight and which do things at night.
- Allow the children to classify what happens during the day and what happens at night by drawing pictures. These pictures can be pinned to the wall under the headings **day** and **night**.
- Discuss which people work during the day and which work at night and why they do so.
- Organise for the children to camp out with some parents and teachers on the school grounds one night and to watch the night sky.
- Children can observe the change in the moon's patterns as it changes from one full moon to the next. This observation can be done for a month. It is not important that children remember the phases of the moon, but that they become aware of the pattern of change. They can make drawings of the moon's shape and discuss these as they occur.
- Children can observe the different colours in the sky at sunrise and sunset. Remember that it is dangerous to look directly into the sun.
- Children can become aware of how the sun travels through the sky by observing shadows. The following are some ideas:
  - Let them find out what kind of shadows they can make with their bodies.
  - Make shadows with different objects such as different box shapes, an umbrella or bicycle.
  - Mark where the shadow of a pole (or any other object) in the schoolyard falls at different times in the day.

Weather (Meteorology)

Children experience changes in the weather on a daily basis. These changes can be observed, described, discussed and recorded by making a weather chart.

Cut a large circle from a piece of cardboard. Divide this circle into four quarters. Draw a cloud, a sun, rain and the wind blowing, each in one of the four quarters. Make a pointer and, using a clip, fasten the pointer in the centre in such a way that it can be turned to a different quarter every morning to indicate the type of weather being experienced. Make extra squares to use if, for example, it is overcast and the wind is blowing.

Every day the weather can be drawn on a home-made calendar. At the end of the month the children can make a graph to indicate how many rainy, windy, cloudy or sunny days there were.

Explore the wind by blowing soap bubbles in the wind or taking kites or small windmills out into the wind.

Wash dolls' clothes and dry them in the sun, the shade and the wind and note how long each takes to dry.

How does the weather affect children's lives? What do they wear in different weather conditions?

Matter and Materials

Properties of materials and how they can change (Chemistry)

Young children believe that magic causes changes in materials, like daisies opening in daylight and closing in the dark. Let them explore materials in their immediate environment. Children may find crayons melted by the sun, and from there experiment with other things that might or might not melt in the sun. This experiment can lead to other similar experiences finding out how materials may change. Do experiments to show:

- which substances will dissolve/not dissolve in water (coffee, tea leaves, sugar, sand)
- how food changes with different cooking methods
- how substances change when they are frozen
- how colours change when mixed.

These experiences will form the foundation for more advanced concept formation. Matter and materials focuses on the properties and uses of materials, and on understanding their structure, changes and reactions in order to promote desired changes.

The easiest way to support young learners to gain concepts about matter and materials is by exposing them to everyday materials in their life world, such as natural materials in their environments and the ingredients in food.

Grouping and Classifying Materials

Learners can find out about materials and their properties; grouping and classifying them; finding out how they change by means of certain processes; making and separating mixtures.

Possible activities for grouping materials:

Learners could:

- use their senses to explore and recognise similarities and differences between materials
- sort materials into groups on the basis of simple properties, including texture, appearance, transparency, and whether they are magnetic or non-magnetic

- recognise and name common types of material e.g. metal, plastic, wood, paper, rocks, spices, and know that some of these materials are found naturally

- find out and understand that materials have different uses, e.g. glass, wood, wool

- discover that materials are chosen for specific uses, e.g. glass for windows, wool for clothing, on the basis of their properties. An activity could entail discussing a collection of kitchen utensils. Learners could be asked why different utensils are made from different materials.

Materials and their properties

Learners could discover that some materials will change their shape or form under certain circumstances.

Learners could:

- find out that objects made from some materials can be changed in shape by processes including squashing, bending, twisting and stretching

- describe the way some materials, e.g. water, chocolate, cheese, bread, dough, spaghetti change when they are heated or cooled.

Possible Activities:

Soil

Collect different types of soils – Examine and describe features of soil – texture, colour, and what can be found in the soil (Martin, 2003:41).

The water tray

The water tray should contain a variety of pouring devices – different types of squirters, such as syringes, washing-up liquid bottles, pumps.

Before setting up activities, learners will need to have been provided with opportunities to handle and play with a variety of different materials. Reception year learners should have ample opportunities to play with water and sand in a sandpit and water tray.

Cooking activities

A variety of cooking activities could provide experiences for young learners to discover how substances may change in various cooking processes – making hot chocolate, jelly, cup cakes, popcorn, etc.

The following simple Chemistry experiments will provide fun and will give surprising and fascinating results to intrigue young children, while developing their natural interest in Science.

At this level it is more important to encourage a child to watch what happens, than to gain a complete understanding of why it happens because it is questionable whether we can measure Chemistry.

Simple instructions are provided for a few simple experiments which may be done in the reception year. These fit in well with themes suitable for this age group. They include:

- making butter

- evaporating water

- making gases

- freezing water

- making invisible ink

- making oobleck (cornflour, water and food colouring)

Making butter

Teacher's notes

This experiment requires full-cream milk to make it work. Milk is an emulsion of tiny fat globules in water and other chemicals. As the soured milk is shaken, the globules of fat stick together to become a larger globule. After lots of shaking all the fat will stick together to form a larger globule that forms the butter. The remaining liquid is called buttermilk and is made up of water and other chemicals. This experiment could form part of a theme (Programme Organiser) about food (dairy products).

Why do the experiment?

It provides children with the opportunity to find out that when milk is shaken (churned), the globules of fat in the milk stick together and become butter.

Learning Outcomes

While doing these experiments, the children:

- practise the skills of predicting, observing, inferring, experimenting

- become aware that globules of fat in milk will stick together and become butter when shaken.

Invisible ink

Teacher's notes

This works because the heat from the radiator causes a chemical reaction so that the lemon juice drawing or writing turns brown. This will also work with milk. This experiment could be done when food, fruit, dairy products, senses or heat are themes/concepts.

Why do the experiment?

It enables children to observe and find out that heat will turn colourless milk or lemon juice brown.

Learning Outcomes

While doing this experiment, the children:

- practise the skills of predicting, observing, experimenting and inferring

- are aware that heat will turn the colourless lemon juice, brown.

What we'll need

- lemon juice in a bowl

- a paintbrush

- a piece of paper

- practise the skills of predicting, observing, experimenting and inferring
- a warm radiator, a burning candle or a hot laundry iron.

How the learners will do it

- They predict what will happen if we paint with lemon juice, as well as what will happen if we heat the painting after the juice/paint is dry.
- They observe what happens during the experiment as they take part in it.
- The children make inferences about what they have seen happening. The teacher can explain that heat will turn lemon juice brown.

Making gases

Teacher's notes

Sometimes when acids and alkalis are mixed, there is a chemical reaction and a gas is produced. This is why baking powder is added to cakes to make them rise. This experiment could be done when air or change is a theme or concept.

Why do the experiment?

It provides children with the opportunity to experience that they can make a gas by mixing baking powder and vinegar.

Learning Outcomes

While doing this experiment, the children

- will practise the skills of predicting, observing, experimenting and inferring
- become aware that baking powder and vinegar will make a gas that will blow up a balloon.

What shall we need?

Vinegar, baking powder, an empty bottle with a narrow neck, a teaspoon and a balloon.

How will they do it?

- They will predict what they think will happen when they mix vinegar and baking powder in a jar.
- They observe what happens once the balloon has been attached to the top of the bottle.
- They make inferences about what they have seen happening: Baking powder mixed with vinegar will make gases that can blow up a balloon.

Freezing water

Teacher's notes

When water becomes ice it expands, becoming less dense than water, so that it floats in water. This experiment can become part of a theme on water. This is why icebergs float in the sea.

Why do the experiment?

Children have the opportunity to see that ice cubes will float in water, even if they contain objects that usually sink in water.

Learning Outcomes

While doing this experiment, the children

- practise the skills of predicting, observing, experimenting and inferring
- become aware that ice cubes will float in water.

What shall we need?

Water, small objects, ice cube tray, bowl.

How will they do it?

- The children will predict what will happen when ice cubes with small objects frozen in them are placed in the water. The previous day the children could have tested the small objects for their floating ability.
- The children observe the experiment.
- They will make inferences about what they saw.

Technology in the Foundation Phase

Only Learning Outcome 1 of the Technology Learning Area is dealt with in this Phase. The Learning Outcome and its associated Assessment Standards have been written so that they reflect an integration of skills, knowledge, attitudes and awareness.

Young children enjoy finding out how things work, making things and trying them out. Through Technology, children can search for ways to develop their ability to control events and to order their environment.

Definition

Technology has existed throughout history. People use the combination of knowledge, skills and available resources to develop solutions that meet their daily needs and wants. Some of these solutions have been in the form of products (e.g. shaping bones into fish hooks and needles, making clay cooking pots), while some solutions have involved combining products into working systems (e.g. bow and arrow, moving water and a wheel, pestle and mortar).

Today people still have needs and wants. However, the knowledge, skills and resources used to find solutions are of a different kind because of accelerating developments in Technology. Today's society is complicated and diverse. Economic and environmental factors and a wide range of attitudes and values need to be taken into account when developing technological solutions. The development of products and systems in modern times must show sensitivity to these issues. It is in this context that Technology is defined as:

Purpose

The Technology Learning Area will contribute towards learners' technological literacy by giving them opportunities to:

- develop and apply specific skills to solve technological problems

- understand the concepts and knowledge used in Technology, and use them responsibly and purposefully

- appreciate the interaction between people's values and attitudes, Technology, society and the environment.

Learning Outcome 1: Technological processes and skills

The learner will be able to apply technological processes and skills ethically and responsibly, using appropriate information and communication technologies.

Assessment Standards in the Foundation Phase

Assessment Standards Grade R	Assessment Standards Grade 1	Assessment Standards Grade 2	Assessment Standards Grade 3
We know this when the learner:	**We know this when the learner:**	**We know this when the learner:**	**We know this when the learner:**
Investigates	**Investigates**	**Investigates**	**Investigates**
▪ Physically manipulates products to explore their shape, size, colour and the materials they are made of.	▪ Investigates why products are made of particular materials.	▪ Describes the past and current uses of different materials.	▪ Finds out about the historical context when given a problem, need or opportunity related to structures, processing, or systems and control.
		▪ Describes the main purpose of different products.	▪ Finds out why given existing products related to a problem, need or opportunity are suitable for their purpose.
Designs	**Designs**	**Designs**	**Designs**
▪ Chooses from a given range, of materials or substances that can be used to make simple products.	▪ Chooses suitable material or substances to make simple products to satisfy a given need.	▪ Chooses suitable materials or substances to make products, and suggests some ways they can be used to satisfy a problem, need or opportunity.	▪ Suggests different possible solutions, chooses one, and uses freehand sketches to represent it.
Makes	**Makes**	**Makes**	**Makes**
▪ Makes simple products from a range of materials provided.	▪ Makes simple products from different materials.	▪ Expresses how products are going to be made.	▪ Expresses how products are going to be made and what will be used to make them.
		▪ Makes products safely from different materials, following given steps.	▪ Makes products safely by joining or combining a range of different materials.
Evaluates	**Evaluates**	**Evaluates**	**Evaluates**
▪ Expresses and expolains own feelings about the products made.	▪ Expresses and explains own feelings about the products made.	▪ Identifies strengths and weaknesses about own products.	▪ Identifies strengths and weaknesses about own products and products of others.

An example of a lesson unit concept map: Trees in my garden

Language (HL)

■ Listening to stories – LO 1

Handa's Surprise (by E Browne)

Handa puts seven delicious fruits in a basket to her friend. Along the way animals sample the fruit. LO 3, 5

■ Listening to sounds – LO 1 Vocabulary: branch, leaves, trunk, branch, leaves – serrated, wavy, smooth, twigs, roots, deciduous, evergreen LO 6

■ Colours: autumn colours – red purple, orange LO 5

What rhymes with trees – sees, bees, wheels LO 3, 6

■ Names of trees LO 5

Mathematics

■ Counting – seeds, acorns, pine cones
■ LO 1
■ One –to one correspondence – leaves LO 3
■ Classify – Seeds, Leaves LO 3
■ Order – leaves (largest to smallest)
■ Patterning – seeds, leaves LO 2
■ Measure girth of trees, age year rings;
■ Plants growth

Measuring – plant an outdoor thermometer in direct sunlight and another beneath the shade of a tree. Compare results LO 4

■ Data handling – Simple leaf graph LO 5

Trees in my garden

Life orientation

■ Value of trees for humans LO 1: Oxygen, food, shade, wood products, clean air.
■ Avoid poisonous plants LO1
■ Make a salad with leaves LO 1
■ Family Tree LO 2.

Cut a tree trunk out of brown paper & treetop out of green paper – Children bring family photo's to display in their tree

■ Relgious Stories – Zaccheus , Parable of the sower LO 2
■ Mime the different ways of moving like
creatures who live in trees – squirrels,
birds, worms, insects LO 4

Natural Sciences LO 1

■ Animal houses (habitat) NS LO 1
■ Go on an outing - explore trees with all senses
■ What do seeds, plants need to grow –sunlight, food water

Experiment with coloured water & celery stalks; plant in dark cupboard

■ How are seeds dispersed?
■ Which seeds, leaves do we eat?

Arts & Culture LO 1

■ Tree rubbings with crayons – bark leaves
■ Twig painting – using twigs as painting tools
■ Printing with pine cones
■ Draw pictures with glue and sprinkle with coloured sawdust
■ Modelling with damp sawdust; paper mache
■ Make music with indigenous wooden insruments marimba, drums, maracas

Economics & Management Sciences

■ Collecting paper to sell E & M LO 1
■ Awareness of value of wood products LO 1

Technology
■ Pine cone bird feeders T LO 1
■ Handmade paper T LO 1

Social Sciences:

■ Sight-seeing and relaxing in a garden SS LO 2
■ A trip to a local park, area where there are many trees SS LO 2

Bibliography

Appleby, S, Bala, B, Celiza & Galant, C. 1996. *Umoyana, the little wind*. Waterfront, Cape Town: Cambridge University

Benbow, A & Mably, C. 2002. *Science Education Press for Elementary Teachers*. Belmont, CA: Wadsworth.

Department of Education. 2002. Revised National Curriculum Statement Grades R – 9. policy. *Natural Sciences*. Pretoria.

Department of Education. 2002. Revised National Curriculum Statement Grades R – 9. policy. *Technology*. Pretoria.

Fleer, M & Hardy, T. 2001. *Science For Children: Developing a Personal Approach to Teaching*. French Forest: Prentice Hall.

Fleer, M & Jane, B. 1999. *Technology for Children*. Sydney: Prentice Hall.

Fleer, M. 1995. *I can make my robot dance: Technology for 3 – 8 year olds*. Carlton, Victoria: TCTP (Technology Curriculum & Teaching Program).

Osborne, R & Freyberg, P. 2001. *Learning in Science: The implications of children's science*. Birkenhead, Auckland: Heinemann.

Harlan, D & Rivkin, MS. 2000. *Science Experiences for the Early Years: An Integrated Approach*. Columbus, Ohio: Merrill.

Chapter

7

Assessment of the reception year learner
Reda Davin

Assessment involves far more than merely testing the learner for the purpose of completing a school report at the end of a term. It is a central part of the whole teaching and learning process. The principles and methods outlined in this chapter will help you to achieve successful assessment of your learners.

OUTCOMES:

After you have read this chapter you should be able to:

■ explain the difference between evaluation and assessment

■ discuss the various reasons for assessing in the reception year

■ understand and apply the principle that will ensure that you conduct reliable and valid assessments of the young learners

■ understand and use the assessment process to have well planned and successful assessment

■ critically discuss the use of tests in the reception year

■ conduct interviews with parents in order to get to know the learner better

■ develop and use portfolios of examples of learners' work as a method to assess the learners' development and learning

■ use observation, applying different observation methods, as a method of assessing the young learner

■ interpret all the information you have collected from and about the learner, in order to complete the assessment process successfully.

Introduction

Assessment is one of the most difficult tasks a reception year teacher is required to carry out, and because it is so difficult, it is often done incorrectly or worse, completely ignored. However, assessment is a vital part of good teaching, whatever the context.

In addition to assessing the learners in their class, teachers should assess themselves, and reflect on their own teaching effort. Assessment is one of the essential building blocks in the planning and presentation of successful, developmentally appropriate presentations and activities for the reception year. Unfortunately, teachers all too often regard assessment as nothing more than an administrative task: something they must do so that they can complete reports for parents, and to keep the principal and parents happy!

The difference between evaluation and assessment

> ### Definition
>
> **Evaluation** means making a value judgement about something according to a specific measurement or set of standards.
>
> It implies that something is being measured against a predetermined unit of measure in order find out whether or not it achieves the standard.
>
> **Assessment** is a process of gathering information to make decisions about (in this case) the young learner. The process should be systematic and based on everyday tasks done by the child.
>
> This implies that assessment happens throughout the school day (not merely during specific 'test periods'). We assess the learner so that we can know the learner better, not to group the child in 'can/cannot' groups. Assessment must therefore be part of every day!

Reasons for assessment in the reception year

Assessment should never be superficial or haphazard. To carry out meaningful assessment, the teacher needs to be clear about the purpose of assessment and how it should be carried out. The three main reasons for assessment when teaching young children are:

1. Assessment of the child's level of development

The most important reason why we assess the reception year learner is to get to know the learner better. There are three main reasons why assessment for finding out the child's developmental level is important. They are:

a) to be able to plan developmentally appropriate themes and activities

b) to identify learners with learning and development barriers

c) to know when to adapt presentations and activities to help learners who experience barriers in their learning and development.

a) Planning developmentally appropriate teaching

You will need to determine the developmental level of every child in your class in order to plan and present developmentally appropriate themes and activities. The themes and activities you present should be based on the interests and needs of the child. Once you have assessed the level of development, potential and behaviour of every learner in your class, you can plan activities geared to each learner's needs.

Assessment gives the teacher a starting point when making decisions such as: suitable Learning Outcomes for *this* group; teaching methods; and planning the classroom layout.

Go to:

Refer back to *Chapter 1: Planning to teach*. The content of Chapter 1 should clearly show that it is impossible to choose relevant themes and activities for learners without *knowing* the child.

b) Identify learners with developmental and learning barriers

By using the information gained during your assessment of the learners, you will be able to identify learners with problem areas in their development. The problems can vary from, for example, struggling to cut with a pair of scissors, to hearing problems (which would indicate special education needs).

When a teacher identifies a learner who may have a serious problem, they should refer the child to specialists, such as a medical doctor, speech therapist or occupational therapist. In situations like these the teacher needs to have detailed documentation of his or her assessment of the learner. Assessment records will serve as a basis for communication with the specialists, as well as with the parents of the child.

c) Adapt teaching methods in order to help learners with developmental and learning barriers

Increasingly, learners with barriers are catered for in the regular school setting. The teacher is therefore an integral member of the team serving the learner with special needs and the learner's family. The teacher's assessment records serve as a source of information for choosing appropriate teaching methods and strategies to help the child, as well as being a starting point for the ongoing assessment of the effectiveness of the interventions planned.

2. Parent guidance and assistance

One of the tasks of teachers of young children is to give parents educational assistance in the upbringing of their child. The school and home environments should be complementary; and therefore it is important to provide feedback to parents regarding their child and to offer advice should the child have a learning barrier.

Unless you have in-depth knowledge about the child you cannot give parents any advice or help regarding the problem. Assessment information serves as a tool to help you to give parents, in a structured and professional way, information about their child's behaviour and development.

Parents play an important role in the assessment of their child. Use them to gain information about the learner. Ask for their opinion regarding their child's progress and behaviour.

3. Improvement of teaching

A very important reason for the assessment of learners is to help the teacher to better his or her teaching. Assessment is in fact the foundation for effective teaching. *Self-assessment* enables the teacher to obtain information about the quality of his or her teaching. By continually assessing your own teaching effort you, can identify your strengths and weaknesses as a teacher. You will grow professionally as you address these shortcomings.

Remember

A teacher teaches and assesses simultaneously.

Principles for true and trustworthy assessment of young learners

One of the most important criticisms against assessment in early childhood is that the teacher makes decisions about learners based on personal feelings. This criticism has some validity, because we use methods such as observation, examples of the child's art and constructions when assessing. There are often no 'right' or 'wrong' answers and one's own background can certainly influence one's decisions. For this reason, following certain rules (principles) can help you to achieve true (valid) and trustworthy (reliable) assessment about the young learner. The following nine principles are particularly significant.

RULE 1: Each child is unique

When assessing a child, one must recognise that each child is unique. This means that the teacher:

- should assess the child's unique, individual pattern of development
- should not categorise or label learners
- should not use words such as 'naughty', 'lazy' or 'highly gifted', to describe a child
- should be careful not to place too much emphasis on certain negative or positive behaviour. A child very seldom repeats certain behaviour consistently!

RULE 2: Assess the whole learner

When assessing a learner it is important to make sure that you assess every aspect of the child. Not assessing the whole learner can lead to oversimplification of the issues. Ensure that you:

- do not have only one assessment of the learner
- assess the learner under different circumstances and during different activities
- assess the learner at different times during the day, as children's behaviour is not necessarily the same throughout the day
- tailor your assessment so that it involves all aspects of the learner and does not reflect a one-sided view.

> **Remember**
> *An unhappy or nervous learner will not be able to perform to his or her full potential. If you are worried about a learner's behaviour or performance in the classroom, assess the learner on the playground as well.*

You can only assess and help learners if you know them as whole human beings, made up of many different facets.

RULE 3: Assess the learner in a variety of situations and use a variety of methods

Your assessment of a learner will be more accurate if you assess the child by using a variety of methods in different situations. This can be compared to looking at a beautiful view from a window. Looking at the same view but from different windows will enable you to see something that you were not able to see before.

When you assess the learner use:

- **Different assessment methods**

  Different methods for assessing learners will be discussed in more detail later in this chapter.

- **Various settings inside and outside the classroom**

  Assess the learner not only in the classroom but also in the outdoor play area. Try to assess the learner in as many different situations as possible – this will enable you to 'see the whole picture'.

- **Various times of the day**

Assess the learner during every part of the day – even in the mornings before school starts and at the end of the day when he or she is going home.

Assessment should be carried out throughout each day and continue throughout the entire year.

RULE 4: Assess both the learning process and the outcome

In traditional examinations and tests, only the end product (or Learning Outcomes) is evaluated. In continuous assessment, however, it is possible, and indeed important, to assess the learning *process*. The teacher should not assess and interpret only the answers or end product of an activity – you should also assess the process of how the learner arrived at the solutions or end product.

By observing the learning process you will be able to find out *why* the learner is making mistakes.

Example

Two learners are building exactly the same puzzle and both of them complete their puzzles. The end result (outcome) is the same – but the process each learner used to get to the end product was different.

Anna struggled to build the puzzle, but kept on trying until she completed it. Nkopodi completed the puzzle with ease, but he had to be reminded by the teacher to focus on the task, as his attention tended to drift away to the other activities in the group.

The same end result can give two different 'messages' about the learners to the teacher, as in the example above. The process the learner follows to reach an answer or end product tells the teacher more about the learner's development than the product ever could. When assessing the process, it is also possible for the teacher to:

- help the learner who struggles with activities
- give extra materials or new ideas to the learner who needs it
- change his or her teaching methods if necessary
- verbalise the learner's learning and by doing so, further the learner's development.

RULE 5: Assessments should be trustworthy (reliable)

Assessments are reliable (trustworthy) if the same interpretations of behaviour can be reached, using the same methods, later on or in different circumstances.

Example

Example of unreliable assessment

Behaviour: Lucy struggles to colour in a picture.

Teacher's assessment: Lucy's small muscle development is not appropriately developed for a five year old.

This assessment is not reliable, because the teacher's assessment was based on a single incident. It does not take into account other possible reasons why Lucy struggles to colour in – e.g. she may have hurt her finger or hand, or the crayons may have been of a very bad quality.

To be able to make reliable assessments the teacher must:

- have more than one assessment of the same behaviour
- limit the negative effects of factors such as environmental distractions, interruptions and unexpected events during the day, and
- take any negative effects that may occur into account in their assessment.

Learners should have more than one chance to show what they know, think, feel or can do. As pointed out above, it is very important not to arrive at conclusions based on limited information about the learner.

RULE 6: Repeat assessment to have valid (true) results

To ensure that the assessment is valid, the teacher should assess what she is supposed to assess and not something else. You need to be conscious of the purpose of each assessment and then ensure that you assess what you set out to assess.

Example

Behaviour: A teacher wanted to assess a learner's ability to complete a pattern using visual perception skills. She planned a manipulative activity where the learners had to complete a pattern using small, coloured beads. Erik struggled to complete the pattern.

Teacher's assessment: Erik has severe visual perceptual problems with regard to skills such as colour recognition, position in space and visual ordering.

The interpretation of the assessment is not valid, because the teacher later realises that the reason for the learner's failure to complete the task is not poor visual perception. Further assessments reveal that the beads were too small for Erik to pick up with his fingers. In her first assessment of Erik's ability to complete a pattern, the teacher unknowingly assessed Erik's small muscle skills and not his visual perception skills. The assessment and interpretation are therefore not valid as the teacher did not assess what she intended to assess.

You can ensure the increased validity of assessments by:

- not overemphasising a single assessment

- checking to see if the assessments obtained in different ways confirm each other.

RULE 7: Remain objective

It may be difficult for you as the reception year teacher to remain objective, as you are so directly and actively involved with your learners. However, it is important not to allow personal experiences or characteristics to influence your perceptions of events, facts or behaviour. You should not allow traits or characteristics in the learner, which either do or don't appeal to you, to affect your objectivity.

To help you achieve objectivity, you should:

- record the events as accurately as possible, without making any value judgement

- avoid judgmental comments such as 'good', 'bad', and 'naughty', as well as labels or jargon

- recognise that no one is totally objective; the information we choose to inform our judgements is influenced by our personal experience, beliefs and interests.

Unfortunately, no teacher can look at a learner in a totally objective way. As the teacher, therefore, you should acknowledge any biases you may have and be aware of them. The most important way to remain objective is to *acknowledge* your feelings and take them into account when you assess a learner.

RULE 8: Know what you are going to assess

Assessment must be goal directed. Before the learner starts an activity, you should determine *what* you want to know about the learner, i.e. what you are going to assess. Assessment without a definite goal will only lead to very superficial knowledge of the learner. Know what behaviour or attitudes of the learner you want to assess.

RULE 9: Assessment must be confidential

Confidentiality is perhaps one of the most important principles of meaningful assessments. The information that you discover about learners when assessing them is potentially sensitive. Do not discuss any information about the learner with any person outside the school. If you feel the need to get expert help or advice regarding handling a learner, ask for the parents' permission.

You can ensure confidentiality by:

- always respecting the rights of the parents in relation to their child

- not using any information to take any action about a learner without written permission (except in cases of suspected child abuse).

You have a legal responsibility to report any cases of suspected abuse or neglect of learners to the authorities . These cases should be handled with the utmost care, as your suspicions may be wrong. Get the help from a social worker before you make any accusations.

> **Remember**
> If you suspect that a learner is abused or neglected and do not report it to the police, you are violating a law. (See the Prevention of Family Violence Act.)

The assessment process

Assessment is a process. Achieving valid and reliable assessment of the young learner requires that you follow certain rules, the most important of which were discussed above. This is however not sufficient in itself, as assessment must be *planned* with care, because high-quality assessment requires a whole process or sequence of activities consisting of certain steps or action.

> The assessment process:
> ■ is systematic
> ■ is well planned
> ■ consists of logical steps
> ■ requires certain action or decisions.
>
> The following steps will help you to conduct well-planned assessment of the learners in your group. This *recipe* consists of four continuous phases, namely:
> ■ Planning (which consists of five steps)
> ■ Implementing ('Doing')
> ■ Interpreting
> ■ Communicating.

The following phases and steps should be followed with care when planning and conducting assessment, especially when you are new at assessing learners. These steps will help you to conduct well-planned assessment and gather valid and reliable assessment results.

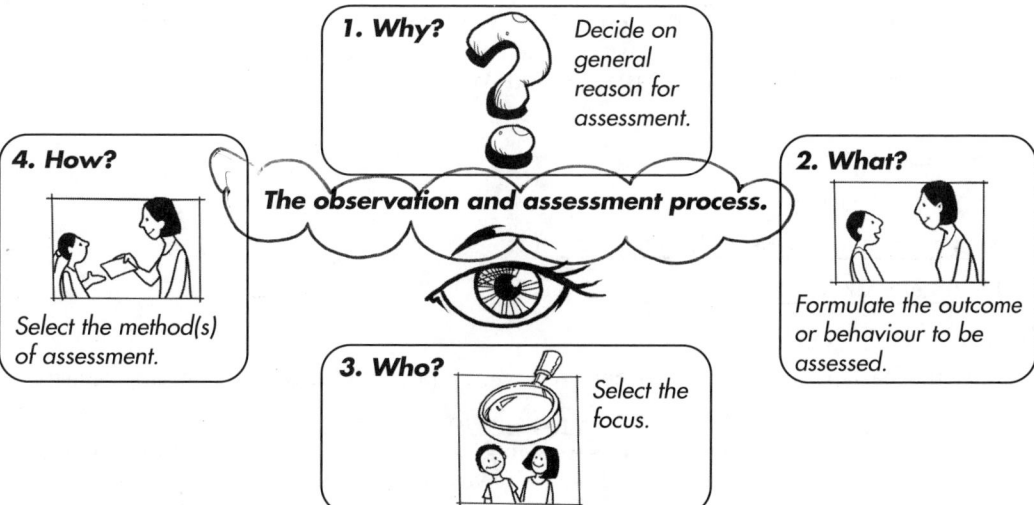

Figure 7.1 – The process of observation and assessment

1. Decide on the general reason for the assessment (WHY?)
2. Formulate the outcome or behaviour that needs to be assessed (WHAT?)
3. Select the focus (WHO?)
4. Select the method(s) of assessment (HOW?)

Phase 1: Planning your assessment

Step 1: Decide on the general reason for the assessment (WHY?)
The first decision to make is to determine the reason for the assessment.

It is important to decide 'WHY' you want to assess the learner or the teaching process.

 **Go to:**

The reasons for assessing were discussed at the beginning of this chapter.

The reason(s) for the assessment will determine the 'WHAT' and 'HOW' of your assessments.

Step 2: Formulate the outcome or behaviour that needs to be assessed (WHAT?)
After you have decided 'WHY' it is important to assess, you need to decide 'WHAT' you want to assess.

When assessment is conducted without a clearly defined reason, and you do not know exactly 'WHAT' you want to assess, assessment is reduced to little more than random and accidental knowledge of the learner.

The 'WHAT' to assess will link to the Learning Outcomes of your teaching. It makes no sense to have certain outcomes that you would like to achieve with your group, but then observe them doing something else.

Step 3: Select the focus (WHO?)
After you have established 'WHY' you want to assess and 'WHAT' you want to assess, you should decide 'WHO' you want to assess. The 'WHO' to assess will vary according to what you have decided for Steps 1 and 2 ('WHY' and 'WHAT'). Depending on these two steps, the focus could be:

- a specific learner
- a group of learners
- the nature and success of the teaching effort
- the organisation of the classroom
- general teaching strategies.

Identify the learners or group of learners you want to assess, during the planning phase.

Trying to assess a large group can pose problems for a teacher. Divide the learners into five groups (between four and eight learners in each group, depending on the number of learners in your class), as this will help you to assess all learners during a one-week period. This will also help you to ensure that you assess all the learners, at different times during the day, and using different methods.

Remember

You have to PLAN your assessment. You must know exactly WHY? WHAT? and WHO? you are going to assess EVERY DAY!

Step 4: Select the method(s) of assessment (HOW?)

Certain 'instruments' or methods can help you to conduct purposeful assessment. The method the teacher uses for the assessments will be determined by all the previous steps:

1. WHY do you want to assess the learner/teaching process?

2. WHAT do you want to assess?

3. WHO do you want to assess?

The four most popular methods used when assessing young children are:

■ **Tests** (which we only use under very rare and specific circumstances; young learners are usually referred to a specialist for testing)

■ **Parent interviews**

■ **Portfolios** (which consist of examples of the learner's Art, Emergent Writing, mathematical experiences and three-dimensional constructions)

■ **Observation of the learner** (using a variety of observation methods such as descriptive methods, developmental checklist and the use of classroom space).

Reliable and valid assessment necessitates using a variety of assessment methods.

Go to:

These above methods of assessment will be discussed in detail in the next section of this chapter.

Step 5: Decide on the time and length of assessment (WHEN? and HOW LONG?)

The time and length of the assessment are mostly a technical decision. They are determined by the assessment method and the teacher's skill and knowledge of assessment.

To determine 'WHEN' you are going to assess you need to keep in mind:

■ 'WHAT' and 'WHY' you want to assess (the reason for assessing, and the outcomes or behaviour you want to assess).

Remember

It is important to make sure that your assessments are at different times of the day.

To work out 'HOW LONG' the assessment should last depends on factors such as:

■ **The objective of the assessment**

For example, if you want to assess whether a learner can cut with a pair of scissors, the assessment will last a few minutes. If you want to work out the learner's level of motor development, your assessment will take at least four weeks. If you want to find out whether a certain teaching method is successful, it will take the duration of the lesson. One would assess the success of a teaching method after the lesson, when assessing whether learners had achieved the outcomes.

■ **The method of assessment**

The method of assessment will also determine the length of it. For example, it can take a whole term to complete a checklist; but a learners' use of classroom space during the course of one day, and other descriptive records may take no more than ten minutes.

■ **The experience of the teacher**

The more experienced teacher can complete the assessments sooner due to her competence in assessing a number of learners.

Phase 2: Implementation of your assessment plan: collecting and storing assessment information

The first five steps are the *planning phase* of the assessment process. After you have decided on each of the five steps outlined above, you can start to assess the class, individual learner, or teaching effort.

This phase involves collecting information about each learner. One assessment of the learner is not enough to make reliable and valid decisions about the learner. To be able to get a complete picture of the learner, you need more than one assessment, and you need to use different assessment methods. You should therefore collect information about the learner through repeated assessments. All the information about the learner must be recorded and stored until you set aside time to INTERPRET it. One of the best ways to do this is to open a *personal file* for each learner.

The personal file for each learner must be divided into sections. The following are suggestions for possible sections:

■ the learner's enrolment form

■ all legal documents signed by the parents (e.g. permission forms for outings and emergency medical treatment.)

■ records of parent interviews

■ all observation records

■ examples from portfolios

■ previous assessment reports.

Remember

Only after you have collected information, using a variety of methods, will you start to interpret *the information. It is only then that you can assess the learner's progress and level of development.*

Phase 3: Interpreting assessment information

During the implementation phase of your assessment you will have collected information about each learner. Arriving at a complete picture in terms of assessing each learner needs to be an ongoing process. All the information you have gathered must be combined to enable you to get a picture of the learner's development and learning progress.

● **Go to:**
Because the interpretation of assessment results is such an important and difficult task, it will be discussed in detail in the last section of this chapter.

Phase 4: Communicate and use the assessment results

Your effort to assess learners will be wasted if you do not USE the assessment results. The answer to the question: 'What can I use the assessment results for'? is very simple. All you have to do is to go back to the reasons ('WHY?') for the assessment process.

You can use assessment results to:

■ guide your teaching plans

■ improve your teaching

■ give better guidance and assistance to parents

■ plan developmentally appropriate Programme Organisers (themes) and activities as you will know the learners' various developmental levels

■ identify learners with developmental and learning barriers

■ adapt your teaching methods to help learners with developmental and learning barriers.

After you have gone through the whole assessment process you also need to INFORM the people who should know about the results. You should prepare the following:

1. Personal assessment report to send to the next teacher who will be teaching the learner.

2. Parent report (this can also be supplemented by a parent interview).

3. Reports to other professionals (such as specialists to whom you may refer a learner with learning or developmental barriers).

4. Report to another ECD-centre or the primary school.

   Each of these reports serves a different purpose and will therefore emphasise different aspects of the assessment results:

1. Personal assessment report
It is advisable to prepare a report on each learner's progress. The assessment report provides an overview of the learner's progress over the year. (At the end of the year this report must be sent to the next teacher or primary school.)

2. Parent report and parent interview
The information in the learner's personal assessment report must also be sent to or discussed with the learner's parents. The parent report, or discussion at a parent's interview, will be a summary of the personal assessment report. The frequency with which parents should receive a report will be decided by the school – it must, however, not be less than twice a year.

When you complete reports to parents, keep to the following guidelines in mind:

■ keep the language clear and simple

■ use words the parents can easily understand. Avoid using 'academic terms' (i.e. jargon).

Example

Do not use words such as 'auditory discrimination' or 'cognitive process', rather say 'the learner's ability to hear differences in sounds' or 'the way the learner thinks'.

- do not label the learner as 'hyperactive' or 'gifted'
- if the parent speaks a different language to your own, try to have the parent report translated into their home language
- be straightforward and supportive in the report. Every learner has strengths and needs; ensure that you share both with the parents.
- it is not helpful or kind to write nothing about a learner's weaknesses
- be sensitive to the impact of what you say on the learner and the family
- do not *wait* to tell parents your concerns about a learner until report time. The moment you identify a concern, discuss it with the parents. It is unfair to parents to have to read in a report that their child has difficulties when they were under the impression that their child was doing well.

<u>The best practice is to discuss the parent report with the parents individually.</u> The teacher and parents should go through all the information about the learner together. This is a particularly important strategy with parents who are illiterate. Try to have an interpreter present if you and the parents speak different languages.

● **Go to:**

In the next section we will discuss parent interviews. The guidelines we will discuss are just as applicable when you report your assessment of the learner to parents.

Remember

Parents can often help you to solve their learner's problem. Giving help and support to a child (however big or small the need may be) is part of their task as parents. It is your task as a teacher, however, to make sure that the parents know WHAT to do and HOW to do it.

3. Reports to other professionals

When you refer a learner to a specialist (depending on the problem this can be, for example, to a medical doctor, a speech or occupational therapist) it is very important that you write a report to the specialist. The fact that you work with the learner in a setting that is different to the one in which the specialist will see the learner, means that the specialist needs your input. Your observations of the learner in a group setting (i.e. the classroom) can <u>give the specialist valuable insight</u> into the learner, which can be very useful when diagnosing the learner's specific problem.

4. Report to another ECD-centre or the primary school

As the learner moves from one ECD-centre to another, or goes on to the primary school, it is important that the new principal receives an assessment report on the learner. Valuable knowledge about the learner can be lost if the new teacher is not informed about possible problems or strengths.

Assessment is very important! How do I go about it?

To be able to assess a learner the teacher needs INFORMATION about the learner.

As said before, the teacher makes use of four different assessment methods to gather information about the learner:

1. Tests
2. Interviews with responsible caregivers/parents
3. Portfolios with examples of learner's work
4. Observation of the learner using different observation methods

Each of these methods helps the teacher to focus on a specific aspect of the child's development and learning. Each method will be discussed in detail in order to help you use them when you assess the learners in your class.

1. Tests

Tests are often used to assess the learner's level of development and to 'screen' them in terms of school readiness. In fact, school readiness tests are the most widely used tests for young learners. These tests are used to screen learners to find out whether they are ready for school or not. The use of these tests is one of the hotly contested areas in early childhood education.

The use of tests is not part of the ordinary assessment procedures in a reception year class due to the following reasons:

Disadvantages related to the young learner

■ Administering a test to young children is a challenge to the teacher and the learners, because the child's behaviour and performance are influenced by the test administrator, the test situation and the unfamiliar nature of the test environment.

■ The young learner's language abilities are limited and this may result in the misunderstanding of instructions, which would, in turn, lead to false test results.

■ The emotional aspect of a young child is a very important component of himself or herself as a young person. It is very difficult to test or assess the learner's emotions during a test situation.

■ Young children are eager to please adults. They may therefore respond in the way they think the adult wants them to respond, instead of trying to answer the questions 'correctly'.

Disadvantages related to the test itself

■ If standardised tests (i.e. tests developed by specialised professionals according to strict statistical principles) are not administered according to stringent rules, under specific conditions as set out in a test manual, the results are useless.

■ Teachers need special training in order to be able to administer standardised tests, and due to the limited use of these tests (particularly in the reception year), teachers are seldom trained for this purpose.

■ Tests do not provide a total picture of the reception year learner, as they tend to focus on abilities that are easy to measure: e.g. the learner's visual (seeing) and auditory (hearing) perceptions.

- Standardised tests are not always valid (true) and reliable (trustworthy) for all cultural groups. Children from poor, rural areas in particular are often discriminated against through the use of such tests. One of the reasons this is so is that often the writers of the test come from a very different world than that of the children taking the test.

- Using tests can also result in 'teaching to the test'. In other words, the test dictates what activities and content the teacher chooses to present to the class. This results in a content driven curriculum, and is just the opposite what we want to achieve in an outcomes-based approach.

> **Remember**
> The decision that a learner needs special educational services or has developmental or learning barriers should not be based on a single test but on the input from a team of experts in the field of early childhood development.

2. Interviews with parents

Interviews with parents are an important source of information about the learner and are also a way of involving the parent in their child's education. The reception year teacher should never underestimate a parent's intuitive feelings about a learner. Always investigate any concerns a parent communicates to you regarding their child.

It may sometimes be necessary to visit the parent's home for an interview. A visit to the parent's home can reveal a great deal about the parent's way of life, economic situation, cultural background and the way they raise their children. However, teachers must be careful not to make inappropriate remarks or ask hurtful questions, particularly about religion or the parents' economic situation (Landsberg 1996 : 9).

Interviews with parents are an important means of communication between school (teacher) and home (caregivers/parents.) However, it is important to remember that if not handled in a professional and caring manner, interviews can block communication between home and school. It is important to plan an interview with parents very well, even if the parent requests the interview.

How to conduct an interview
The planning stage

- Know *why* you want to talk to the parents (or why they want to talk to you). Make sure you are sure *what information* you would like to get from them.

- Give parents at least two weeks' notification of the interview, by writing a letter. The letter should inform the parent (or caregiver) of the reason for the interview and explain what you will expect from them during the interview. Suggest a few possible dates and times and ask them to confirm these with you.

The interview

- Help the parents to feel comfortable by establishing a warm, friendly environment. Arrange chairs in a circle in such a way as to include both them and yourself – do not sit behind a desk.

- Ensure as far as possible that your talk with the parents will be uninterrupted.

- Parents must feel that they are valued people with helpful ideas and insight into their child. Avoid displaying a 'know-it-all' attitude. Your interaction with parents should leave them feeling that they are important partners in their child's education.

- Trust and mutual respect between teacher and parent are essential ingredients for a successful interview.

- Be sensitive to the needs of the parents.

- Listen to the parents and look directly at them when they are speaking to you. Listening is more important then talking!

- Give the parents a chance to say why they think their child has a problem or displays certain behaviour. Ask them to share information about their child's behaviour at home.

- Let the parents decide on a plan of action to help their child; guide them if they are unsure. The plan will work better if they propose it.

- Use language the parents will understand. Do not talk down to them, but also avoid using educational jargon to impress them.

- End the interview on a positive note.

Remember

Parent interviews are an important means of communication between school and home. However, if not handled in a professional and caring manner, interviews can actually block communication between home and school. Be careful not to have a 'know-all' attitude and be sensitive to language and cultural differences.

After the interview

It is important to follow up after an interview – if there is no follow up, the interview is nothing more than a friendly 'chat' between parent and teacher. The teacher must make notes of the interview and put them on the learner's file.

An example of the information noted for the learner's file:

Notes on parent interview

Name of child:.. Date: .... Time ....

Participants: ....

....

....

Concerns expressed by parents ....

....

....

....

....

Concerns expressed by teacher ....

....

....

....

....

Plan of action ....

....

....

....

Overall assessment of interview ....

....

....

Portfolios of learners' work

Keeping samples of learners' work is a visual method of gaining knowledge about a learner's development and learning. This kind of record is called a portfolio.

Definition

A portfolio is an organised, purposeful compilation of evidence documenting a child's development over time (McAfee and Leong 2002: 96).

Portfolios of reception year learners' work consist of examples of:

- art works – drawings, paintings and cutting activities
- three-dimensional constructions with building blocks or other construction materials (take photos or make sketches from these)
- Emergent Writing
- dictation of own stories to teacher with pictures drawn by the learner
- data collected for science, e.g. a drawing after an outing, simple graphs of learner's observations
- best or first attempts, e.g. photos of times where the learner is completing a special tasks; laying the table correctly for lunch on his own.

Portfolios are characterised by a great variety of examples from the learner's work.

Portfolios are important assessment tools as they:

- provide a _visual_ progress report of the learner. The teacher (or anyone who looks at the portfolio) can see how the learner's work has changed
- can be used to answer questions about the learner's development, such as 'Are the learner's cutting skills getting better or not?'
- illustrate progression or regression in the learner's development. Is the learner developing or is the learner deteriorating in certain ways?

The teachers' analysis the learner's work samples, together with information from parents' interviews and observations of the learner, will provide a record of the learner's learning and development. With this record it is possible for the teacher to clearly *see* how each learner is progressing and where possible problem areas could be occurring.

Guidelines

The following guidelines are useful when using portfolios as a method of obtaining assessment information:

- Never make any deductions based on a single example of the learner's work. The quality of learners' work will not be constant – a single excellent picture or construction does not necessarily mean that the child is gifted, nor can a single incident below the learner's normal behaviour indicate regression (i.e. where the learner is not developing and certain behaviour is actually deteriorating).
- Don't compare one child's work with that of another child. Rather assess a learner's work against their own previous efforts.
- Do not assess the learner's work according to adult standards. Use the accepted development of a five- to six-year-old as a guideline. (*See Chapter 2: Know the child.*)
- Do not use 'popular psychology' to analyse learners' pictures – e.g. black does *not* always mean depression; and a human figure without arms does *not* indicate a cold and loveless mother! Always ask learners to explain their pictures and write their 'story' down as they tell it to you.
- Sort the samples of the learner's work into categories. Ensure that each sample has a date and add any additional information that may be relevant for later interpretations of the samples. A standard form can be very helpful when assessing examples of the learner's

work. See the following examples of standard forms: 'Assessment of the learner's Art' and 'Assessment of constructions'. Complete these forms for the art and construction examples you collect. Staple the completed form to the sample. You will refer to it when interpreting all the assessment information (data) you have gathered for the learner.

Assessment of example of learner's art

Name of learner .... Date of birth .... Date..............

	Yes	Sometimes	No
Is able to draw a straight line			
Is able to snip with scissors			
Is able to cut 2 cm on a straight line			
Does uncontrolled scribbling			
Does controlled scribbling			
Draws a sun face figure			
Draws a head-foot, hair-pin figure			
Draws a figure with a torso			
Draws a figure with double lines and details			
Draws a picture with a base-line			
Draws a picture with a sky-line			
Draws a picture where all lines meet neatly			
Colours picture in			
Make use of unrealistic colours			
Make use of realistic colours			

Assessment of example of learner's three-dimensional analysis

Name of learner .... Date of birth .... Date..............

	Yes	Sometimes	No
Starts building horizontal / vertical rows			
Builds a three block bridge			
Builds a circle			
Makes decorative patterns but not "buildings"			
Imitates structures form the environment			
Builds structure and uses it in fantasy play			

Bear in mind that collecting and assessing portfolios is a time consuming process. You need time to collect samples of the work done by each learner in your class, and then to assess each sample. The best way to do this is to collect one example from each learner once a month. Each week, assess one sample of work from four to eight learners. This will help you to get samples of all learners' work in a manageable way.

> ### Remember
> *Do not keep all art, or other work samples of the learners in your class. These portfolios will be too big to handle and will become unmanageable. Keep only one example a month. This amount will be manageable and you will still be able to have visual representations of their development and learning.*

Observation

The most useful and important method for obtaining information about the young learner is by OBSERVING the child. By using observation the teacher obtains first hand information about the learner in everyday situations.

> ### Definition
> Observation is to take notice, to watch attentively, and to focus on one particular aspect of the learner with a specific reason in mind. Observation is therefore more than mere looking and seeing, it is looking with a specific reason.

You can use three methods to assist in directing your observation of the learners in your class. They are:

1. Descriptive records,

2. Developmental checklists, and

3. Participation charts.

The use of these methods will be discussed in more detail below.

> ### Remember
> *The best way to get to know the different observation methods is to use them. Use these methods in your class and you will realise the more you use them, the easier they are to use!*

1. Descriptive records

The most common way of gathering information about learners is to watch and listen to them. Descriptive records are therefore an excellent method of recording information about the learners in your class. This method has also been referred to as 'pictures written down' (McAfee and Leong 2002: 103).

> ### Definition
> Descriptive records are continuous written records of everything said or done during the observation period.

When creating descriptive records, the teacher writes down in detail his or her observation of what happens to and with the learner.

Through focused observation the teacher:

- listens for *verbal* responses. This includes not only what the learner says but also the tone of the voice, pronunciation of words and the use of words.

- watches for *nonverbal* responses. This includes gestures and facial expressions.

- describes the circumstances or context in which the behaviour takes place.

Advantages of the 'descriptive records' method of observation:

- it is a direct way to obtain information about a learner

- it enables the teacher to assess the learner's reactions as a complete person under different situations (i.e. the information gained much richer than that obtained if the learner were merely to write a test)

- it gives the teacher insight in the learner as a *unique* person

- it is an unobtrusive method. Learners do not have to be aware that they are being observed.

- descriptive records take place during normal daily activities and lessons – no changes are necessary in or to the daily routine

- it requires minimal equipment

- these records preserve information in a form that is the closest to what really happens to the learner in the classroom and the outside play area

- it helps the teacher analyse the effectiveness of the teaching effort.

Disadvantages of descriptive records:

- they are time-consuming

- good descriptive records need to be completed without interruption

- one needs lots of information to be able to make reliable interpretations. One observation is not enough.

- using language as the descriptive tool requires a large vocabulary and a skilful recorder (i.e. person who writes the records)

- descriptive records recorded after the actual observation may not be reliable.

Guidelines for recording descriptive records

- The simplest way to write down descriptive records is to use large index cards, one for each learner. Each card should have the following information:
  - the learner's name
  - birth date
  - date of each new entry
- Make a habit of keeping note cards and a pencil in your pocket.
- Observe each learner for not longer then ten minutes at a time.
- Each time you observe a learner, make sure that the observation is at a different time and lesson/activity.

- Focus on a specific learner, behaviour or problem – know what you want to observe.

- Describe the surrounding environment and what happened immediately before the observation and what followed it (i.e. a brief description of the context).

- Observe verbal and nonverbal behaviour.

- Use words conveying exactly what the learner says and does (i.e. quote the learner verbatim where possible).

- Records must be as accurate as possible an account of what you have observed. Avoid using labelling words, such as hyperactive, naughty, good, gifted, etc.

- Use a tape recorder or a camera to take pictures if you cannot write down the information immediately. This makes the descriptive record more reliable

- Interpret descriptive records written *after* the observation with caution, because your memory may not be reliable.

Examples of correct and incorrect descriptive records:

Example of correct descriptive record

Learner's name: *Sipho Masola*

Birth date: *22 April 1999*

Date of observation: *15 June 2004*

Place: *Inside the classroom in the block play area.*

Context: *Sipho finishes a painting at the easel. He walks over to the block area where Peter is playing.*

Observation: *Sipho builds a construction using fifteen blocks. He stops five times to look at his construction from a distance, before adding additional blocks. Peter is playing next to him. Peter takes a red block from a heap near Sipho. Sipho takes the block from his hands saying firmly, 'I need this block'. Peter tries to take the block from Sipho but Sipho said firmly that he sorted out the blocks and he needs this one. Peter starts to cry while Sipho puts the block on his construction. He looks at his construction from all sides. He lifts his shoulders and then he kicks the construction over. He starts building a new construction immediately. Jan calls him to play with him at the games-table. He leaves the construction area.*

Example of an incorrect descriptive record

Learner's name: *Sipho Masola*

Birth date: *22 April 1999*

Date of observation: *15 June 2004*

Observation: *Sipho builds a very advanced construction for his age, using a lot of blocks. It is clear that he plans his construction very carefully and thinks before he builds. Peter who is playing next to him, is not as advanced. Peter is a selfish learner as he tries to take a block from Sipho. Peter is also immature as he starts to cry when Sipho does not want to give the block to him. Sipho is cross and kicks his construction over. He lost interest and he left the area as soon as Jan called him.*

As illustrated in the above example, descriptive records are not easy to complete. It is however, an important assessment method and every teacher should be encouraged to gain the necessary skills to use it successfully.

2. Developmental checklists

Developmental checklists help the teacher to focus on a specific aspect or skill in the learner's development.

Definition

A developmental checklist is a prepared list of important developmental milestones. At various times the teacher indicates on the list whether or not a specific milestone has been reached.

When using developmental checklists, the teacher records what kind of behaviour is expected of the learner. Before the observation begins, the teacher identifies the behaviour they expect or would like to observe, and develops a checklist of this behaviour. Checklists can be compiled by using sources such as:

- the Learning Outcomes of the reception year
- characteristics of tasks or activities learners are expected to perform
- developmental milestones.

 **Remember**

Checklists are not tests! They are merely a way of tracking a learners' progression.

Advantages of using developmental checklists to record observations:

- Large amounts of information can be recorded quickly.
- Checklists are flexible and versatile. They can be changed and adapted to fit specific circumstances.
- They are easily analysed and interpreted.
- Teachers can be easily trained to use checklists.
- Checklists help teachers to keep track of a learner's progress and achievements at a specific time.

Disadvantages of using developmental checklists to record observations:

- Checklists that contain only a few items must be interpreted with caution.
- Checklists can oversimplify behaviour and learning, which are in fact rather difficult to interpret.
- Unexpected behaviour (those not identified in the checklist) may not be recorded.

Principles for compiling checklists

Follow the principles below to help you compile a developmental checklist. You can also use these principles to *evaluate* commercially available checklists, or any other checklists that you may want to use in your reception year class.

- The checklist must have space for the following information:
  - dates of observation
  - a column for remarks (to write down any information that may affect the observation)
- The identified behaviour must be well defined. You must be able to note clearly what behaviour or activity.

Example

Two items in a checklist were:

The learner shows aggressive behaviour

The learner hits other learners

These are not suitable items as aggressive behaviour and hitting overlap, i.e. hitting can be counted as aggressive behaviour.

- The identified behaviour must not overlap with other behaviour.
- The items in the checklist must be grouped under appropriate headings (this helps when you fill in the checklist).

Example

When you compile a checklist for observing block building, you will use the development of skills for block building as a guideline.

- The different items must follow the sequence of normal development

---

Example

Incorrect item on a checklist: Knows numerals 1 to 5.

Correct items on a checklist:

Points to a numeral when asked.

Says the name of a numeral when asked.

Volunteers the name of a numeral between 1 and 5.

- Behaviour must be listed in small steps or levels

Example

Incorrect item on a checklist: Cannot jump on one foot.

Correct items on a checklist:

Jumps on the right foot.

Jumps on the left foot.

- The <u>items must be stated in the positive to avoid confusion.</u>
- The checklist must include <u>behaviour below and above what is expect</u>ed of learners in the reception year.

Guidelines for filling in a checklist

- Before you start to fill in a checklist, make sure that you are familiar with the contents of the whole list.
- Not all learners have to be observed simultaneously. <u>Divide the group on</u>ce again and observe the learners over a period of a week.
- Develop your <u>own coding system t</u>o fill in the checklist. The following are a few hints to help you with your own coding system:
  - Items that the learner can do or has mastered, or cannot or hasn't mastered: These items can be marked by a check (✓), X or Yes/No.
  - Items performed partially: These items can be marked by a slash (/) that can be made into an (✓) when the learner masters the item. Another possibility is to use a B for beginning or a P for partial.
  - Items not observed because the learner was absent or the target behaviour was not observed: Use a blank (no mark) or a special code such as A for absent and N/O for not observed.
- <u>Write down the date</u> when you observe the specific skill. This will enable you to compare later observations. Only with written records will you be able to determine whether or not the learner is progressing.
- A good checklist will have <u>space for 'Remarks'</u>. Write down notes on the learner's behaviour and the circumstances surrounding it (if necessary).

Example

A checklist's aim is not to determine the mental age or IQ of a learner or to predict future development of performance of the learner, but to help you to determine the learner's unique development and areas of strength.

Remember

Checklists that are filled in over a period create a record of the learner's development.

3. Participation charts

Participation charts involve a plan of the classroom or outdoor playground on which the areas and length of learners' visits are indicated.

Participation charts are useful to record whether and how often learners participate in certain activities.

Records of the use of space provide insight into:

■ a learner's preferences in terms of different activities

■ patterns of a learner's participation

■ the group social structure and interactions. For example, are there learners who are *always* playing alone; or that are being 'pushed' aside by the group?

■ a learner's preferred activity(ies) over a period (if the chart is filled in over a period)

■ activities or areas in the playroom that are under or over used.

■ the success of the layout of the classroom.

Advantages of participation charts:

■ They are a simple and quick way of recording participation.

■ They are easy to interpret.

■ They provide information about social structures and interactions that other methods may overlook.

Disadvantages of participation charts:

■ The rate of participation may not necessarily reflect how much a child is learning.

■ A teacher needs to repeat the observations a number of times in order to make valid interpretations.

■ As with descriptive records, participation charts need to be filled in while observing the children, otherwise the records may not be reliable.

How to observe the use of space inside and outside the playroom:

■ Draw a plan of the playroom or outdoor play area that you want to observe.

■ Decide on the learners you want to observe before you start observing them. (Tip: Divide your class into ten groups and observe all ten groups during free play indoors and free play outdoors every day for a week. Ensure that you observe all learners during that week.)

■ While observing the learners, write down their names and the time they spend in the different play areas. (Tip: Make use of a code for learners, e.g. use their initials rather than their full names, unless this will result in confusion.)

■ Write down where each learner is, every ten to fifteen minutes. Decide before you start how long the intervals are going to be.

■ Repeat your observation of the use of space at least once a month.

■ Do not interpret your findings after one observation. Rather go back to previous participation charts of the learners and see if you can find any patterns in their participation.

Remember

This exercise may sound time consuming but, in fact, all it involves is looking around every ten or fifteen minutes and noting down where the learners you have decided to observe that day are playing.

You should aim to identify the following information from observing the learner's use of space:

- those learners who do not <u>stay at an area for more than five minutes</u>
- the area that a s<u>pecific learner never or very seldom visits</u>
- <u>areas in the playroom that are never or very seldom</u> visited by the learners in your class
- <u>learners that spend a whole period in only one area</u>
- establish the *traffic flow* in your playroom. This information will help you to plan your playroom better.

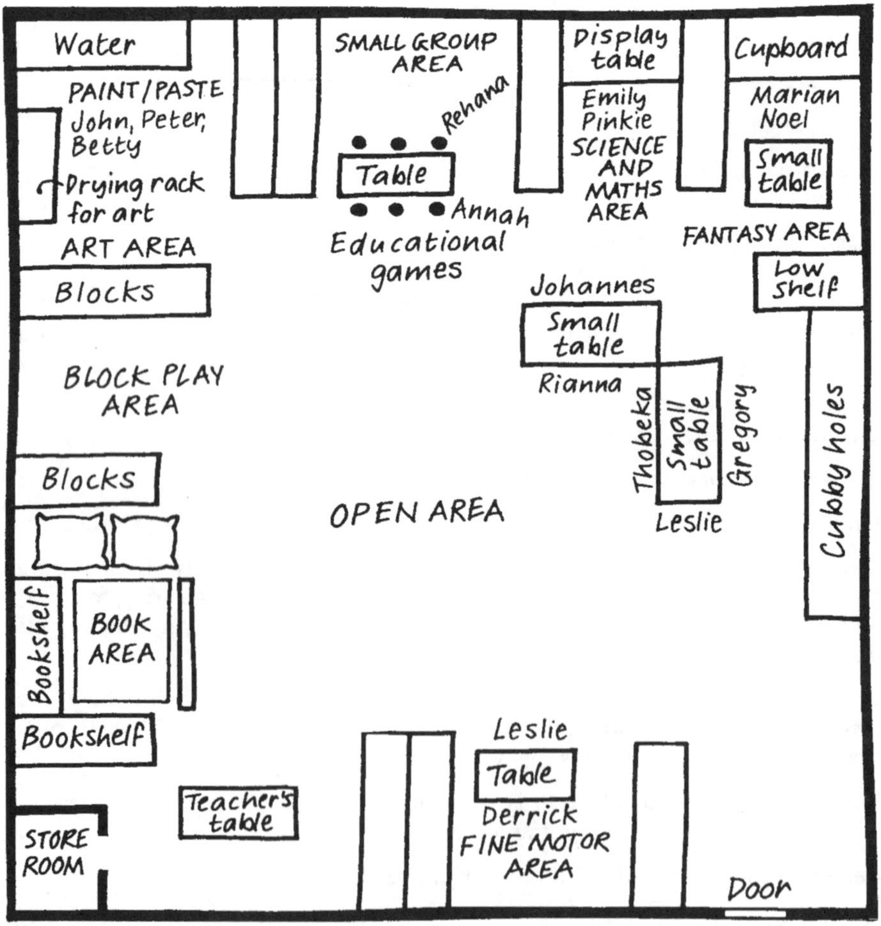

An example of the use of a participation chart

Using other methods of recording observations

When reading textbooks on assessment and when talking to other teachers, you will find that there are many other methods of recording observations that can be used in the observation of young learners. The three methods explained above are the most important methods, and they are also easy to use and to interpret. As a reception year teacher, you may naturally use any method of recording your observations, as long as the methods are valid and reliable.

Principles for interpreting assessment results

The assessment process requires that the teacher interprets the information that he or she has collected about the learner. Interpretation of information is *the most important phase* in assessment. Many teachers unfortunately think that gathering and storing information about the learner is where the assessment stops. In fact, the information that you have collected about the learner is of no use if not *interpreted* and *used*.

We discussed the rules (principles) to guide you when you assess the learner on page 227. Bearing the nine principles in mind will ensure that you can achieve true and trustworthy interpretations of assessment information.

RULE 1: Base interpretations on all available information on the WHOLE learner

When you start to interpret the information, ensure that you take all available information into account and that you look at the whole learner. Do no focus only on certain skills or aspects of the child.

One way to achieve this is to look at information collected from different sources.

For example:

- Look at your notes and find out whether during the *parent interview* the parents spoke or asked about aspects of the learner that you were also worried about.

- Look at *examples of the learner's work* and use different examples over a period of time. Try to identify whether the examples show improvement (an indication of growth and development) or regression.

- Look at the *observations records* you have made of the learner, using the different recording methods. The information from developmental checklists, descriptive records and the participation charts will each tell you something more about the learner.

- Has the learner ever been *tested* by a specialist? What was the reason for the test(s)? What were the results of the test(s)? Do you agree with the results of the tests(s)?

When you add all the information together, ask yourself whether it makes a complete picture of the learner, or are there still some unanswered questions? If so, identify the areas and assess the learner further.

RULE 2: Normal behaviour can vary greatly

Even the best books on learner development differ on the question of 'What is normal behaviour?' Normal behaviour can vary greatly and each learner has a unique and individual pattern of development. Be careful not to identify 'developmental problems' too hastily. Ensure that your interpretation is correct by using different methods and sources of information.

RULE 3: Interpretations are tentative

Interpretations of information should always be tentative. Learners change rapidly. Even under the best circumstances the assessment of a learner is based only on a small sample of what the learner can do. Many important kinds of information about the learner are difficult to observe and to interpret. Interpretations should only reflect what the teacher really *knows* about the learner and not merely what he or she thinks.

> ### Remember
> *Attitudes such as motivation, willingness, and encouragement are difficult to assess and, together with factors such as family support, can have a major influence on a learner's future development.*

RULE 4: Interpretations are not easy to make

The interpretation of a learner's behaviour is never easy. When you interpret information keep the following in mind:

■ Human behaviour is not fixed, but changes over time and in different circumstances. The young learner's behaviour is easily influenced and your observations or work examples of the learner are never a full indication of the learner's developmental level.

> ### Remember
> *We are not the same every day – some days we feel on top of the world and other days nothing seems to work out. The young learner's behaviour is even more erratic than that of an adult.*

■ Young children's development and learning cannot be pinpointed precisely. What we may know about a learner is only an *indication* of what the learner is capable of. (A learner's behaviour at a certain point can vary within a larger interval, which reflects the upper and lower limits of his capabilities at that point.)

■ Information about a learner can have different meanings because human development is complex. We cannot say that because a learner does certain things, the only possible interpretation is X and that there is no other possibility.

> ### Example
> *Nkopodi is a shy and quiet boy.*
>
> This can be interpreted that Nkopodi is respectful (a positive interpretation). It can also be interpreted that Nkopodi lacks self-confidence (a negative interpretation). These are two very different interpretations of the same behaviour.

RULE 5: Teachers have to make decisions

The previous principle stressed that all interpretations are tentative. This does not mean that you should never make a decision about a learner. When you interpret the information, you have to make a decision about the learner's developmental level and behaviour, and one of the most important reasons for assessment is to make decisions about the learner.

> **Remember**
>
> Our decisions about the learner are not:
>
> ■ fixed and never to be changed
>
> ■ to exclude a learner from any opportunity (in any form).

Assessment should not be phrased in unqualified terms, such as 'the learner can/cannot … '. In other words, interpretations need to be explained.

To be able to make decisions about the learner we have to:

■ identify what the learner's level of development is;

■ identify possible problems and/or strengths of the learner.

Sometimes it is difficult for a teacher to admit, even to him- or herself, that a learner has a possible developmental or learning barrier. As discussed before, it is not always easy to decide whether a learner's behaviour is unique but still within the 'normal development' range, or whether the behaviour or development is a 'red light' (i.e. signifying a learning or developmental barrier).

Often the reception year teacher will be the first person to identify a possible learning barrier. No teacher has all the knowledge necessary to deal adequately with all learners and all problems. Some learners, as discussed previously, need to be referred to specialists.

Learners who need referral typically have repeated patterns of behaviour that alert the teacher. One or two incidents of behaviour that cause alarm will require the teacher's attention, but it is consistent patterns of 'problem' behaviour that call for further action.

RULE 6: Be aware of the 'halo' effect

The 'halo' effect occurs when we interpret a learner's behaviour as being wholly favourable or wholly unfavourable because of certain exceptional behaviour. It is very easy for a teacher working with young children to fall into the trap of the 'halo' effect.

> **Example**
>
> It is easy to interpret all behaviour in a positive way if a learner has an exceptionaly sweet and cute personality.

Learners who are exceptionally competent with certain skills, or more advanced than the rest of the group, are not necessary better at everything else. It is important to bear in mind that learners develop unevenly, both with regard to a given developmental area and as a whole person. Again, you should base your assessment on all possible information.

RULE 7: Remember that you are biased

All the knowledge, values, attitudes and experiences that you have act as filters though which you interpret assessment information. Your interpretation of the information can never be totally objective, as it will always be influenced by these factors to some degree. Since no two individuals are exactly alike, no two persons will interpret the same information in the same way. Having said this, one of the most effective ways of working towards achieving some measure of objectivity is to acknowledge that you are biased, and to try to identify exactly how you are biased, whether positively or negatively, regarding the learner you are assessing. These biases then need to be taken into consideration when you make your final assessment.

RULE 8: A team approach results in better interpretations for assessment

The best way to interpret assessment is to use a team approach. Your team should consist of the school principal and all teachers involved with the learner. A team approach is not always possible, but is always something worth working towards. This is an excellent way to counteract being biased for or against a learner, and to have more objective interpretations, as the information is being interpreted by different people with different viewpoints.

Example

You cannot tell a parent that a learner definitely is for example hyperactive, gifted or hard of hearing. As the reception year teacher, your role is to *identify* that the learner's behaviour suggests a possible problem and to advise that further investigation, by a specialist, is needed.

RULE 9: We cannot *diagnose* a problem

Our assessment methods are not diagnostic tools and we cannot therefore diagnose a barrier in learners. We can only *identify* possible developmental or learning barriers. Any diagnoses (if any is necessary) must be made by a relevant specialist (e.g. paediatrician, neurologist, occupational therapist, speech therapist, etc).

Conclusion

Assessment is one of the cornerstones of successful teaching in the reception year. It is, however, not an easy task and we hope that the practical guidelines and tips in this chapter will help to make this task easier. The saying 'Practise makes perfect' applies to assessment – keep trying, keep improving and above all, keep learning! We hope you will find this an exciting journey of discovering more about each learner in your class.

Bibliography

Ackers, J. 1994. 'Why involve me?' Encouraging children and their parents to participate in the assessment process. In: Abbott, L & Roger, R. (Eds) *Quality education in the early years.* Buckingham: Open University Press. (pp55 – 75)

Airasian, P W. 1994. *Classroom assessment.* New York: McGraw-Hill.

American Academy of Pediatrics. Committee on School Health and Committee on Early Childhood, Adoption and Dependent Care. 1995. The inappropriate use of school "readiness" tests. In: *Pediatrics* (Vol 95 no 3) (pp 437 – 438)

Baker, E L. 1994. Making performance assessment work: The road ahead. In: *Educational Leadership.* (Vol 51 no 6) (pp 58 – 62)

Beaty, J. 1994 (3rd ed). *Observing development of the young child.* Engelwood Cliffs: Merrill.

Bentzen, W R. 1985. *Seeing young children. A guide to observing and recording behavior.* Albany: Delmar.

Bergan, J R & Feld, J K. 1993. Developmental assessment: New Directions In: *Young Children.* (Vol 48, July) (pp 41 – 47)

Bergman, A B. 1993. Performance assessment for early childhood. What could be more natural? In: *Science and Children* (Vol 30 no 5) (pp 20 – 22)

Bracey, G W. 1991. Tests and kindergarten entry. In: *Phi Delta Kappan.* (Vol 73, Dec.) (pp 335 – 336)

Bronfenbrenner, U. 1979. *Ecology of human development. Experiments by nature and design.* Cambridge: Harvard University Press.

Burgess-Macey, C. 1994. Assessing young children's learning. In: Keel, P (Ed) *Assessment in the Multi-Ethnic Primary Classroom.* Trentham Books: Staffordshire. (pp 47 – 60)

Cartwright, C A & Cartwright G P.1984. (2nd ed). *Developing observational skills.* New York: McGraw-Hill.

Cassel, R N. 1995. Accountability for early childhood education. (Assessing global functioning) In: *Reading Improvement.* (Vol 32 no 1) (pp 32 – 37)

Chittenden, E. 1991. Authentic assessment, evaluation, and documentation of student performance. In: *Expanding student assessment*, edited by V. Perrone, Alexandria: Association for Supervision and Curriculum Development (pp 22 – 31).

Cole, M & Cole, S R. 1993. (2nd ed.) *The development of children.* New York: Scientific American Books.

Department of Education. (Not dated). *Draft recommendations for the development and implementations of assessment policy.* Ongepubliseerde werksdokument

Department of Education. 1996 (a). *Interim Policy for Early Childhood Development.* Pretoria: Government Printers.

Department of Education 1996 (b). Draft Document. *Curriculum Framework for General and Further Education and Training* Amended document revised by the Curriculum Development Working Group of the NCDC.

Department of Education. 1997 (a). *Curriculum 2005. Lifelong learning for the 21st century.* Cape Town: CTB Books.

Department of Education. 1997 (b). *Foundation Phase. (Grades R to 3) Policy Document.* October 19997. Pretoria: Government Printers.

Department of Education. 1997 (c). *Norms and standards for teacher education, training and development.* Technical committee on the revision of norms and standards for teacher education. Pretoria: Department of Education.

Department of Education. 1997 (d). *Outcomes based education in South Africa. Background information for educators.* Pretoria: Department of Education.

Department of Education. 1997 (e). *Towards a policy framework for assessment in the general and further education and training phases in South Africa.* Discussion document. Pretoria: Department of Education.

Department of Education. 1999. *The Early Childhood Development sector and the National Qualifications Framework: Norms and standards for Early Childhood Development practitioners.* Unpublished.

Department of Education. 2001. *Education White Paper 6. Special needs Education. Building an inclusive education and training system.* July 2001. Pretoria: Department of Education.

Department of Education. 2002. (a). *Foundation Phase Learning Programme Policy Guidelines: Strenghtening Policy-in-action.* Pretoria: Department of Education.

Department of Education. 2002. (b). *Revised National Curriculum Statement Grades R – 9 (Schools) Policy: Overview English.* Pretoria: Department of Education.

Department of Education. 2003. *The Revised National Curriculum Statements Foundation Phase Learning Programme Policy Guidelines.* (Draft). Pretoria: Department of Education.

Drummond, M J & Nutbrown, C. 1996. (2nd ed.) Observing and assessing young children. In: Pugh, G (Ed) *Contemporary issues in the early years. Working collaboratively for children.* London: Paul Chapman. (pp 102 – 118)

Ebbeck, M & Ebbeck, F. 1994. Account ability in the early childhood profession. In: *Australian Journal of Early Childhood.* (Vol 19, March) (pp 16 – 20)

Elkind, E. 1996. Early Childhood Education: What should we expect? In: *Principal.* (Vol 75 no 5) (pp 11 – 13)

Ellwein, M C, Walsh, D J, Eads II, G M & Miller, A. 1991. Using readiness tests to route kindergarten students: The snarled intersection of psychometrics, policy, and practice. In: *Educational Evaluation and Policy Analysis.* (Vol 13 no 2) (pp 159 – 175)

Essa, E L. 1999. (3rd ed.) *Introduction to early childhood education.* Albany: Delmar Publishers.

Faber, R J. 1996. *Assessment in the reception year. Module 4.* Unpublished. *Study Guide for the Certificate in Reception Year Teaching* Pretoria: University of South Africa.

Farr, R & Tone, B. 1998. (2nd ed.) *Portfolio and Performance Assessment. Helping Students Evaluate their Progress as Readers and Writers.* Orlando: Harcourt Brace College Publishers.

Feeney, S, Christensen, D & Moravcik, E. 2001 *Who am I in the lives of children?* Columbus: Merrill.

Feuer, M J & Fulton, K. 1993. The many faces of performance assessment. In: *Phi Delta Kappan.* (Vol 74 no 6) (p 478)

Glazer, M S. 1995. Are those alternatives to grades honest alternatives? In: *Teaching K – 8* (Vol 24 no 8) (pp 98 – 101)

Gordon, A & Williams-Browne, K. 2001. *Beginnings and Beyond.* Albany: Delmar.

Grace, C & Shores, E F. 1992. *The portfolio and its use. Developmentally appropriate assessment of young children.* Little Rock: Southern Association on Children Under Six.

Greurin, G R & Maier, A S. 1983. *Informal assessment in Education.* Palo Alto: Mayfield.

Gronlund, G. 1998. Portfolios as an Assessment Tool: Is Collection of Work Enough? In: *Young Children.* (May) (pp 4 – 10)

Gultig, J. 1997. *Understanding Outcomes-based Education. Knowledge, curriculum & assessment in South Africa.* Learning guide. South African Institute for Distance Education. Pretoria: Government Printers.

Gultig, J. 1998. *Understanding Outcomes-based Education. Teaching and assessment in South Africa.* Learning guide. South African Institute for Distance Education. Cape Town: Oxford University Press South Africa.

Hargreaves, L. 1995. Seeing clearly. Observation in the primary classroom. In: *Beginning teaching: Beginning learning in primary education.* Moyles, J.(Ed) (pp 41 – 63)

Hartman, A. 1995. Diagrammatic assessment of family relationships. In: *Families-in-Society.* (Vol 76 no 2) (pp 111 – 122)

Hendrick, J. 1994. (4th ed). *Total learning. Developmental curriculum for the young child.* New York: Merrill.

Hendrickson, J M. 1992. Assessing the student-instructional setting interface using an eco-behavioral observation system. In: *Preventing School Failure.* (Vol 36 no 3) (pp 26 – 31)

Hills, T W. 1993. Assessment in context – Teachers and chidlren at work. In: *Young Children.* (Vol 48, July) (pp 20 – 28)

Hunter-Carsch, M. 1995. Keeping track. Assessing, monitoring and recording children's progress and achievement. In: *Beginning teaching: beginning learning in primary education.* *Moyles*, J. (Ed.) Buckingham: Open University Press. (pp 195 – 216)

Hurst, V. 1994. Observing play in early childhood. In: *The excellence of play.* Moyles, J. (Ed) (pp 173 – 188)

Hurst, V & Lally, M. 1992. Assessment and the nursery curriculum. In: *Assessment in Early Childhood Education.* Blenkin G. M. & Kelly, A.V. (Eds) (pp 46 – 68). London: Paul Chapman.

Jervis, K & McDonald J. 1996. Standards: The philosophical monster in the classroom. In: *Phi Delta Kappan.* (Vol 77 no 8) (pp 563 – 569)

Johnson, S. 1996. What is alternative assessment? In: *Gifted Children Today Magazine.* (pp 12 – 13; 49 – 50)

Kagan, S L. 1992. Readiness past, present and future: Shaping the agenda. In: *Young Children.* (Vol 48, No 1) (pp 48 – 53)

Kelly, V. 1992. Concepts of assessment: An overview. In: *Assessment in Early Childhood Education.* Blenkin, G. M. & Kelly, A.V (Editors) (pp. 1 – 23). London: Paul Chapman.

Kemp, J. 1994. Failing the first year. Challenges facing South African education. In: *Information update.* (Vol 4 no 2) (pp 17 – 22)

Kingore, B. 1995. Introducing parents to portfolio assessment. A collaborative effort toward authentic assessment. In: *Gifted Children Today Magazine.* (pp 12 – 13)

Kronowitz, E L. 1999. *Your first year of teaching and beyond.* New York: Longman.

Lally, M & Hurst, V. 1992. Assessment in nursery education: A review of approaches. In: *Assessment in Early Childhood.* Blenkin, G V & Kelly, AV (Eds). London: Paul Chapman. (pp 69-92)

Landsberg, E. 1996. *Identification and informal assessment of learners with special educational needs in the regular classroom.* Paper read at the 21st National Conference of the South African Association for Learning and Educational Difficulties, 1 – 3 April 1999; University of South Africa. (Unpublished)

Lavadenz, M. 1996. Authentic assessment: Toward equitable assessment of language – minority students. In: *New Schools, New Communities.* (Vol 12 no 2) (pp 31 – 35)

Leavitt, R L & Eheart, B K. 1991 Assessment in early childhood programmes. In: *Young Children* (Vol 46 no 5) (pp 4 – 9)

Le Roux, S. 1992. Moet ek my kind laat toets vir skoolgereedheid? In: *Die Departement Sielkundige Opvoedkunde Simposium;* Van kleinkind tot skoolkind V. "Die beste vir my kind" (pp 63 – 80). Pretoria: Universiteit van Suid-Afrika.

Lubisi, C; Wedekind, V; Parker, B & Gultig, J. 1997. *Understanding Outcomes-based Education. Knowledge, Curriculum and Assessment in South Africa. A Reader. A pilot module for the SAIDE Study of Education. South Africa Institute for Distance Education and the National Department of Education.* Cape Town: CTB Book Printers.

Mattaini, M A. 1995. Visualizing practice with children and families. In: *Early Child Development and Care.* (Vol 106, Feb) (pp 59 – 74)

May, D C & Kundert, D.K. 1992. Kindergarten screening in the New York state: Tests, purposes, and recommendations. In: *Psychology in the Schools.* (Vol 29 no 1) (pp 35 – 41)

McAfee, O & Leong, V G. 2002. *Assessing and guiding young children's development and learning.* Boston: Allyn & Bacon.

Mindes, G Ireton, H & Mardell-Czudnowski, C. 1996. *Assessing young children.* Albany: Delmar.

Morrison, G S. 2001. (6th ed.) *Early childhood education today.* New Jersey: Merrill-Prentice Hall.

Pahad, M. 1997. *Curriculum 2005. Assessment and the National Qualifications Framework. A guide for teachers.* Johannesburg: Heinemann.

Penning, R J. 1986. *'n Didaktiese analise van die informele onderrigbenadering in die preprimêre skool.* Ongepubliseerde M Ed – verhandeling. Universiteit van Suid Afrika.

Penning, R J. 1987. Die bepaling van skoolgereedheid: waarneming of toetsing. In: *Kleuterklanke.* (Vol 12 no 1) (pp 7 – 9)

Pidgeon, S. 1992. Assessment at Key Stage 1: Teacher assessment through record-keeping. In: *Assessment in Early Childhood Education.* Blenkin, G.M. & Kelly, A.V. (Eds.) London: Paul Chapman. (pp. 122 – 143)

Pike, K & Salend, S J. 1995. Authentic Assessment Strategies. Alternatives to norm-referenced testing. In: *Teaching Exceptional Children.* (Vol 28 no 1) (pp 15 – 20)

Pope, C A. 1990. Indirect teaching and assessment: Are they mutually exclusive? In: *NASSP Bulletin.* (Vol 74 no 527) (pp 1 – 15)

Privett, N B. 1996. Without fear of failure. The attributes of an ungrated primary school. In: *The School Administrator.* (Vol 53 no1) (pp 6 – 11)

Puckett, M B & Black, J K. 1994. *Authentic assessment of the young child. Celebrating development and learning.* New York: Merrill.

Qualter, A. 1990. Assessing five year olds – Where do we start? In: *Education 3-13.* (Vol 18 no 3) (pp 20 – 26)

Republic of South Africa. 1998. Department of Education. *National Education Policy Act, 1996 (Act No. 27 of 1996) Assessment policy in the general education and training band, Grades R to 9 and ABET.* (Vol 402 No 19640) 23 December 1998. Pretoria: Government Printers.

Republic of South Africa. 2001. Government Gazette. *Department of Education. Education White Paper 5 on Early Childhood Education. Meeting the challenges of Early Childhood Development in South Africa.* Pretoria: Government Printers.

Smidt, S. 1998. *A Guide to early years practice*. London: Routeledge.

Sperling, D H. 1994. Assessment and reporting: A natural pair. In: *Educational Leadership*. (Vol 52 No 2) (pp 10 – 13)

Stewart, S C, Choate, J S & Poteet, J A. 1995. The revolution in assessment within and across educational settings. In: *Preventing School Failure*. (Vol 39 no 3) (pp 20 – 24)

St James-Roberts, I, Singh, G, Lynn, R & Jackson, S. 1994. Assessing emotional and behavioural problems in reception class children: factor structure convergence and prevalence using the PBCL. In: *British Journal of Educational Psychology*. (pp 105 – 118)

Thurman, S K & Widerstrom, A H. 1985. *Young children with special needs. A developmental and ecological approach.* Boston: Allyn and Bacon.

Tindal, G A & Marston, D B. 1990. *Classroom-based assessment. Evaluating instructional outcomes*. New York: Macmillan.

Valencia, S W. 1997. Authentic classroom assessment of early reading: Alternatives to standardized tests. In: *Preventing School Failure*. (Vol 41 no 2) (pp 63 – 70)

Van der Horst, H & McDonald, R. 1997. *OBE Outcomes-Based Education. A teacher's manual*. Pretoria: Kagiso.

Van Rooyen, A E & Engelbrecht, P. 1997. Die effektiwiteit van enkele skoolgereedheids-toetse vir die voorspelling van skolastiese prestasie by die skoolbeginner. In: *South African Journal of Education*. (Vol 17 no 1) (pp 7 – 10)

Van Staden, C J S. 1987. *Die Aard en Struktuur van Kleuterkuns: 'n Didaktiese Perspektief*. M Ed Verhandeling. Universiteit van Suid-Afrika: Ongepubliseerd.

Weade, G & Evertson, C M. 1991. On what can be learned by observing teaching. In: *Theory Into Practice*. (Vol 30 no 1) (pp 37 – 45)

Wiggins,G. 1993. Assessment: Authenticity, Context, and Validity. In: *Phi Delta Kappan* (Vol 75 no 3) (pp 200 – 214)

Wilkens, F. 1999. Implementering van Kurrikulum 2005. In: *Ongepubliseerde simposiumbundel* (pp 1 – 7) SAOU Referate. Skoolhoofdesimposium

Willer, B & Bredekamp, S. 1990. Redefining readiness: An essential requisite for educational reform. In: *Young Children*. (Vol 45, July) (pp 22 – 24)

Willis, S & Kissane, B. 1997(a). *Achieving outcome-based education: premises, principles and implications for curriculum and assessment*. Deakin West: Australian Curriculum Studies Association.

Willis, S & Kissane, B. 1997 (b) Systematic approaches to articulating and monitoring student outcomes: are they consistent with outcome-based education? In: *Studies of Educational Evaluation*. (Vol 23 no 1) (pp 5 – 30)

Wilmot, D. 1999. Portfolios as a tool for course work assessment within the context of pre-service teacher education. In: *South African Journal of Education*. (Vol 19 no 4) (pp 257 – 266)

Wortham, S C.1995. (2nd ed.) *Measurement and evaluation in early childhood education*. Englewood Cliffs: Merrill.

Worthen, B R. 1993. Critical issues that will determine the future of alternative assessment. In: *Phi Delta Kappan*. (Vol 74 no 6) (pp. 444 – 550)

Zessoules, R & Gardner, H.. 1991 Authentic assessment beyond the buzzword and into the classroom, in *Expanding student assessment*, edited by V Perrone. Alexandria: Association for Supervision and Curriculum Development (pp 63 – 65).

Chapter

8

Putting it all together: A practical example of integrating in context

Christie van Staden

OUTCOMES

After working through this chapter you should be able to:

■ choose Learning Outcomes for a lesson, and develop a suitable topic to place Learning Outcomes and activities in context

■ understand why and how to research a topic

■ implement the Learning Outcomes to develop activities for the three Learning Programmes

■ identify the Critical and Development Outcomes which should be covered in each of the three Learning Programmes

■ integrate activities with the eight Learning Areas

■ develop a concept web, a curriculum web and a Learning Unit.

> Please note that the following abbreviations are used in this chapter:
>
> LO: Learning Outcome
>
> AS: Assessment Standard
>
> HL: Home Language
>
> FAL: First Additional Language

Placing Learning Programmes in context

The first task of a reception year teacher is to choose suitable themes as vehicles for teaching through the year. These themes should be able to place the Learning Outcomes in a context that makes sense to reception year learners.

When choosing a theme, you should pay attention to the following:

■ Will it be of interest to young children?

■ Is it a part of their life experience?

■ Can it be explored in depth?

- Will it be able to place the three Learning Programmes in context?
- Will it provide a suitable vehicle for covering some of the Learning Outcomes for the three Learning Programmes?
- Can it be integrated with the eight learning areas?

Choosing a topic

The focus of this chapter is a practical example of using a theme, in this case, *Bugs in Wonderland*, to organise Learning Outcomes for the three Learning Programmes. This is an appropriate topic to use in the reception year because these creatures are part of all children's *life experience;* whether they live on a farm, in the city or in a township. You will probably have seen *children showing an interest* in these tiny creatures, noticing ants carrying crumbs to their nests, spiders spinning their webs, a ladybird sitting on flowers, butterflies flitting between plants, moths buzzing around a light and snails making trails on the ground.

Young learners should be given the opportunity to observe some of these small creatures in the natural world, and this can be done almost anywhere in the school playground, a garden, a field adjacent to the school, a wasteland at the edge of a pond, at the edge of a shoreline, or wherever is the most practical for your specific school.

Real examples are always preferable to pictures. If you have to rely on pictures, ensure that the proportions are correct, e.g. a fly should not be the same size as a crab.

It is both difficult and impractical for children to make detailed studies of large animals in their own environments (unless they are at a farm school), so a close look at 'mini-beasts' (insects) may be more practical.

Researching the topic

It is important that educators find out as much as possible about the topic themselves, to provide a rich background against which to plan a Learning Programme for a reception year class. Background information on your theme is also helpful when planning how to integrate and realise the Learning Outcomes of the different Learning Areas.

The following are suggestions for doing your research:

1. **Visit the library**

   Visit your local library and ask the librarian to assist you to find the following for your theme:

   - information
   - stories
   - rhymes, poems and songs
   - Science activities
   - other sources available in print.

2. **Check the World Wide Web**

   If you or somebody you know has access to the Internet, do a search on the Web. This could also be done at your library, if the facilities are available.

3. Start a portfolio

Start a portfolio of all your different topics. Keep the following in your portfolio:

- a summary of the main facts and concepts you have found on your topic

- concept and curriculum webs on your topics (more about this later in the chapter)

- a Unit on each theme with the Learning Outcomes covered in the different Learning Areas

- a list of the Critical Outcomes you have addressed in each theme

- a list of the skills learners will acquire by working through the theme

- a list of the values and attitudes that are addressed

- activities for the Learning Outcomes that you plan to write out in more detail

- a collection of stories, rhymes, poems, riddles, games, puzzles and pictures

- any experiments that you find which relate to this theme.

Every time you repeat your topic, add more information, activities, etc to your portfolio. See Appendix 1 (p.299) for examples of research for the theme *Bugs in Wonderland*.

Planning and developing the three Learning Programmes

Choose the Learning Outcomes to be covered in the three Learning Programmes

Compare the Learning Outcomes in the curriculum web and Llearning Units.

Indicate which Critical and Developmental Outcomes will be realised

The Critical and Developmental Outcomes are prescribed from the Constitution (see The South African Qualifications Act, 1995) and describe what kind of citizen the Constitution envisages. You should indicate clearly which Critical and Developmental Outcomes you plan to focus on when planning Programmes. You may emphasise different Critical and Developmental Outcomes for each Programme. The following table indicates the different emphases of the different outcomes for the topic *Bugs in Wonderland*.

Critical and Developmental Outcomes for the theme: *Bugs in Wonderland*

Critical Outcomes envisage learners who will be able to:	Emphases
■ identify and solve problems and make decisions using critical and creative thinking	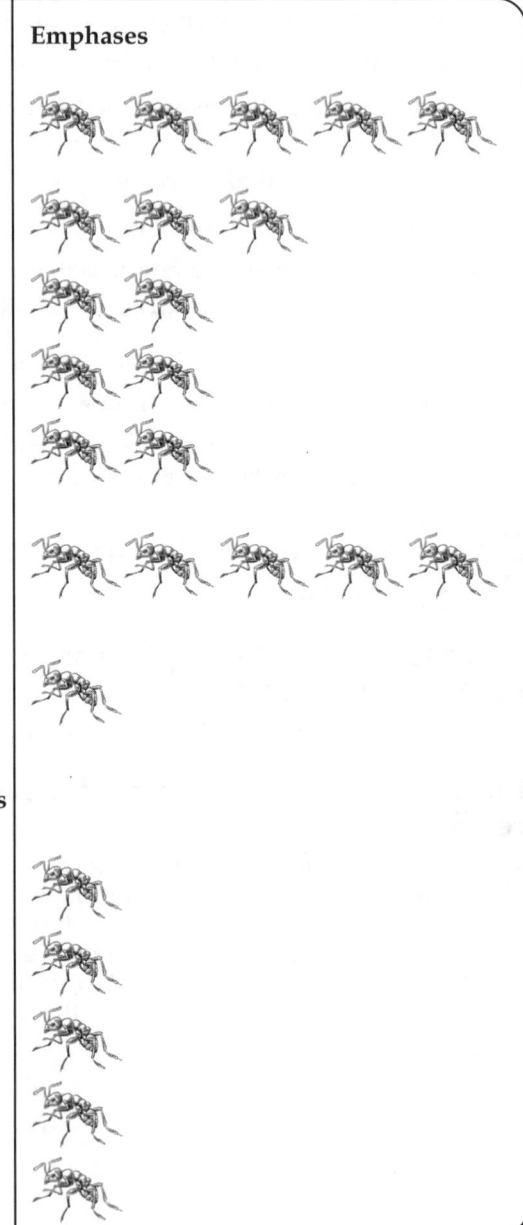
■ work effectively with each other as a team or group	
■ organise and manage themselves and their activities responsibly and effectively	
■ collect, analyse, organise and critically evaluate information	
■ communicate effectively using visual, symbolic, and/or language skills in various modes	
■ use Science and Technology effectively and critically showing responsibility towards the environment and the health of others	
■ demonstrate an understanding of the world as a set of related systems by recognising that problem-solving contexts do not exist in isolation.	
Developmental Outcomes envisage learners who will be able to:	
■ reflect on and explore a variety of strategies to learn more effectively	
■ participate as responsible citizens in the life of local communities	
■ be culturally and aesthetically sensitive across a range of social contexts	
■ explore education and career opportunities	
■ develop entrepreneurial opportunities.	

Integrating the eight Learning Areas into the three Learning Programmes by means of a Curriculum Web

The integration of subject matter helps children perceive learning as a whole. Instead of developing and working with separate subject matter and skills, the reception year teacher should present various ideas, issues and skills in an integrated way (Sunal, Powell, McClelland, Rule and Smith 2000).

1. Decide which Learning Outcomes from the eight Learning Areas will be covered in each of the three Learning Programmes.

2. Find activities that will act as vehicles for helping learners achieve the Learning Outcomes you have chosen. Then arrange the Learning Outcomes for the different Learning Areas with the accompanying activities into a web, so that you can see at a glance what you have planned and whether all the Learning Outcomes have been covered.

3. Bear in mind that the National Curriculum Statements prescribe the amount of time each Learning Programme should be given, out of the total amount of time you have with the learners: Literacy (40%); Numeracy (35%); Life Skills (25%).

Example of a Curriculum Web
Literacy

Listening LO 1

- Listening to stories

- Names of mini-creatures: ant, bee, fly, wasp, flea, moth, beetle, spider, cricket, aphid, grasshopper, ladybird, butterfly, dragonfly.

Thinking and reasoning LO5

- Learn the meaning of the words for changes in life cycles: pupa, cocoon, chrysalis, maggot, grub, etc.

- Learn similes/proverbs:

    - as joyful as a fly

    - as lively as a cricket

    - as faint as the hum of distant bees

    - as persistent as a mosquito

    - as elastic as a caterpillar

    - as angry as a wasp

    - to make a bee-line

    - as busy as a bee

    - to have a bee in your bonnet

    - as jumpy as a grasshopper

Reading and viewing (English Home Language LO 3)

■ Picture of *Bugs in Wonderland* displayed at interest table.

Reading and listening (First Additional Language LO 3):

■ Clap and classify words according to syllables

■ Label objects on interest table

■ Sequence life cycle pictures and match word to cycle

■ Teacher reads books and tells stories, e.g.:

The Very Hungry Caterpillar (E Carle)

'n Ruspe Kan Nie Vlieg Nie

Aesop's Fables 'The ant and the dove'; 'The ant and the grasshopper'

The Bad-Tempered Ladybird (Eric Carle)

The Snail and the Whale (J Donaldson and A Scheffler)

Mr McGee and the Biting Flea (P Allen)

■ Label diagrams of mini-creatures with word cards.

■ Draw and construct own storybooks about mini-creatures. Teachers write the labels and children read back.

Writing LO 4:

■ Teacher writes down what the learners know in their own words in a concept web at the beginning of the discussion about the topic, and again at the discussion at the conclusion of the Learning Programme.

Speaking LO 2:

■ Conversation and discussion around the large background picture at the interest table.

■ Learning and reciting rhymes.

Numeracy

Count LO 1:

■ Count parts of insects, number of legs, body parts, feelers, etc.

■ The Snail Game (Counting on and counting back)

■ Insect sums: If you have two ants how many legs would they have?

■ Link Language Learning Area with Mathematics Learning Area with poem *Feet* (see below) where the poem is used to demonstrate mathematical concepts.

Classify LO 2:

■ Categorise and classify a selection of mini-creatures into those who sting, fly, crawl, help in the garden.

Order/seriate LO 2:

■ Seriate mini-creatures according to sizes, shapes or patterns

Measure LO 4:

▓ Measure the time it takes an ant to carry a breadcrumb a certain distance.

Data handling LO 5:

▓ Simple graph

Shapes LO 3:

▓ Complete puzzles with mini-creatures cut into tangram shapes.

▓ Make a game with different insect body parts. Four children play the game. Each child gets a certain insect to complete. Different body parts have got a different value on a dice (head 5; thorax 4; abdomen 3; wing 2; leg 1).

Arts and Culture LO 1

Dance:

▓ How bees dance to relay messages.

Drama:

▓ Dramatise an insect story.

Visual Arts:

▓ Make a bookmark from the silk created by silkworms' spinning

▓ Make your own insect with waste products (i.e. recycling used products)

▓ Butterfly blot painting

Music:

▓ Learn a song about insects: *Spider in my bath*

▓ Choose musical instruments to represent insect sounds and create a music story with insect characters

▓ Moving to *'Boogie-woogie bugs'* by Don Cooper

Life Orientation:

Health promotion LO 1:

▓ Grouping insects into those we like and dislike and why

▓ Cleanliness. Disease spread by insects (mosquitoes – malaria)

▓ Talk by SPCA official on fleas, and why hands need to be washed after handling pets

Physical Development and Movement LO 4:

▓ Moving like different insects

Economic and Management Sciences LO 1:

▓ Bee-keeping

▓ Products that can be made from bee-keeping and selling those products

▓ Silk. Where it comes from and what can be done with it.

▓ Make your own insect with waste products

Human and Social Sciences:

History LO 1:

- Usefulness of insects for humans and in history (e.g. fossils)

Natural Sciences LO 1:

- Life cycle of a butterfly/silkworm
- Insects in the food chain
- Insect habitats
- An outing to look for insects
- Keeping an ant farm
- Keeping earthworms to see how they mix soil

Technology LO 1:

- Plan and design an insect home to observe and keep insects safely
- Plan and design a garden that attracts insects

Example of a Concept Web

Brainstorm which main ideas (concepts) you could develop from your theme in order to cover the Learning Outcomes you have chosen. The following is an example of a concept web for the theme *Bugs in Wonderland*.

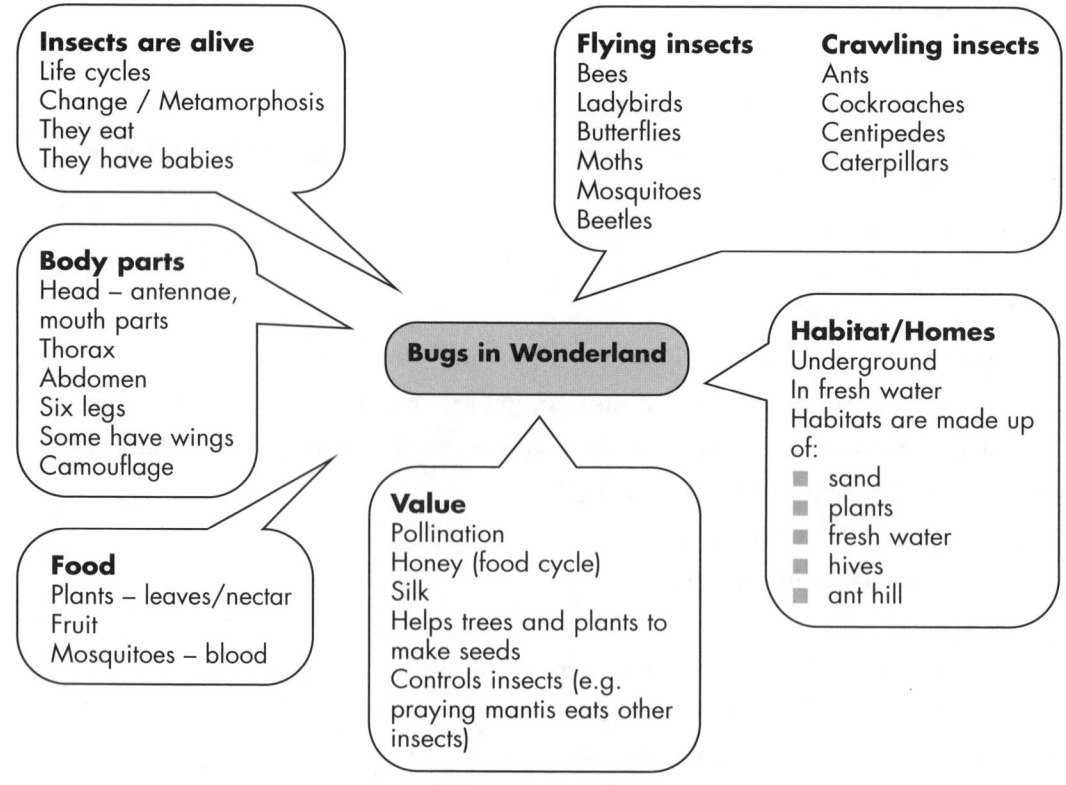

Activities to cover the three Learning Programmes (Literacy, Numeracy and Life Skills) and eight Learning Areas

Learning programme: Literacy

Language use based on viewing a picture (Language LO 3)
LO 1: LISTENING

a) AS 4 (HL): Learners will develop phonic awareness and distinguish between different sounds.

b) AS 2 (FAL): Learners will be able to understand simple oral instructions by responding physically.]

ACTIVITY 1

Languages LO 3: The learner will be able to view for information and enjoyment.

Assessment Standard: We know this when the learners:

■ Use visual cues to make meaning.

Instruction: Look carefully at the picture and try to identify common objects and experiences.

Resource: Large picture of *Bugs in Wonderland*.

Open and closed questions:

What do you see in the picture?

What do they look like?

What colours are they?

How are they the same/different?

What are they doing?

What do you think they will be doing next?

Integration: Arts and Culture LO 1:
Draw your own garden with bugs with felt pens and colour in with crayons.

Figure 8.1 Bugs in Wonderland

ACTIVITY 2

Figure 8.2 The interest table

Game: 'I spy with my little eye'

Start the game by saying: 'I spy with my little eye something starting with b'. The children look at the picture displayed at the interest table where different mini-creatures are illustrated, and try to find a bug whose name starts with b, e.g., bee or butterfly. They point to the mini-creature on the picture or pick it up if it is on the interest table. The game can be continued in two ways depending on the abilities of learners. If the children are less able, the teacher makes the statement every time. e.g. 'I spy with my little eye something starting with g' and the children try to identify the correct mini-creature. If the children are more able, the teacher can start the game, and then encourage the child who gave the correct answer to make the next statement themselves. Whoever gives the correct answer gets a turn to make a statement.

ACTIVITY 3
LO 2 Listening

AS 1 (HL): Learners will be able to listen with enjoyment to oral texts (simple stories) and show an understanding by drawing a picture of the story.

AS 1 (FAL): Learners will be able to understand short, simple, dramatised stories and draw a picture of the story.

Learners first listen to a story, for example, *Betty Butterfly: FBI (Eye)* (see Appendix 2.). Thereafter, they draw a picture of the story. Note that there are two versions of the story. One has been simplified and should be used for FAL learners.

ACTIVITY 4
LO 2: SPEAKING

AS 3 (HL): Learners will be able to sing and recite simple songs and rhymes

AS 2 (FAL): Learners will be able to memorise and perform songs and action rhymes with the right intonation, rhythm and pronunciation.

Learners memorise a simple song, e.g. *Garden Visitors' Song* (see Appendix 3) and/or one of the other poems or rhymes included with the right intonation, rhythm and pronunciation.

ACTIVITY 5
LO 2: SPEAKING

AS 8 (HL): Learners will be able to retell a story e.g. *Betty Butterfly* (see Appendix 2).

LO 1: LISTENING

AS 2 (HL): Learners demonstrate appropriate listening behaviour by listening without interrupting, showing respect for the speaker and taking turns to speak.

Learners listen to the story and thereafter retell the story. To give more learners an opportunity to participate and enhance overall level of concentration amongst learners, a 'chain-story' can be told. The teacher starts the story and each learner gets an opportunity to add a part to the story. Throughout the activity, learners demonstrate appropriate listening behaviour by listening without interrupting, showing respect for the learner who is telling his or her part and taking turns to speak.

ACTIVITY 6

LO 3: Reading and viewing

AS 1a (HL): Learners will be able to use visual cues to make meaning by looking carefully at the picture to recognise common objects and experiences.

LO 1 (HL): LISTENING

AS 4b: Learners will able to distinguish between different sounds, specially at the beginning and end of words.

Learners look at the picture of 'Bugs in Wonderland' where the mini-creatures are living in their garden. They identify the different mini-creatures (AS 1a). This activity can be linked with the game 'I spy with my little eye' as explained earlier on (AS 4b).

ACTIVITY 7

LO 3: Reading and Viewing

AS 4 (FAL): Learners will be able to learn rhymes and songs which develop phonic awareness.

Learners learn the action rhyme *Beetles,* as it contains repetitive words. Alternatively, they learn the Garden Visitors' Song as it also contains repetitive words (see Appendix 4).

ACTIVITY 8

LO 4: WRITING

AS 1i (HL): Learners show a beginning awareness of directionality.

AS 1l (HL): Learners manipulate writing tools such as crayons and pencils.

Learners complete pre-writing activities such as the following:

Creepy crawlies

Beetle (straight line)

Earthworm (wavy line)

Butterfly (zigzag line)

ACTIVITY 9
LO 5: THINKING AND REASONING

AS 2c (HL): Learners will be able to classify things.

AS 1 (FAL): Learners will be able to identify similarities.

Give learners pictures of mini-creatures/bugs to classify. For example, instruct learners that all the pictures of mini-creatures that can fly could be put in the left-hand column of a graph while the pictures of those that cannot fly are placed in the right-hand column. See the example below. Learners could also classify mini-creatures can also be classified according to size or colour.

Can fly	Cannot fly

ACTIVITY 10

AS 1 (FAL): Learners are able to draw a picture on which teacher writes labels.

Each learner draws a mini-creature of their choice, using crayons. Thereafter, they tell you what they have drawn and you label the drawing. The pictures are then pasted on a large sheet to create a picture or wall frieze.

ACTIVITY 11
LO 6: LANGUAGE STRUCTURE AND USE

AS 3 (HL): Learners will be able to communicate ideas using descriptions and action words.

Learners are asked to describe the mini-creatures in the pictures pasted on the large sheet (from the previous activity) and identify the actions being performed in the picture. For example, the brown bee and the yellow butterfly are flying. The fat, soft earthworm is sliding along the ground. The red, round lady bird is eating aphids. The snail is making a slimy trail on the stone. Afterwards, each learner should get a turn to imitate an action that has been described, and the rest of the class must say what he or she is doing. For example, 'You are sliding like the fat, soft earthworm.'

ACTIVITY 12
LO 6: LANGUAGE STRUCTURE AND USE

AS 1 (FAL): Learners show some understanding of question forms in oral texts.

The teacher asks simple questions based on the picture, e.g.

'What is this?'

'How many ladybirds can you see?'

'What is the frog doing?'

'Can the worm fly?'

'Which one is the biggest: the snail or the ant?'

ACTIVITY 13
LO 6: LANGUAGE STRUCTURE AND USE

AS 4 (FAL): Learners show some understanding of modal verbs in oral texts.

The teacher gives an instruction to the class, the instruction being something that either the mini-creature can or cannot do. If the mini-creature can perform the action, the learners imitate the action. If not, they stand still. For example, when the teacher says, 'Fly like a butterfly', the learners should imitate the action. When the teacher says, for example, 'Swim like a worm', the learners should stand still.

Learning Programme: Mathematics

ACTIVITY 1
LO 1: NUMBERS, OPERATIONS AND RELATIONSHIPS

AS 1: Learners will be able to count ten objects reliably.

The teacher prepares large pictures of mini-creatures or three-dimensional mini-creatures. Learners count:

- their legs
- how many are green / black
- how many can fly/cannot fly.

ACTIVITY 2

The teacher provides a Numeracy game where learners count on and count back.

The snail game:

Select a token and start at the arrow.

Roll the dice in turn and move the token forward according to the number shown on the dice. If you land on a 'sun' move backwards the number on the dice. If you land on clouds move forward the number on the dice. Be the first to land in the middle where there is a lettuce for the snail to eat.

ACTIVITY 3

LO 1: NUMBERS, OPERATIONS AND RELATIONSHIPS

AS 3: Learners will be able to match number names and symbols for the numbers 1–10.

AS 4: Learners will be able to compare objects using the words *more, less* and *equal.*

Learners are given a worksheet containing mini-creatures. They count specific features of the mini-creature, for example, the spots on the ladybird, the legs of the spider, the segments of the centipede, etc. Next to the mini-creature, they write the relevant numeral.

ACTIVITY 4

The teacher compiles a simple graph on a worksheet showing different mini-creatures that can be seen in the picture. Learners draw the same amount of mini-creatures under the relevant heading. They count the number of each of the mini-creatures and write down the number as well as the number name. Thereafter, the teacher asks questions that include words such as *more, less, fewer* and *equal.* For example: *Are there more ants than snails? Which rows are the same (equal)? Are there fewer spiders than moths? Which other row is equal to this row? If not, how many must we add or take away to make them equal.*

Bees	Ants	Snails	Spiders	Moths
5 five	2 two	4 four	2 two	8 eight

ACTIVITY 5
LO 1: NUMBERS, OPERATIONS AND RELATIONSHIPS

AS 7b: Learners will be able to double numbers.

Teach the concept of doubling by:

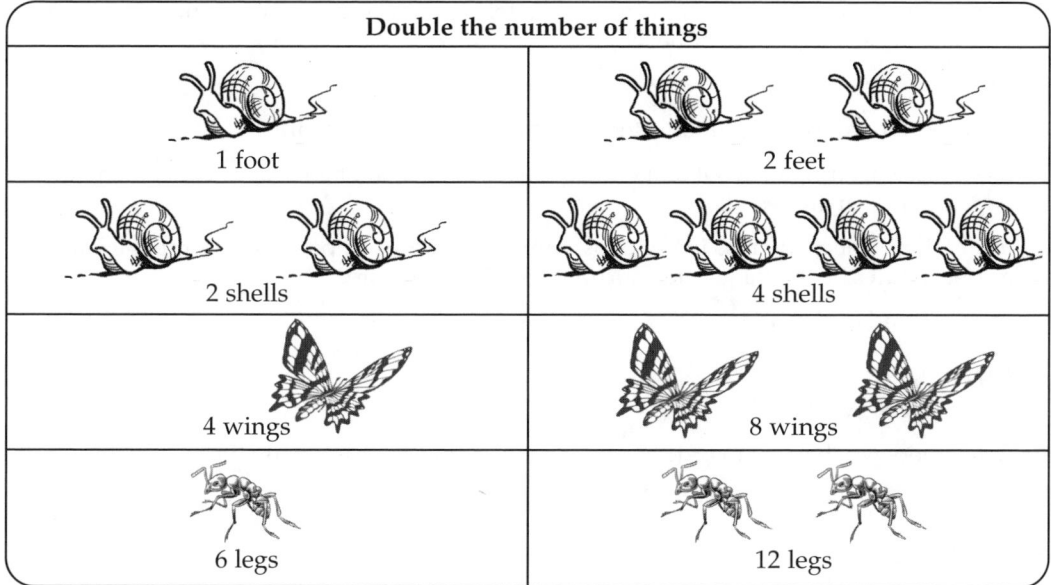

Double the number of things	
1 foot	2 feet
2 shells	4 shells
4 wings	8 wings
6 legs	12 legs

ACTIVITY 6
LO 2: PATTERNS, FUNCTIONS AND ALGEBRA

AS 1: Learners will be able to copy and extend physical objects using colours and shapes

Three-dimensional:

Learners extend the given pattern of toy mini-creatures on the interest table, e.g. ant, bee, moth, centipede.

Two-dimensional:

Learners colour in a given pattern on a worksheet containing mini-creatures, e.g. red ant, black ant, red ant, black ant or colour in the spaces on the butterfly's wings red, blue, yellow, purple, red, blue, yellow, purple, etc.

ACTIVITY 7
LO 3: SPACE AND SHAPE (GEOMETRY)

AS 3: Learners will be able to build a three-dimensional object using concrete materials.

Learners construct a mini-creature using waste materials, e.g.

- they can make spiders using empty egg-boxes, pipe-cleaners (or thin wire covered with wool);
- they can make butterfly kites using scrap paper, pieces of wood and string or wool
- they can make ants out of papier-mâché.

Each learner creates an imaginary mini-creature using waste material. The learner names it and the teacher labels it. All the mini-creatures are put on display.

ACTIVITY 8
LO 4: MEASUREMENT

AS 4c: Learners will be able to work concretely comparing and ordering objects using appropriate vocabulary to describe length.

Learners can:

■ use a cardboard earthworm or caterpillar as an arbitrary measure;

■ use a piece of string or wool to measure the winding trail of a mini-creature, then glue on paper and compare results;

■ use various objects such as paper clips, counters, buttons or pegs to measure the length of mini-creatures' legs/wings, etc., portrayed on large picture.

■ compare and order mini-creatures according to length.

ACTIVITY 9
LO 4: MEASUREMENT

AS 2: Learners will be able to order recurring events in their own daily life.

Learners observe the life-cycle of silkworms.

ACTIVITY 10
LO 5: DATA HANDLING

AS 3: Learners will be able to draw a picture as a record of collected objects.

AS 4: Learners will be able to answer questions based on the picture.

Learners go on a nature walk in the school garden. They make a 'rough sketch' of the mini-creature that they see. Back in class, they hand in their pictures. The teacher compiles a graph displaying the number of mini-creatures seen by the learners. Then the teacher asks questions such as:

■ Which mini-creature was seen by the most children?

■ Which mini-creatures were seen by the same number of children?

ACTIVITY 11
The following activity can be used to link Literacy outcomes with Mathematical outcomes. This is demonstrated in the following poem.

FEET
Feet of snails
Are only one.
Birds grow two
to hop and run.
Dogs and cats
and cows grow four.
Ants and beetles
add two more.

> Spiders run around
> on eight,
> which may seem
> a lot, but wait –
> centipedes
> have more than thirty
> feet to wash
> when they get dirty.

(From *Cricket in a Thicket* by A Fisher)

Numeracy concepts that can be covered by using this poem

Provide pictures of insects on cards so that learners can work with insects in a concrete way.

a) Counting (Math LO1)

■ Four snails have four feet – counting on by one.

■ Two butterflies have eight wings – counting on by four.

■ Two insects have 12 legs – counting on by six.

b) Matching (Math LO 5); (Natural Sciences LO 2)

Prepare an insect domino game for learners, where the number of insects match the number in the opposite block.

c) Classifying (Math LO 4 and 5)

Instruct learners to classify bugs according to number of feet they have, their colours, their value, whether they fly or crawl.

d) Ordering according to size from smallest to largest (Math LO 2)

e) Patterning (Math LO 2)

Carry on with the pattern.

■ What bug has been left out of the pattern?

■ Learners create their own patterns

f) Measuring (Math LO 4)

How long does it take a snail to move from one point to another (see Problem on p.283).

g) Data handling (Math LO5)

Create a picture graph on which learners can record, by means of bottletops, which creature in the poem learners would most like to be. Learners can personalise the bottletops by drawing faces on them.

Snail	Spider	Bee	Butterfly	Ant
☺	☺	☺	☺	☺
☺	☺	☺	☺	☺
☺	☺	☺	☺	☺
☺	☺	☺	☺	
☺	☺		☺	
☺	☺		☺	
☺				
7	6	4	6	3

Learning Programme: Natural Sciences

Knowledge Strand: *Life and Living*

LO1 Scientific Investigations: *The learner will be able to act confidently on curiosity about natural phenomena, and to investigate relationships and solve problems in scientific, technological and environmental contexts.*

Science concepts young learners could grasp:

a) Concept: Bugs eat, grow and change

- Bugs grow to a definite size and shape according to their species. For example, an ant will never grow as large as a locust, and a spider will never have six legs like an insect.

- Bugs need food for growth, energy and replacement of tissue. Different bugs eat different kinds of food.

b) Concept: Bugs are living creatures because they eat

As introduction, ask your learners, 'Did you have a nice bowl of acorns and a plateful of grass and a ladybug for breakfast today? Why not? What did you have?' Whether in urban, suburban, small town or urban settings there are rich opportunities to observe what bugs eat – see the following activity.

ACTIVITY 1: An ant picnic

Natural Sciences LO 1; Language LO 5

Plan:

■ Ants are usually found in all settings. In order to discover which foods ants prefer, attract them to an area by taking a spoonful of honey or jam, a spoonful of tuna and a piece of fruit and arranging the different foods on the ground, 10 cm apart. Put the honey on a leaf and the fruit and tuna directly on the ground.

Do:

Ask learners the following questions to guide the scientific investigation:

Learners making predictions:

■ Which food do you think ants will go to first?

■ Do you think ants will go to their favourite food, or to the food closest to them?

Observing/comparing:

■ Which food do the ants choose to eat?

■ Do they eat the food where they find it, or do they move it first?

Recording observations:

■ Ask learners to tell you what they saw. Write down their observances in simple phrases and sentences, in the form of a mind map.

■ Get learners to draw what they saw.

■ Make a simple pictograph recording results and classifying the foods.

Review: Interpreting observations/making inferences

■ Which food did the ants like the most? Which food did the ants like the least?

■ Did all the ants choose the same food?

■ Did the ants carry the food to where they live, or did they eat it where they found it?

■ Did some ants leave the area without eating? Why do you think they did this? (Sometimes ants act like messengers. When they find food, they go back to their nest and tell the others; then everybody comes to share the food.)

■ How do you think the ants knew where to find their food? Can they hear the food; see the food; or smell the food?

Explain to learners that as the ant runs to tell about the picnic, it leaves a trail for the others to follow.

ACTIVITY 2: A scent trail

Children can follow a scent made by the teacher as the ants would do: Makea a scent trail outside for the children to follow. Use several distinctive scents such as peppermint, cinnamon or lemon to create a trail on the playground. Children choose one of the scents each and follow that trail.

(c) Concept: Bugs are alive because they grow and change

Young children can be introduced to the fact that growth and change are characteristic of living things and that, in some cases, the changes may be so remarkable that the 'baby' bears little resemblance to the 'adult' (e.g. tadpole to frog; caterpillar to moth).

Most children in South Africa are fascinated by the life cycle of silkworms. Teachers may make use of this opportunity to illustrate the concept of change using the silkworm.

(d) Concept: Bugs need shelters (homes/habitats)

All people live in some type of shelter. Homes are shelters that people live in to protect them from the weather. A family group usually shares the same house. There are many types of homes.

Ask the children what kind of shelter they live in. Also ask them if they think bugs need homes.

ACTIVITY 3

Children could go on a hunt in the garden or playground to find bug homes.

ACTIVITY 4: Experiments:

Do some experiments (Natural Sciences LO1) to find out more about snails and answer some of the questions children àsk about them.

Problem 1 – Do snails like dark places or light places?

(Natural Sciences LO 1; Language LO 5)

Plan:

You will need:

A cardboard box with a small door cut out at one end

Some snails

Do:

Turn the box upside down, either in the garden or playground. Place the snails at the door created in the box. Stay and watch until the snails move.

Figure 8.3 Do snails like dark or light places?

Review: What did you find out?

Did most of the snails stay in the dark or go out into the light?

Problem 2 – How do snails move?

(Natural Sciences LO 1; Language LO 5)

Plan:

You will need:

A large glass bowl or an empty fish tank

Some snails

Do:

Put snails at the bottom of the bowl in a cool, shady place. Wait until the snails begin to move. Look through the glass to see how the snails manage to move without legs.

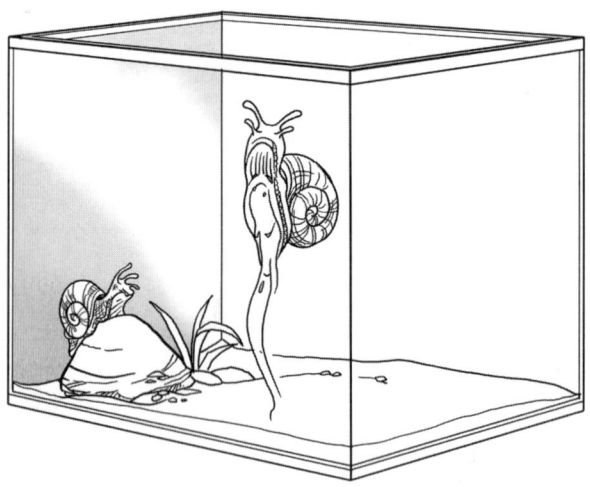

Figure 8.4 How do snails move?

Review: What did you see?

Problem 3 – Do snails like damp places or dry places?

(Natural Sciences LO 1; Language LO 5)

Plan:

You will need:

A cardboard box

Some damp newspaper

Some dry newspaper

Some snails

Do:

Place the dry newspaper at one end of the box. Place the damp newspaper at the other end.

Place the snails in the middle.

Review:

To which end do most snails move?

ACTVITY 5

Integrating Literacy with Natural Sciences using process skills

(Language LO 5 and Natural Sciences LO 1)

The following poem can be used to link Literacy outcomes with Natural Science outcomes. List the Science Process Skills and try to apply them to the poem. This is demonstrated for you below.

THE SILKWORM
I saw a tiny silkworm
It had a funny name
My teacher called it larva
But it wriggled all the same.

One day it changed from hairy to smooth
From black to very white.
Its body was much larger too
And it did it overnight.

It changed just three more times
And always in between
It ate and ate and ATE
Mulberry leaves so green.

One day it stopped and started to spin
A shiny silken thread
Around and round in figure eight
It moved its little head.
It made a cocoon snowy white,
Its neighbours made theirs yellow and bright,
And the inside where none could see,
A pupa formed my teacher told me.

One day it pushed from its cocoon
How different it looked now.
It fluttered about on weak little wings –
A silkworm moth. But how?

It laid so many golden eggs
Near its empty white cocoon.
I wondered when the larva would hatch,
Would it be very soon?

Eggs to larva to pupa to adult
Is a strange way
To change from being born
Into a grown up moth –
I'd say!
(Author unknown)

Science Process Skills:

1. Observing

   Observe real worms and pictures of worms, moths and butterflies, notice their colours and other characteristics.

2. Comparing

   Compare worms, butterflies and moths – point out similarities and differences. Look at external characteristics, including their appearance and diet.

3. Classifying

   Classify the bugs according to their appearance and diet.

4. Experimenting

   Find out what leaves silkworms prefer to eat. Provide the silkworms with edible leaves (water cress, beetroot leaves, mulberry leaves).

5. Predicting

   Get learners to predict which leaves silkworms will eat.

6. Inference

   After observing silkworms feeding, get learners to infer which leaves silkworms prefer to eat.

7. Measuring

   Use a calender to measure the number of days it takes for silkworms to move through the different stages in their development cycle.

8. Communication

   ■ Learners reflect on what they observed as they worked through the Science Process Skills.

   ■ Learners draw what they understand about the life cycle of the silkworm.

   ■ Make a concept web with the learners at the beginning of the process to see what they know about silk worms. Do another web with them after you have worked through the processes above.

Learning Area: Technology

What is a Learning Unit?

ACTIVITY 1
Technology LO1

Plan, make and test an insect home where insects can be safe. Keep this insect home in your classroom for a day, or longer. Provide learners with waste materials from which containers can be devised.

A sample Learning Unit

The following is an example of a Learning Unit based on the theme *Bugs in Wonderland.*

A Learning Unit should contain the following:

- A day-to-day arrangement of facilitation and learning for a period of time.
- Activities to help learners achieve predetermined Learning Outcomes and Assessment Standards
- Clear integration with other Learning Areas and Learning Programmes.
- Assessment strategies
- A list of the skills, knowledge, values and attitudes (SKVA's) to be covered in the unit
- An indication of how the specific needs of learners will be addressed.

Reception year teachers should develop Learning Units for all three of the Learning Programmes, i.e. Literacy, Numeracy and Life Skills.

Example of a Literacy Learning Unit for Grade R

Context: *Bugs in Wonderland* (Unit organiser)

Duration: 10 to 15 days

Learning Outcome	Assessment Standard	Skills, Knowledge, Values and Attitudes	Learning Activities	Resources	Assessment
Languages: LO 1 Listening The learner will be able to listen for information and enjoyment and respond appropriately and critically in a wide range of situations.	**We know this when the learner:** 1. Listens attentively to questions and announcements and responds appropriately. 2. Demonstrates appropriate listening behaviour by listening without interrupting, showing respect to the speaker. 3. Listens with enjoyment to oral texts, and shows understanding: a) acts out parts of the story, song or rhyme; b) joins in choruses at the appropriate time; c) draws a picture of the story, song or rhyme; d) notes details and gives the main idea of an oral text; e) puts pictures in the right sequence. 4. Develops phonic awareness: a) recognises that words are made up of sounds; b) distinguishes between different sounds, at the beginning and end of words;	**Skills:** Communication Gains listening skills as stated in LO 1. **Knowledge:** Knows the sequence of what happens in stories – a story has a beginning, middle and end. **Values:** Picks up values illustrated in stories – e.g. 'sharing' in *The Bad-tempered Ladybird*. **Attitude:** Consideration for small creatures in the environment.	**AS 1 and 2** Listens to stories told and read by educator; as well as questions asked about stories. Puts pictures of stories in the right sequence (flash cards). **AS 1, 2 and 3** Listens to rhymes *(Butterfly)*: a) Acts out parts of the rhyme 4 a) and b) Finds beginning and ending sounds of words – words starting and then ending with **s**; starting with **h**; c) claps syllables: (one) wings, cups, day, flies (two) ti-ny, gol-den, sum-mer, hap-py, soft-ly (three) but-ter-fly	**AS 1 and 2** *The Very Hungry Caterpillar* (Eric Carle) **Wall hanging with concrete objects made of felt** *'n Ruspe kan nie vlieg nie* **Stories to read from Aesop's Fables:** *The ant and the dove'; 'The ant and the grasshopper'* **Book to read and show pictures** *The Bad-Tempered Ladybird* (Eric Carle) **Flash cards** *The Snail and the Whale* (J Donaldson and A Scheffler) **Book** *Mr McGee and the Biting Flea* (P Allen)	**Form:** Rhymes, stories. **Method:** Observation. **Tools:** Observation sheet, Check lists, Assessment grid. **Purpose:** Baseline, Diagnostic.

Learning Outcome	Assessment Standard	Skills, Knowledge, Values and Attitudes	Learning Activities	Resources	Assessment
	c) segments oral sentences into individual words of one syllable first; d) segments spoken multi-syllabic words into syllables; using clapping or drumbeats; e) recognises some rhyming words in rhymes and songs.		d) recognises rhyming words – wings, swings; day, away.	**Rhyme** The Butterfly I know a lovely butterfly With tiny golden wings He plays among the summer flowers And up and down he swings. He dances on the honey cups So happy all the day And then he spreads his tiny wings And softly flies away. (See more examples of rhymes in the appendices)	
LO 2 Speaking The learner will be able to communicate confidently and effectively in spoken language in a wide range of situations.	**We know this when the learner:** 1. Talks about personal experiences and news. 2. Sings and recites simple songs and rhymes. 3. Recounts own personal experiences. 4. Tells own stories and retells stories of others in own words.	**Skills:** Communication Recalling and retelling stories they have listened to. **Knowledge:** Recites known rhymes. **Values:** Realises the value of the spoken word to communicate.	• Learners talk about the insects they found and brought to the interest table. • Learners sing songs and recite rhymes they have learnt about bugs (see Appendix 2).	Learners catch insects with their parents and bring them to school in containers. Keep these for one day on the interest table, and release them at the end of the day.	**Form:** Rhymes, stories, drawing. **Method:** Observation. **Tools:** Observation sheet, Checklists, Assessment grid.

Learning Outcome	Assessment Standard	Skills, Knowledge, Values and Attitudes	Learning Activities	Resources	Assessment
	5. Participates confidently and fluently in a group. 6. Shows sensitivity when speaking with others. 7. Role-plays different kinds and manners of speech.	**Attitudes:** Respects the person speaking – takes turns to speak.			**Purpose:** Baseline, Diagnostic.
LO 3 Reading and Viewing The learner will be able to read and view for information and enjoyment and respond critically to the aesthetic, cultural and emotional values in texts.	**We know this when the learner:** 1. Uses visual cues to make meaning: a) looks carefully at pictures and photographs to recognise common objects and experiences; b) identifies a picture or figure from a background; c) makes sense of picture stories; d) uses illustrations to understand simple captions in story books; 2. Role-plays reading: a) holds book the right way up, turns pages, looks at words and pictures and understands relationships between them, uses pictures to construct ideas;	**Skills:** Finds out about books by looking at their covers. Gains knowledge and insight by 'reading' pictures. **Knowledge:** Knows that a picture provides information and that you can find out about what a book contains by looking at its cover. **Values:** We should care about and handle books with respect. **Attitudes:** Ability to share with and respect peers.	• Viewing and discussing background picture to interest table with different kinds of bugs in a garden. • Viewing and discussing covers of story books and talking about what they see and think the story will be about. • Learners draw their own stories while the teacher writes down what the learners say. This is read back to the learner. • Learners role-play reading. • Learners 'read' rhymes that they know, from charts on the wall.	Background picture against wall for interest table. Picture contains different bugs found in a garden. Provide simple story books about this topic in the book corner. Books should have large colourful pictures with very little print (one line per page); run finger along the line being read. Learners are usually very interested in story books which have been read to them.	**Form:** Observation, Interviews. **Method:** Observation; Questions and answers. **Tools:** Observation sheet; Assessment grid. **Purpose:** Baseline, Formative, Diagnostic.

Learning Outcome	Assessment Standard	Skills, Knowledge, Values and Attitudes	Learning Activities	Resources	Assessment
	b) distinguishes pictures from print. 3. Makes meaning of written text: a) understands the purpose of print – it carries meaning; b) 'reads' in a group with the teacher; c) makes links to own experience when reading with the teacher, viewing television or pictures; d) describes and gives opinions of characters in stories or television. 4. Starts recognising and making meaning of letters and words: a) recognises that written words refer to spoken words; b) recognises print in the environment; c) 'reads' picture books with simple captions. 5. Begins to develop phonic awareness: a) recognises initial consonant and short vowel sounds; b) recognises and names some letters of the alphabet;				

Learning Outcome	Assessment Standard	Skills, Knowledge, Values and Attitudes	Learning Activities	Resources	Assessment
	c) recognises some rhyming words.				
LO 4 Writing The learner will be able to write different kinds of factual and imaginative texts for a wide range of purposes.	**We know this when the learner:** 1. Experiments with writing: a) creates and uses drawings to put across a message, and as a starting point for writing; b) forms letters in various ways (e.g. own body writing in sand); c) understands that writing and drawing are different; d) 'writes' and asks others to give the meaning of it; e) talks about own drawing and 'writing'; f) role-plays writing telephone messages, shopping lists; g) uses known letters and numerals to represent written language; h) reads own emerging writing.	**Skills:** Recognises known print in the environment. **Knowledge:** Knows some of the words connected with bugs. **Values:** Recognises that drawing and writing can be used to communicate.	• Learners draw and role-play writing. • Teacher writes down what learners say under their drawings, i.e. captions.	Provide writing materials such as crayons, pencils, kokis and paper in a writing area.	**Form:** Rhymes, stories. **Method:** Observation. **Tools:** Observation sheet, Checklists, Assessment grid. **Purpose:** Baseline, Diagnostic.

Learning Outcome	Assessment Standard	Skills, Knowledge, Values and Attitudes	Learning Activities	Resources	Assessment
LO 5 Thinking and reasoning The learner will be able to think and reason, as well as to access, process and use information for learning.	**We know this when the learner:** 1. Uses language to develop concepts: a) demonstrates developed concepts such as quantity, size, shape, etc. 2. Uses language to think and reason: a) identifies and describes similarities and differences; b) matches things that go together; c) classifies things; d) identifies parts from the whole. 3. Uses language to investigate and explore: a) asks questions and searches for explanations; b) gives explanations and offers solutions. 4. Processes information: a) Picks out selected information from a description.	**Skills:** Acquires skills to solve problems by thinking and reasoning. Using questions, offers solutions. **Knowledge:** Acquires knowledge about bugs by thinking and reasoning. **Values:** Becomes aware of the needs of small creatures and our interaction with them.	• Solving riddles. • Solving problems.	**RIDDLES: What am I?** I fly. I am yellow and black. I make honey. I live in a hive. I am a ... (Find more riddles in the appendices) **SOLVING PROBLEMS: Review:** • How do snails move? • Do snails like damp or dry places? • Do snails prefer dark or light places? • Which food do ants prefer?	**Form:** Rhymes, stories. **Method:** Observation. **Tools:** Observation sheet, Checklists, Assessment grid. **Purpose:** Baseline, Diagnostic.

Learning Outcome	Assessment Standard	Skills, Knowledge, Values and Attitudes	Learning Activities	Resources	Assessment
LO 6 Language structure and use The learners will be able to use sounds, words and grammar of the language to create and interpret texts.	**We know this when the learner:** 1. Relates sounds to letters and words: a) recognises that words are made up of sounds; b) recognises the sounds at the beginning of some words. 2. Works with words: a) groups words (e.g. words whic rhyme); b) identifies a word, a letter and a space in print. 3. Works with sentences: a) communicates ideas using descriptions and action words. 4. Works with texts – talks about stories using terms like beginning, middle and end. 5. Uses meta-language (e.g. sound, word, letter, rhyme, beginning and end).	**Skills:** Acquires the skill to work with language structure nd use. **Knowledge:** Knows words of rhymes; words to describe; and action words: e.g. Rhyming words: Play – day; By – sky. Action words: running, singing, jumping, leaping, holding tight, letting go.	Teacher reads the story of *Mr McGee and the Biting Flea*: • run fingers along the text while reading so that learners can see what you are reading; • find sounds at beginning of words and match with other words of the same sound; • find rhyming words; • find action words and imitate the actions. • Ask learners to describe the mini-creatures in the picture and identify the actions being performed in the picture.	***Mr McGee and the Biting Flea (P Allen)*** *Mr McGee went out to play,* *Down to the beach one windy day.* *Mr McGee was running along,* *Flying his kite and singing a song.* *Just then a dog came racing by,* *frightening the birds up into the sky.* *Mr McGee was having fun,* *Flying his kite up close to the sun,* *When jumping and leaping the dog joined in,* *Chasing the kite and making a din.* *Mr McGee was holding on tight until....* *Suddenly he felt a bite.* *That was when he let go of the kite.* Picture on wall behind interest table.	**Form:** Rhymes, stories. **Method:** Observation. **Tools:** Concept web completed for learners, Observation sheet, Checklists, Assessment grid. **Purpose:** Baseline, Diagnostic.

Learning Outcome	Assessment Standard	Skills, Knowledge, Values and Attitudes	Learning Activities	Resources	Assessment
Integration: Linking Learning Areas – Natural Sciences **LO 1** **Language structure and use**		**Knowledge:** Covers the knowledge strand Life and Living in Natural Sciences. **Skills:** Acquires Science Skills: • Science process skills; and plan, do and review. **Values:** Gains respect for helpful insects and values the tiny creatures in our environment.	• A variety of activities covering science concepts, as set out in text.	Real bugs are brought to the classroom for a day and then released where they were found. Magnifying lenses to observe the bugs in detail. Pictures of bugs. A variety of reference books providing facts and colourful pictures of bug to put on the interest table.	
Arts and Culture **LO 1**	Visual Arts 1. Freely creates images of own world in various media.		• Learners draw pictures of the bugs in their gardens. • Learners create a three-dimensional model of their favourite insect.	Koki's, paper, crayons. Waste material: toothpaste boxes, egg cartons; variety of paper of different textures; pipe cleaners, etc.	
Mathematics **LO 1** **Numbers Operations and Relationships**	Sequences events in the story within one day. (See the curriculum web for other examples)		• Learners count body parts (including legs) of ladybirds and other animals featured in the story (LO 1).	*The Bad-Tempered Ladybird* (Eric Carle)	

Learning outcome	Assessment Standard	Skills, Knowledge, Values and Attitudes	Learning Activities	Resources	Assessment
LO 4 **Measurement**			• Ladybird meeting different animals at different times in one day (LO 4).		
Life Orientation **LO 1** **LO 2** **LO 4**			• Learn about cleanliness and diseases carried by some insects (LO 1). • Learn about respecting all creatures.	Picture of a kitchen with garbage and dirty dishes visible. **Hurt No Loving Thing** (Life Orientation LO 2) *Ladybird nor butterfly,* *Nor moth with dusty wing,* *Nor cricket chirping cheerily,* *Nor grasshopper, so light of leap,* *Nor dancing gnat,* *Nor beetle fat,* *Nor harmless worms that creep.* (Cristina Rossetti) Moving like different insects LO 4: The Centipede Dance (Learners form a long line to represent a 'centipede'. They translate the words into actions.)	

Learning outcome	Assessment Standard	Skills, Knowledge, Values and Attitudes	Learning Activities	Resources	Assessment
				Can you do the centipede dance? *Well come on everyone, hitch on. Hang on, everyone! Three stomps with your left foot, Three stomps with your right, Now wiggle and jiggle with all your might! Two stomps with your left foot, Two stomps with your right. Now wiggle and jiggle with all your might! One stomp with your left foot, One stomp with your right. Now wiggle and jiggle with all your might!* (Yvonne Winer and Lyndall Stewart)	

Conclusion

This chapter provided an overview of some frameworks and strategies to plan integrated Learning Programmes for Reception Year around a theme. These were discussed with the purpose of encouraging teachers to think critically about their choices of activities for programmes and the ultimate consequences of these choices for the learners in their class.

Bibliography

DoE. 2002. *Revised National Curriculum Statement*. Pretoria.

Filmer, MR. 1999. *Southern African Spiders*. Cape Town: Struik.

Carlson, L. 1993. *Eco Art*. Charlotte, Vermont: Williamson Publishing.

Greaves, N. 2000. *When Lion Could Fly and other tales from Africa*. Cape Town: Struik.

Jacobs,J & Terblance, R. 2003. *Hoe hoog kan 'n sprinkaan spring?* Pretoria: LAPA Uitgewers.

Leroy, A and J. 2000. *Spiderwatch in Southern Africa*. Cape Town: Struik.

Potter, JP. 1995. *Science in Seconds for kids*. New YorkWiley & Sons.

Reid, J. 2000. *Butterfly Gardening in South Africa*. Pretoria: Briza Publications.

Reys, RE. Suydam, MN. 1995. *Helping children learn mathematics*. Needham heights, MA: Allyn and Bacon.

Sunal, C, Powel d, Rovgno,I, Smith C, Sunal, D. 2000. *Integrating Academic units in the elementary School curriculum*. New York: Harcourt.

Websites (for further information on the insects and other creatures discussed in this chapter)

www.alienplanet.com/ecology/p38.html

www.howstuffworks.com

www.insecta-inspecta.com/bees/honey

www.insecta-inspecta.com/ants

www.naturewatch.ca/english/wormwatch

www.uky.edu/Agriculture/Entomology/ythfacts/bugfun

www.ricgroup.com.au

Appendix 1

Background information

Bugs can be classified as *arthropods*. An arthropod can reproduce, grow, and develop. An arthropod needs food and uses energy. In these ways arthropods are very much like human beings.

An arthropod is an invertebrate, because it does not have a backbone. A backbone is an important part of a skeleton (a framework providing support to a body like ours). Some of them have developed a hard external support called an exoskeleton. Here an arthropod is very different from humans!

An arthropod has certain characteristics which makes it different from other invertebrates. It has jointed legs and a segmented body. It has an exoskeleton. It also has a heart, blood system and a nervous system.

Arthropods are divided into five basic classes: centipedes, millipedes, crustaceans, insects and arachnids.

Tables, such as the one below, are a useful tool for summarising and comparing information.

	Insects	Arachnids	Crustaceans	Centipedes	Millipedes
Body parts	3	2	2	2	2
Number of legs	6	8	10	30 or more	60 or more
Number of antennae	2	0	4	2	2
Parts for movement	Legs; Wings	Legs	Legs	Legs	Legs
Habitat	Land, water, air	Land	Water (few on land)	Land	Land
Example	Fly	Spider	Crab	Centipede	Millipede

Facts about particular insects

Focus on specific examples that will be of interest to your learners.

Aphid facts

Habitat: Aphids live in house plants and homes and gardens.

Food: Aphids like to eat roses, beans, cabbages and other plants.

Enemies: The ladybird bug is their main enemy.

Camouflage: Aphids are usually green. This helps them blend with the green leaves they eat.

Did you know? Aphids have spear-like mouths that help them to drink sap (liquid) from plants.

Ant facts

Habitat: Ants live and work in colonies. They are found in deserts, woods, fields, and gardens.

Types of ants: There are four kinds of ants in a nest. The workers dig tunnels and chambers, look for food and look after the eggs and larvae. The soldier ants protect the nest. The winged male ants mate with the queen. The queen lays eggs.

Food: Ants eat honeydew made by aphids, as well as seeds and food that humans eat.

Enemies: The anteater

Way of 'talking': Ants touch each other to pass on the smell of their nest.

Did you know? Ants can lift objects that weigh more than they do!

Bee facts

Habitat: A beehive can be home to more than 50 000 bees.

Food: Bees suck nectar with their tube-shaped mouth parts.

Way of 'talking': A worker bee 'dances' by waggling her abdomen. This is how she tells other bees where the nectar is.

Queen bee: The queen bee spends her life laying eggs.

Did you know?

- A bee can only sting once.

- Every bee colony has its own scent.

- Visitors from other colonies will be pushed out.

- Bees were around in prehistoric times with the dinosaurs.

Beetle facts

Habitat: Beetles can be found on mountains, in deserts, in ponds, and in trees.

Food: Some beetles eat only vegetables. Underwater beetles eat tadpoles. Beetles clear up dead plants and animals.

Enemies: Birds and fish

Did you know? The scarab was a sacred beetle in ancient Egypt.

Butterfly facts

Habitat: Butterflies live in grasslands, mountains and rain forests.

Food: Butterflies eat liquid nectar from flowers.

Enemies: Birds and lizards.

Way of 'talking': They use sight and smell to find their mates.

Did you know? Butterflies use their front pair of legs for cleaning their eyes, rather than for walking.

Spider facts

Habitat: Spiders can be found everywhere.

Food: Spiders eat insects and other spiders, which they trap in their sticky webs. Without spiders there would be too many insects in the world. Spiders use their silk for binding prey and making webs and cocoons.

Enemies: Birds eat spiders.

Way of 'talking': Spiders are good listeners. They can work out the size of their enemies by the sounds they make.

Did you know? A spider is an arachnid and has eight legs, two body parts, and six or more eyes than us. Spiders usually have four pairs of eyes.

Centipede facts

Habitat: Centipedes can be found in caves, deserts, forests and gardens.

Food: Centipedes eat insect larvae, slugs, snails and worms. Large centipedes eat mice, birds and lizards.

Enemies: Certain birds and ants eat centipedes, but most centipedes taste horrible, so many insects won't eat them.

Did you know? Most centipedes have 35 pairs of legs. (Centipedes are not insects – insects only have six legs).

Ladybird facts

Habitat: Ladybirds can be found in field and gardens.

Food: They love to eat aphids. One ladybird can eat 100 aphids in a day. Ladybirds help us by eating many harmful insects.

Enemies: Birds are one of their enemies.

Did you know? Not all ladybirds are ladies. Males are called ladybirds too.

Snail facts

Habitat: Cool, moist places in the garden.

Food: Snails eat plants.

Enemies: Birds eat snails.

Snails are molluscs: They have a soft body and a shell, which they use for protection. The shell grows as the snail grows. A snail moves using its foot, which is a large, muscular part of its body. It has very sensitive feelers and eyes on stalks at the top of its head. These eyestalks retract when faced with danger.

Did you know? Snails hatch from eggs and look like young adults.

Interesting and helpful Insects

Some insects do more harm than good to humans and plants. Among these are flies, mosquitoes, cockroaches, black widow and brown recluse spiders, miller moths and clothes moths. Many insects that sting or bite to defend themselves will not bother people if they are not disturbed. Among these are wasps, hornets, bees and spiders. Look at the following table listing interesting, helpful insects.

INSECTS	FUNCTION	INTERESTING FEATURES
ANTS	Ants are scavengers who clean their surroundings. Newly discovered function: pollinators of flowers	Social insects who live in colonies with individual jobs to perform: some nurse young; some gather food.
BEES	Bees are highly valued pollinators of plants. Producers of honey and beeswax.	Social insects that live in colonies with specialised jobs to perform.
BUTTERFLIES	Pollinators of plants. (Explain to learners that they help plants make seeds.)	Slender bodies. Antennae have ball tips. Fly by day. Fold wings straight up when resting. Usually form a chrysalis.
MOTHS	Some are pollinators. Silk moths spin strong, lustrous fibres that are made into fabric.	Fat, furry bodies. Feathery antennae. Wings spread flat when resting. Usually spin cocoons. Fly at night.
BEETLES	Some kinds are scavengers who tidy up. Gardeners value ladybug beetles for pest control. Some beetles destroy crops.	Many pretty varieties: striped, spotted, and iridescent.

CRICKETS	Serve as food for other animals. They are destructive to some crops.	Only male crickets chirp. They raise and rub their hard wing covers together to make vibrations.
FIREFLIES (soft-bodied beetles)	Appreciated for adding charm to summer nights.	Fireflies signal to one another with flashes of light.
GRASSHOPPERS/ LOCUSTS	Destroy some crops, but also serve as food for other animals.	Wings are barely visible when flying. Use hind pair of legs to jump. Hearing area is in the abdomen.
PRAYING MANTIS	So valuable for pest control that egg cases of these are sold to gardeners.	Almost 10 cm long. Eat other insects by tearing them apart.
WASPS and HORNETS	Some wasps pollinate fruit trees. Some eat destructive larvae.	Hornets and some wasps chew dead wood to make paper nests. Some wasps use mud.

Appendix 2

Telling a story: Betty Butterfly

Listen! Can you hear it? Can you hear something or somebody crying? (The teacher turns up the sound of the recording of someone crying softly.) Let's go and see who or what it is so that we can help. (The learners look around. While the children are looking around, the teacher puts Betty Butterfly onto a flower.)

'Look, children! It's Betty Butterfly who is crying.'

Betty Butterfly looks up. Big tears roll over her cheeks.

'Why are you crying, Betty Butterfly?'

'All the creatures say I am not a real butterfly and I am ugly.'

'That is very, very unkind of them! But tell us why you have to wear glasses.'

Betty Butterfly stops crying and dries the tears from her eyes.

'I cannot see well. I bump into things and hurt myself. Look at this bump on my head. I flew into a big tree and bumped my head so I had to have stitches. Look at my left wing. I hooked it on a thorn and it tore my wing.'

'Shame, you poor little butterfly. Please don't cry anymore. We will be your friends from now on. Look! Even Sipho is wearing glasses because he can't see well either.'

Every day, the children play with Betty Butterfly. She is happy again.

A few days later, the children go out to play with Betty Butterfly. She is not at the flower where she always waited for them. They call and call: 'Betty Butterfly, where are you?' But there is no answer. They are very worried and sad.

'Let's go and look for her!' says Sipho.

Just then, they hear all the other mini-creatures singing: 'Betty Butterfly is our hero! Betty Butterfly is our hero!'

The bees are carrying her on their little shoulders.

'What happened?' the children ask.

The beetle says: 'A naughty little girl pushed me over onto my back and I could not get up. Nobody could see me because I was lying in a bush. Betty Butterfly saw me and came to help me back onto my feet again. If she did not help me, I would have died!'

The bees say: 'That's not all! Someone has been stealing our honey. Betty Butterfly was sitting near our hive this morning. She saw the thief coming and called us. We all flew out and stung the man. It is her glasses that help her to see so well.'

The children clap their hands and so do all the other mini-creatures. Wiggly Worm stands up and says: 'Dear Betty Butterfly, please forgive us for being so unkind to you. We promise to be your friend and to look after you. We will never say unkind things again.'

They give her a badge which says: BETTY BUTTERFLY: FB EYE. Betty Butterfly loves the badge.

The spider says: 'We can now call you BETTY BUTTERFLY FB EYE because you can see so well!'

(Explain that the FBI are detectives hence the name Betty Butterfly FBI but because she can see so well, they have changed FBI into FB EYE.)

Appendix 3

Garden Visitors' Song

(Composed by Esmé Prinsloo – used with permission)

> Note:
>
> - The number of garden visitors included in the song should be determined by the abilities of the learners. This means that the number of garden visitors can be reduced for a young group of learners or for learners who cannot memorise the whole song. The number of garden visitors should also be reduced for FAL learners.
>
> - The sound of the letter must be used, not the alphabet name. For example, the *a* should sound like the *a* in *ant* and the *b* like the *b* in *butterfly*.)

A is for the little black ant

I wonder why he goes pant, pant, pant.

B is for butterfly, bug and bee

I wonder what it is they see, see, see.

C is for the cricket that makes a noise

I wonder if they are boys, boys, boys.

D is for dragonfly flying low

I wonder where he wants to go, go, go.

F is for the fly on the wall

I wonder why he worries us all, all, all.

G is for the grasshopper watch him hop

I wonder when he'll stop, stop, stop.

L is for ladybird black and red

I wonder why she's in bed, bed, bed.

M is for the moth flying around

I wonder why he never makes a sound, sound, sound.

S is for spiders and the snails

I wonder if they've got tails, tails, tails.

W is for wasps and worms so fat

I wonder why they're like that, that, that.

Variation:

The song can be accompanied by percussion instruments. Each mini-creature plays a certain instrument, for example:

- **Ants:** small triangles
- **Bees, bugs and butterflies:** tambourines
- **Cricket:** castanets
- **Dragonfly:** base drum
- **Fly:** shakers
- **Grasshopper:** rhythm sticks
- **Ladybird:** bells
- Spiders and snails: small drum
- **Wasps and worms:** big triangles
- **Moth:** triangles, but tap them lightly with their fingers so that no sound is produced when you say the words *never makes a sound*.

Divide the class into different mini-creatures. Each group gets a specific type of percussion instrument. They listen for the mini-creature that they represent and play the instruments on the three words that are repeated in the last line. For example, the ants will play the small triangles when they sing the words *pant, pants, pant* while the butterflies, bugs and bees will play the tambourines when they sing the words *see, see, see*.

Appendix 4

Beetles (Action Rhyme)

Learners translate words into actions.

When beetles go a-walking
I wonder what they say,
Because they nod their little heads
'Good-day! Good-day! Good-day!'
When beetles go a-flying
I wonder what they sing,
Because their wings make whirring sounds
A-zing, A-zing, A-zing!

When beetles go a-munching
I wonder what they munch,
Because the little nibbly sounds
Go crunch, crunch, crunch!

When beetles go to bed
I don't wonder any more,
Because I hear the tiniest sounds
Go snore, snore, snore!

(Yvonne Winer and Lyndall Stewart)

Appendix 5

Riddles and Rhymes

Riddles:

What am I?
I am long.
I wriggle.
I live in the ground.
I mix the soil to make it healthy.

I am an …

Who am I?
I am very pretty.
I can fly.
People always think I'm a lady – but I'm not!
I am red and black.

I am a …

> **Who am I?**
> I have a large foot, a soft body and a shell to protect me.
>
> I am an …

Rhymes

CATERPILLARS

Wiggling, woggling up and down
Painted as gay as a circus clown
Clinging to twigs with tiny feet
Always looking for something to eat
Some have bristles and some have spots
Some have patches like polka dots
They're brown and yellow, green and blue
But mostly green like the leaves they chew.

(By Eric Slayter)

THE CATERPILLAR (Finger play)

I can see a caterpillar wriggling on a leaf,
wriggling on a leaf.
It wriggles on the top and wriggles underneath.

(Use left hand as leaf,
and fingers of RH to wriggle on
top & underneath hand)

Then one day it's very still,
I stand quietly watching till,
It changes shape and falls asleep.

(Finger curls in half moon shape)

Every day I take a peep,
Then at last it moves about –
I'm so surprised I give a shout!
For now there's a butterfly sitting on a leaf.
It spreads its wings and flies about.

(Palms of hands together and
fly around)

THE FLY

I try my best to watch him, naughty little fly
But always he escapes me, however hard I try.
He settles on my finger, still I can't succeed,
He dances on my nose, till I'm very cross indeed.
He creeps along the ceiling, then upon the wall,
You cheeky little insect, we get no peace at all.
But wait you little rascal, see what I have found,
with this I soon will swat you, and knock you to the ground.
Now all of us are insects, catch us if you can
But flies like us will never make sad the heart of man!

- Marching movements are made.
- Body awareness – settles on fingers; dances on nose.
- Appeals to children's sense of humour.

OUR SNAIL

He cannot run
This snail of ours
A short walk takes him
Simply hours!

He'll never win
A running race –
Slow and steady
Is his pace.

I don't mind
If he takes his time,
'Cos this slimy snail
Is a friend of mine.

Cecile Levin (in *Take Note*)

SAKKIE SLAK

Sakkie Slak, waarheen gaan jy
al sleep-sleep by my verby?
op jou rug dra jy jou huis:
Te lekker, jy is altyd tuis.

(G.S. Engelbrecht, in *Trompettertjie* deur PW Grobbelaar)

IF I WERE A BUG

If I were a bug
I would be raspy and round,
Covered with spots
And creep all around.

I'd like to have feelers
Ever so thin,
And wings that would make me
Spin and spin.

Perhaps I would have
Great spiky horns
That cover me over
Like sharp nasty thorns.

So people will tremble
And people will say:
I SAW THE MOST …
TERRIBLE BUG TODAY!

(Yvonne Winer & Lyndall Stewart in *Of Beetles and Bugs*)